Leadership Embodied

A Gift from the U.S. Naval Academy Class of 1978

LEADERSHIP EMBODIED

THE SECRETS TO SUCCESS OF THE MOST EFFECTIVE NAVY AND MARINE CORPS LEADERS

Edited by Lieutenant Colonel Joseph J. Thomas

A joint publication of the Naval Institute Press and the Naval Historical Center

Naval Institute Press
Annapolis, Maryland

Naval Institute Press
291 Wood Road
Annapolis, MD 21402

Library of Congress Cataloging-in-Publication Data

Leadership embodied : the secrets to success of the most effective Navy and Marine Corps leaders / Joseph J. Thomas, editor.
    p. cm.
 Includes bibliographical references.
 ISBN 1-59114-860-X (alk. paper)
 1. Naval biography—United states. 2. United States. Navy—Biography. 3. United States. Marine Corps—Biography. 4. Leadership. 5. Command of troops. I. Thomas, Joseph J.
 V62.L43 2005
 359.3′3041′0973—dc22

                                                                        2005004972

Printed in the United States of America on acid-free paper ∞
12 11 10 09 08 07 06 05   9 8 7 6 5 4 3 2
First printing

*To Marines and Sailors everywhere
who man the lonely ramparts of freedom.
The generation currently engaged in the Global War
on Terror takes a backseat to no one.
Many future authors will chronicle the
remarkable deeds that these brave men and women
do on our behalf. I stand in awe of them now and
am confident future generations will learn
from their exploits.*

Contents

Foreword

I attribute the successful outcome of many significant decisions in my professional career to the reading and understanding of the experiences of historic naval officers and leaders.

While in command of USS *Cavalla*, a nuclear attack submarine, I faced a situation reminiscent of one that Rear Admiral Eugene B. Fluckey (U.S. Naval Academy Class of 1935) and his crew encountered during a war patrol in World War II. As commanding officer of USS *Barb*, a fleet submarine, then–Commander Fluckey would go on to earn the Congressional Medal of Honor, three Navy Crosses, one Presidential Unit Commendation, and three Navy Unit Commendations, all before his ten-year Naval Academy reunion. In January 1945, *Barb* was operating deep in Japanese-held waters off the coast of China, wreaking havoc on the Japanese supply lines in the Pacific. Approaching a Chinese harbor under cover of darkness, Commander Fluckey saw a great opportunity to deal a crushing blow to a Japanese convoy at anchor in the harbor. However, prior to launching the attack, and despite having already distinguished himself as one of the submarine force's greatest combat leaders, Commander Fluckey walked through his entire ship to discuss his assessment of the situation and gather inputs on the impending attack. He clearly recognized the importance of involving the entire crew. Commander Fluckey and the USS *Barb* subsequently sailed directly into the harbor on the surface that night and aggressively attacked the anchored convoy, sinking or damaging seven Japanese ships.

Fifty years later, while in command of USS *Cavalla*, I too found myself approaching unfriendly waters with an opportunity to collect significant operational intelligence against another nation's navy. While not at war, *Cavalla's* special operations and intelligence-gathering missions were of vital importance to our national security, and the stakes were as high as any wartime operation. My mission was to operate in the vicinity of their fleet, remain undetected for several weeks, and observe and

gather intelligence on their activities. The officers and crew of *Cavalla* approached such missions as seriously as they would offensive combat
operations for, at a minimum, to be unsuccessful
is to invite counter-detection and possibly pro-
voke an international incident. Approaching our
operating area, I was concerned that a vital piece
of sonar gear was still not fully operational.
Despite my technicians' best efforts, it appeared
we would be forced to operate without it for the
foreseeable future. The question before me was
should I allow *Cavalla* to proceed into the operating area with less than her full capability?
While the decision rested exclusively upon my
shoulders as commanding officer, I nonetheless
recalled Commander Fluckey's decision to seek
the counsel and advice of his crew before entering the Chinese harbor in 1945. During discussions with my officers, chiefs, and crew, a
number of ideas to mitigate risks and compen-
sate for the deficient sonar equipment were pre-

sented that I would not have otherwise considered. Given the benefit of time and the knowledge of Commander Fluckey's approach to such
decisions, I was able to fully evaluate the situation and, ultimately, proceed into the operating
area and successfully complete the mission.

Throughout my career, I have actively sought
insights on leadership through the challenges
faced by our historic naval leaders. At other
times, I recalled key events from my professional
reading and was able to draw invaluable lessons
relevant to an impending mission, as I did in
recalling Commander Fluckey's attack. I trust
this leadership book, coupled with a lifelong passion for reading and the never-ending pursuit of
professional knowledge, provides you these same
opportunities.

Keep charging!!!

Captain Charles J. Leidig Jr.
80th Commandant of Midshipmen

Preface

Leadership is a most demanding undertaking. How do some people make it seem so simple, so natural and instinctive? In the age-old debate as to whether leaders are born or made, I unequivocally, indisputably believe the answer is "both." Great leaders throughout history were born with certain capabilities. Preparation honed those capabilities. Then that ability and preparation were combined with a will to lead. When circumstances demanded, the great leaders of history pulled these attributes together to create results that drove the course of history.

While leaders are present in every aspect of human undertaking, we chose to illustrate each of the components of leadership through the most dramatic and demanding of all human undertakings—war and the preparations for war. Wartime leaders are "writ with a darker pen." Wartime challenges are, because of the life-and-death nature of the affair, more monumental and exacting. In the selection of individuals to illustrate each point, we chose wartime leaders as well as those who guided their subordinates and organizations in preparation for combat. Furthermore, we chose American leaders with a distinct and obvious bias toward the U.S. Navy and Marine Corps.

Multiple reasons led us to our approach for *Leadership Embodied*. First, biography is perhaps the most effective method for imparting leadership lessons. Simple listings of prescriptive traits or descriptive qualities are patronizing and, frequently, boring. Second, our biographical examples are familiar to most—or at least they should be. Finally, all of these historical selections have dramatically shaped today's institutions, practices, and customs within the naval services. These are not marginal figures with marginal influence. The individuals included here, and their respective leadership attributes, should be required reading for any student of leadership. Each has a particular lesson for midshipmen on their journey to becoming a U.S. Navy or Marine Corps officer.

This book does not promise to be a panacea.

There is no shortcut. Leadership does not follow a prescribed path. We study examples to inspire us to become better, to be strong when it is easy to give in, and to know that others have gone before us and faced insurmountable odds. Leadership, as an ill-defined social science, crosses boundaries with several disciplines including sociology, psychology, philosophy, and history. We have selected a method that combines the psychological "profile" of effective leaders and the historical context of the impact their leadership brought to organizations and events.

Our hope for this book is that these case studies illustrate the basic elements—in themselves the very essence—of leadership. It is through inherent talent, arduous preparation, and practical experience that we become capable leaders. The reader brings the first to the table, and then we offer a small token in the second pursuit; circumstances enable the third. We all wish you good luck on your journey.

Acknowledgments

This book merges the concepts behind James C. Bradford's *Quarterdeck and Bridge: Two Centuries of American Naval Leaders* and Karel Montor's *Naval Leadership: Voices of Experience*. Bradford's *Quarterdeck* was published in 1997 as a naval history text and included brief biographies of twenty seminal figures from the history of the U.S. Navy. It continues to be one of the most widely used naval history texts at the U.S. Naval Academy, Naval ROTCs, and elsewhere.

Montor's *Naval Leadership* is an exhaustive, multiyear effort to introduce the prescriptive advice of contemporary naval leaders (published in 1987) and is an equally cherished reference. Its Preface and Acknowledgments states: "This book was designed to be the final leadership text for those who are to be commissioned into the Naval Service; to provide instruction in leadership needed by junior officers who did not have the opportunity to review this material prior to being commissioned; and to provide information to junior officers who wished to review the concepts inherent in leadership in the Naval Service. Work on the book spanned three decades and involved input from 1,000 officers covering 15,000 years of leadership experience." In many ways, Montor's magnum opus remains such a "final leadership text" for naval officers.

Just as *Naval Leadership* offers prescriptive advice from great figures in the field, this book, *Leadership Embodied*, hopes to provide *descriptive* advice from equally admired professionals from the history of the U.S. Navy and Marine Corps. The contributing authors have attempted to condense the essential traits and principles that enabled the success of their subjects. Whether professional historian or student of naval history, each author reviewed the life and accomplishments of his or her subject and highlighted the most prominent leadership characteristics. The selfless work of the authors is intended to help shape and inform tomorrow's Navy and Marine Corps officers and will inevitably leave an indelible impression.

Many others also provided invaluable contributions to the publication of this book. Commander Tom Cutler of the Naval Institute Press provided sage advice and editorial assistance throughout the process of bringing the concept of this book to fruition. Commander Cutler is a consummate professional who continues to contribute his talents to the nation and naval service. Dr. Edward J. Marolda, senior historian of the Naval Historical Center, was also vital to the publication of this text. He marshaled the collective talent of the Naval Historical Center, dedicated a substantial portion of his already overburdened schedule to editing, and offered further assistance for Sailors and Marines to tap into the legacy and treasure trove of information that is the Naval Historical Center. His summary of resources available at the Naval Historical Center (Appendix A) at the end of this book serves as a road map to more complete lessons in naval leadership. Both Commander Cutler and Dr. Marolda also authored excellent pieces in *Leadership Embodied.*

As is the case in the fleet, the truly hard work was left to particularly talented junior officers. Ensign Nicholas Pinkston, USN, awaiting Basic Underwater Demolition School and assignment to the SEALs, traveled to the Marine Corps History and Museums Division to research the most appropriate photographs to be added to the biographies. (As a Midshipman First Class, Nick also coauthored the essay on William B. Cushing included in this collection.) Second Lieutenant Katharine E. Folz, USMC, on temporary assignment to the Naval Academy while awaiting graduate school in chemistry at Cambridge, dedicated hundreds of hours to editing, researching photographs, and compiling recommended reading. This book is a testament to her attention to detail and unflagging willingness to see an important project through to completion. She is an absolute rising star. Both officers wore "big stripes" and were leaders within the Brigade of Midshipmen for a reason. Both have bright futures in their respective communities and will undoubtedly be the subject of future studies on "the most effective Navy and Marine Corps leaders."

Finally, this book would have been impossible without the generous contributions of the great U.S. Naval Academy Class of 1978. Their steadfast dedication to the professional development of future generations of U.S. Navy and Marine Corps officers is an impressive example of their continuing national service.

About the Publisher

Naval Institute Press

The Naval Institute Press is a private, nonprofit, membership society for sea service professionals and others who share an interest in naval and maritime affairs. Established in 1873 at the U.S. Naval Academy in Annapolis, Maryland, where its offices remain today, the Institute has members worldwide. Membership includes the influential monthly magazine *Proceedings* and discounts on books, photos, and subscriptions to the Institute's bimonthly magazine *Naval History*, as well as reduced admission fees to Institute-sponsored seminars. The Naval Institute Press publishes books of general military, maritime, and national security interest. Nearly nine hundred titles are currently available online and at bookstores. For further information, please visit our Web site, www.navalinstitute.org.

Naval Historical Center

The Naval Historical Center, located in the Washington Navy Yard not far from the U.S. Capitol, holds the keys to the history and heritage of the U.S. Navy from its creation in 1775 to the present. With good reason, the Naval Historical Center has been called "the Navy's Smithsonian Institution." The Navy Department Library, Navy Art, and United States Navy Museum branches maintain thousands of books, artifacts, photographs, and paintings, and the Operational Archive holds the Navy's most important records from 1945 to the present. In support of the operating forces and their global mission, Center civilian staff historians, curators, and artists deploy with uniformed members of Naval Reserve Combat Documentation Detachment 206 to capture the vital history of the U.S. Navy in the twenty-first century. For further information, please visit the Naval Historical Center Web site at www.history.navy.mil.

Leadership Embodied

1

Lambert Wickes
Initiative

Charles E. Brodine Jr.

Lambert Wickes joined the Continental Navy in April 1776. Over the next eighteen months, he compiled an enviable record of service that included two diplomatic missions, the first operations by a continental cruiser in European waters, and the capture of twenty-eight prizes. His exploits won him the admiration of Congress and established his reputation as one of the infant Navy's top commanders. Regrettably, the career that began with such promise ended tragically when Wickes perished in a storm off the coast of Newfoundland in October 1777. Because death cut short Wickes's naval service, his deeds are not as well known today as are those of his brother officers John Barry and John Paul Jones, who served over the entire course of the Revolutionary conflict. Yet Wickes's contributions to the Continental Navy's early successes were important and merit recognition. Those successes were rooted in Wickes's sterling qualities as an officer, most especially his initiative and desire for active command.

Lambert Wickes was born in Tidewater, Maryland, to a family with deep roots in the colony's history. Bred for the sea, Wickes had risen within his profession to become captain and shipowner on the eve of the Revolution. In April 1776, the Continental Marine Committee appointed the Marylander to command *Reprisal*, a ship-rigged vessel mounting eighteen six-pound carriage guns and carrying a crew of 130. Wickes first saw action in *Reprisal* in early May, when he assisted the Pennsylvania State Navy in driving off several British warships in the Delaware River. He then joined three other continental vessels patrolling Delaware Bay to protect inward- and outward-bound American shipping from enemy attack. Dissatisfied with this duty, Wickes wrote to the Marine Committee, soliciting a more active assignment.

Wickes's initiative was rewarded with orders to convey Continental Agent William Bingham to the French island of Martinique. Wickes distinguished himself on this mission by capturing three prizes, battling a more powerful British warship to a draw, and carrying home to Philadelphia sorely needed supplies of arms and military stores.

The Marine Committee was so impressed with Wickes's spirited execution of its instructions that it designated *Reprisal*'s commander for an even greater assignment, one that would lead to his most memorable accomplishments. On 24 October 1776, the Continental Committee of Secret Correspondence directed Wickes to convey American Commissioner Benjamin Franklin to Nantes, France. After setting Franklin ashore safely in France, Wickes was to cruise against enemy shipping off the English coast. If the cruise proved successful and if the French proved willing to grant *Reprisal* and her prizes the protection of their ports, then Wickes was to mount an aggressive campaign of short, seaborne strikes aimed at the British merchant fleet. Lest Wickes mistake the purpose of his cruise, his orders declared them emphatically: "Let Old England See how they like to have an active Enemy at their own Door, [for] they have Sent Fire and Sword to ours."

Operating in the waters off the English coast entailed considerable risk to Wickes and his crew. The Royal Navy's major naval bases were situated along or near the English and Irish Channels, *Reprisal*'s likely cruising grounds, thus increasing her chances of discovery, pursuit, and capture by the enemy. Moreover, should *Reprisal* become damaged by storm or in combat, she would be far from harbors offering sanctuary for repairs. It was also unclear what kind of assistance the Continental warship would receive in France. By treaty, French ports were closed to vessels of nations at war with Great Britain unless they were in distress. It remained to be seen whether French authorities would be willing to stretch this rule in *Reprisal*'s favor thereby jeopardizing relations with England.

Wickes arrived at Saint-Nazaire, France, on 17 December 1776. He set about preparing *Reprisal* for her first cruise in European waters with characteristic energy, putting to sea again on 24 January 1777. Over the next three weeks, he captured five prizes including a sixteen-gun British government packet that was carried by a boarding action. The arrival of the American cruiser and her prizes at Port Louis, France, on 13 February caused a diplomatic furor. British ambassador to France, Lord Stormont, protested Wickes's violation of French neutrality and demanded the expulsion of *Reprisal* and the restoration of her prizes. Before the French government could act, Wickes, with the assistance of Franklin, arranged for the clandestine sale of the prize vessels. He also avoided French demands to leave port by claiming his ship was unseaworthy and unable to depart.

The obstructionism Wickes met from port officials following his cruise led him to question the value of continued operations in Europe, especially if French willingness to support the American cause covertly was faltering. Therefore he wrote to Franklin requesting permission to return to America where *Reprisal* could operate less fettered by the strictures of international law. But the American commissioners decided to order Wickes on one more cruise before sending him home. In conjunction with the commissioners, Wickes laid plans to attack the Irish linen fleet. To assist Wickes, the commissioners purchased a cutter, *Dolphin*, and placed the recently arrived continental brigantine *Lexington* at his disposal.

Wickes sortied from Saint-Nazaire on his second and final cruise in European waters on 28 May. He sailed with his squadron to the British Isles taking a clockwise trek around the coast of Ireland, entering the Irish Sea via the North Channel. Beginning on 19 June and over the next week, Wickes bagged eighteen prizes. The Continental captain's daring raid plunged Britain's shipping industry into temporary turmoil, delaying the sailing of the Irish linen fleet and prompting a sharp rise in insurance rates.

Reprisal's return to Saint Malo, France, at June's end precipitated a major diplomatic crisis.

Mariner's Museum

Lord Stormont accused the French of aiding and abetting American privateering operations and threatened war if the continental ships were not expelled. Although France sought to support the patriots secretly, they could not appear to condone raids on British shipping on the scale of those launched by Wickes. To avert hostilities, French officials ordered Wickes's squadron sequestered. After receiving assurances that he would return home, the French government lifted Wickes's detention, permitting him to sail for America in mid-September. On 1 October Lambert Wickes's brief career in the Continental Navy came to a close when *Reprisal* sank in a gale off the coast of Newfoundland.

Lambert Wickes exemplified a number of outstanding qualities as a naval officer. He was an accomplished seaman; he had a genuine interest in the welfare of his men; he was deferential to civilian authority; and he was a resolute quarterdeck warrior. These attributes contributed in important ways to his success as *Reprisal*'s commander, but it was Wickes's initiative, his desire for active and enterprising service, that underlay his Revolutionary War achievements. Wickes's initiative first singled him out in the eyes of Congress for important and increasingly challenging assignments. And Wickes's initiative later enabled him to persevere over the numerous obstacles that constantly bedeviled his efforts to be an "active enemy" at England's door. Had Wickes been less motivated, less resourceful, and shown less pluck, his European operations would likely have ended in failure or capture. His success demonstrated what a brave, capable officer unafraid to seize the initiative can accomplish even in the face of long odds.

Suggested Reading

Bowen-Hassell, E. Gordon. "Lambert Wickes." In *Sea Raiders of the American Revolution: The*

Continental Navy in European Waters, by E. Gordon Bowen-Hassell, Dennis M. Conrad, and Mark L. Hayes. Washington, D.C.: Naval Historical Center, 2003.

Clark, William Bell. *Lambert Wickes, Sea Raider and Diplomat: The Story of a Naval Captain of the Revolution.* New Haven, Conn.: Yale University Press, 1932.

Plummer, Norman H. *Lambert Wickes: Pirate or Patriot?* St. Michaels, Md.: Chesapeake Bay Maritime Museum, 1991.

About the Author

Charles E. Brodine Jr. is a historian with the Early History Branch of the Naval Historical Center on whose staff he has served since 1987. He is one of the editors of the documentary publication series, *The Naval War of 1812: A Documentary History.* He has also assisted in editing *Naval Documents of the Revolutionary War.* Mr. Brodine holds a master's degree in history from the University of North Carolina at Chapel Hill.

2

John Paul Jones
Tenacity

Dr. Dennis M. Conrad

U.S. Naval Institute Photo Archive

In all my life, I have never seen such a person; sweet like a vine when he wished, but when necessary, like a rock. . . . And how one trusted him! One movement of his hand you obey like a commanding voice.

> *Ivak, a Cossack sailor who rowed Jones, then serving as an admiral in the Imperial Russian Navy, on a personal reconnaissance among the vessels of the enemy Turkish fleet just prior to the Second Battle of Liman, 17–18 June 1788.*

Every officer of our Navy should feel in each fiber of his being an eager desire to emulate the energy, the professional capacity, the indomitable determination and dauntless scorn of death which marked John Paul Jones above all his fellows.

> *President Theodore Roosevelt, address at the John Paul Jones commemoration, Annapolis, Maryland, 24 April 1906.*

It was a climactic moment in the most memorable naval engagement of the American War of Independence. HMS *Serapis* and the Continental Navy ship *Bonhomme Richard*, a converted French East India merchantman, had battled for over two hours. The newer, faster, more heavily armed *Serapis* had pounded *Bonhomme Richard*, whose largest guns had been disabled in the opening minutes of the battle. In desperation, Captain John Paul Jones, in a daring act of seamanship, had run *Bonhomme Richard* close to *Serapis*, lashing his ship to the British frigate and neutralizing somewhat *Serapis*'s advantages of firepower and mobility. But even with the warships locked together, the eighteen-pounders on *Serapis* continued to pummel the American warship, punching holes in its sides large enough, according to one American officer, to drive a large carriage and four-horse team through. British cannon fire had also nearly severed the mainmast, shot away a main pump, and left the hold of the *Bonhomme Richard* half full of water. In short, the American warship was a battered, sinking wreck. Moreover, almost half its crew lay dead or wounded.

Alarmed, Gunner Henry Gardiner, the senior warrant officer, and Carpenter John Gunnison went looking for Jones to report the dire situation of the ship. Arriving on the quarterdeck, they could find neither Jones nor the first lieutenant. (Jones was forward, acting as gun captain for one of the few remaining serviceable cannon; Lieutenant Richard Dale was checking damage to the gun deck.) Convinced that both officers were dead, Gardiner and Gunnison prepared to surrender the ship. They began shouting, "Quarters, quarters, our ship is sinking," and ran to haul down the American ensign. Apprised of their actions, an enraged Jones pursued them shouting, "Shoot them, kill them." Seeing their captain charging at them, Gunnison and Gardiner let go of the pendant halyard and fled. Jones, finding his pistols empty, hurled them at the pair, hitting Gardiner and knocking him unconscious.

Meanwhile, Captain Richard Pearson of *Serapis*, hearing the surrender calls, shouted, "Have you struck? Do you call for quarters?" Reportedly, Jones then heatedly replied, "I have not yet begun to fight," and the battle resumed, according to Jones, "with double fury."

Forty-five minutes later, there was a second call for quarters, this time by Pearson. A grenade thrown from *Bonhomme Richard*'s top had gone down *Serapis*'s partially open main hatch, ignited spare powder cartridges that had been carelessly left on the gun deck, and created a firestorm that killed or disabled the British gun crews and silenced *Serapis*'s big guns. To prevent further slaughter, Pearson surrendered.

Thus ended the greatest single-ship engagement in U.S. Navy history. It ended victoriously for the Continental Navy because of John Paul Jones's ability as a seaman, his decisiveness, his courage, but most of all, because of his tenacity in the face of incredible odds. He won this battle even though he fought with an inferior ship and crew. He won despite the fact that his ship's company suffered an appalling number of casualties and that some of his own officers despaired and tried to surrender. He won because he willed his men to continue the fight and because they

responded to that tenacity. In fact, Jones's entire naval career was a testament to perseverance.

He was born John Paul, the fifth child of a gardener working on an estate on the shores of Solway Firth in Scotland. Without "connections," in a world dominated by class and status, John Paul made his own way and went to sea at age thirteen as an apprentice mariner. Through hard work, application to his craft, intelligence, and some luck, he became master of a ship by age twenty-one. In 1773 while captain of the merchant ship *Betsey*, he killed a mutineer in the waters off Tobago. Fearing he would not receive a fair trial, John Paul fled to America and changed his name to John Paul Jones.

He arrived in America as relations between the colonists and England were in crisis. When fighting broke out in April 1775, Jones traveled to Philadelphia to offer his services to the new Continental Congress, and in December 1775, he was commissioned senior lieutenant in the newly established Continental Navy.

Though his rank qualified him for command, Jones chose to serve as an officer on *Alfred*, the flagship of Esek Hopkins's squadron. He believed that he had much to learn about fleet maneuvers and battle tactics. Throughout his career, Jones tenaciously pursued professional knowledge, all in the hope that he would be appointed the American Navy's first flag officer, a dream he never realized.

In 1776, he received his first independent command and conducted two highly successful cruises as a commerce raider. Anticipating that his performance would get him promoted to squadron commander, Jones was hurt and disappointed when Congress placed him eighteenth on the seniority list. He complained bitterly about this slight, but he persevered, remaining in the service rather than abandoning it for a more lucrative career as a privateer.

In 1777, Jones proposed a new strategy for the American Navy. Recognizing that the Navy was too weak to protect America's coasts and believing that commerce raiding produced minimal strategic benefits, Jones advocated taking the war to Britain's shores and forcing the enemy to divert

U.S. Naval Institute Photo Archive

resources from America. Soon after, when Jones arrived in Europe with the Continental Navy ship *Ranger*, he implemented that strategy by attacking the British coastal town of Whitehaven. Although unpopular with his officers and crew, who were hungry for prize money to augment their meager wages, Jones persevered. Through cajolery and force of character, he convinced his men to conduct a raid that stunned Britain. The following year, Jones encountered *Serapis* while leading a small squadron of vessels on a second such mission.

After the Revolution, Jones tried to interest Congress in establishing a strong Navy. He tenaciously, but unsuccessfully, promoted the idea. Frustrated, Jones, with the blessing of American officials, entered the Imperial Russian Navy as a rear admiral. He won two important victories against Turkish naval forces, but lost the battle for influence in the Russian court and left the Russian service. He then returned to France where he died in 1792.

Throughout his career Jones vigorously promoted himself and the American Navy. It was in battle, however, that his tenacity came most notably into play. His determination inspired his crews to perform better and more heroically than would otherwise be expected.

Suggested Reading

Morison, Samuel Eliot. *John Paul Jones.* Boston: Little, Brown, 1959.

Reaveley, Peter. "The Battle." In *John Paul Jones and the* Bonhomme Richard, edited by Jean Boudriot. Paris: Jean Boudriot, 1987.

Thomas, Evan. *John Paul Jones: Sailor, Hero, Father of the American Navy.* New York: Simon and Schuster, 2003.

About the Author

Dr. Dennis M. Conrad is with the Early History Branch of the Naval Historical Center. Before coming to the Center, he was editor and project director of the *Papers of General Nathanael Greene*, a thirteen-volume documentary series. Greene was also the subject of Conrad's doctoral dissertation at Duke University. At the Naval Historical Center, Conrad helps edit the *Naval Documents of the American Revolution* series. He recently published an essay on John Paul Jones in *Sea Raiders of the American Revolution: The Continental Navy in European Waters* (Naval Historical Center, 2003).

3
Stephen Decatur
Boldness and Resourcefulness

Christine F. Hughes

U.S. Naval Institute Photo Archive

A twenty-minute clash on 16 February 1804 conferred a lifetime of glory on Lieutenant Stephen Decatur Jr. On that day, he led seventy-five Sailors to snatch victory from defeat in a bold raid in the harbor of Tripoli on the coast of North Africa. The Tripolitans had captured the American frigate USS *Philadelphia*, which earlier had grounded on an underwater shoal about three miles from the port.

Born in 1779, Decatur grew up in the bustling seaport of Philadelphia, Pennsylvania. Tales of his father's privateering exploits during the American Revolution attracted the son to a seafaring life. He got his chance when corsairs commissioned by the Barbary States on the North African coast preyed on American merchant ships in the Mediterranean. These attacks, as well as British and French neutrality violations, prompted the U.S. Congress on 27 March 1794 to authorize construction of a navy. On 30 April 1798—the same day Congress established the Department of the Navy—Decatur became a midshipman in the U.S. Navy. The young officer's sterling performance during a short, undeclared war with France assured him a position in the much-reduced postwar Navy.

When the Barbary powers increased attacks on American trade during the first decade of the nineteenth century, President Thomas Jefferson dispatched U.S. naval forces to the Mediterranean. The first two naval squadrons sent by Jefferson failed to settle the issue. When Commodore Edward Preble assumed command in 1803, he accelerated the war's tempo. American forces suffered a setback, however, on 31 October when the Tripolitans captured *Philadelphia*, which constituted half of Preble's frigate force.

Preble chose Decatur to recapture the frigate because he recognized the young lieutenant as a leader who planned operations meticulously but also carried them out with boldness and flexibility. In addition, Preble saw that Decatur was an inspirational motivator who could stir his men to follow him on the most dangerous missions. All of the men chosen for the operation were volunteers.

In early February 1804, Decatur and his men crowded onto a captured Tripolitan ketch, renamed *Intrepid* by Preble, which had been designed to hold only a crew of twenty or thirty. The filthy vessel's other passengers were rats and lice. The men were condemned to endure the vermin and crowding longer than they expected because foul weather delayed the operation at Tripoli. While battling gale force winds to remain on course, Decatur used encouraging words to bolster the flagging spirits of his Sailors. On the evening of 15 February, *Intrepid* and its consort *Siren* entered Tripoli harbor, but Decatur delayed ordering the attack because he needed to verify their position. He was not dissuaded by grumbling from his sleep-deprived, malnourished crewmen, who feared discovery by the Tripolitans.

When Decatur eventually decided to attack, he moved with dispatch. He did not wait to bolster his force with men from *Siren*, as planned earlier. Trusting in his judgment, Decatur's shipmates accepted the lieutenant's reasoning that "the fewer the men, the greater share of honor."

Decatur slowly navigated *Intrepid*, disguised as a Maltese trader, toward the moored *Philadelphia*, whose small Tripolitan crew slept on deck. Approaching the captured ship, Decatur's harbor pilot, a native of Palermo, Italy, spoke in Arabic to one of the enemy guards. The Italian told the Tripolitan in Arabic that his ship had lost an anchor and needed to tie up to *Philadelphia* for the night. Just before *Intrepid* reached the frigate, however, the Tripolitan realized it was a ruse and exclaimed, "They are Americans!" The pilot panicked and voiced an order to board the *Philadelphia*, but Decatur instantly countermanded him. Only when the two vessels touched did Decatur shout, "Board!" The brave officer jumped into the enemy-held ship with his men right behind him. After subduing the enemy sailors, Decatur calmed his victorious men and ordered them to prepare the ship for destruction by fire. He had his men place combustible materials at each hatch from stem to stern and when satisfied all was ready shouted, "Fire!" Surgeon's Mate Lewis Heermann later recalled the scene:

> Enveloped in a dense cloud of suffocating smoke, the officers and men jumped on board the ketch, and Captain D., bringing up the rear, was literally followed by the flames, which issued out of the hatchways in volumes as large as their diameters would allow. . . . But, notwithstanding the most imminent danger of being consumed by the devouring element they had kindled, the crew were so delighted with the "bonfire" that, perfectly careless of danger, they indulged in looking and laughing and casting their jokes. But Captain D., seeing the utmost peril of his situation, leapt upon the companion [way] and, flourishing his sword, threatened to cut down the first man that was noisy after that.

After Decatur and every one of his daring compatriots safely withdrew from the scene, word of his exploit reached Europe and the United States. This raid electrified the young American nation. Great Britain's Horatio Lord Nelson pronounced it "the most bold and daring act of the age." Preble immediately recommended his young lieutenant for a captaincy, which the Secretary of the Navy granted, making Decatur the youngest captain in the U.S. Navy at twenty-five years of age. That accomplishment has never been equaled.

For the remaining sixteen years of his naval career, Decatur continued to embody the leadership qualities he developed as a young lieutenant. Whether in peace or war, Decatur always saw to the welfare of his crew, earning him their trust, respect, and loyalty. Many of his men followed him from one ship to the next. During the War of 1812, Decatur demonstrated exceptional courage and leadership, not only in his victory over HMS *Macedonian* but also in his loss of USS *President*. Killed in a duel at the age of forty-one, Stephen Decatur had already earned a reputation as a U.S. naval officer of exceptional bravery and resourcefulness.

Naval Historical Foundation

Suggested Reading

Allison, Robert. *Stephen Decatur: American Naval Hero, 1779–1820*. Amherst: University of Massachusetts Press, forthcoming 2005.

De Kay, James Tertius. *A Rage for Glory: The Life of Commodore Stephen Decatur, USN*. New York: Free Press, 2004.

Leiner, Frederick C. "'The Greater the Honor': Decatur and Naval Leadership." *Naval History*, 15 (October 2001): 30–34.

Tucker, Spencer. *Stephen Decatur: A Life Most Bold and Daring*. Annapolis, Md.: Naval Institute Press, 2004.

About the Author

Christine Hughes is the assistant branch head of the Naval Historical Center's Early History Branch and coeditor of the four-volume series, *The Naval War of 1812: A Documentary History*. Her other publications include entries on naval figures for the *Dictionary of National Biography* and essays on Lewis Warrington for *The Early Republic and the Sea: Essays on the Naval and Maritime History of the Early United States* and on Joshua Barney for the forthcoming *Against All Odds: U.S. Sailors in the War of 1812*. She is currently studying for her doctorate in history at George Mason University.

4

Joshua Barney
Perseverance and Resourcefulness

Dr. William S. Dudley

U.S. Naval Institute Photo Archive

Of all the naval leaders of the early sailing Navy, Joshua Barney may have been the most unusual. When confronted with many turns of fortune, he persevered. His skills, bravery, and resourcefulness carried him through several difficult assignments. All these qualities prepared him for the magnificent leadership he displayed during the War of 1812. His naval career commenced before the American Revolution. He gained early experience in merchant sail, and when the war against Great Britain broke out, he volunteered for service in the fledging Continental Navy. He served in the Navy sloop *Hornet* under Captain William Stone and Captain Charles Alexander and was in the Navy ship *Andrew Doria* when she received the first salute from a foreign nation, rendered to the Continental Navy from the Dutch fort at St. Eustatius in 1776.

He sailed as first lieutenant of the U.S. Navy ship *Saratoga* commanded by Captain John Young in 1780. Young put him in command of the prize *Charming Molly*, but HMS *Intrepid* captured her. Barney was sent as a prisoner of war to Mill Prison in England from which he soon escaped. After many adventures, he returned to the United States in 1781. He joined the Pennsylvania navy and received command of the ship *Hyder Ally* to escort trading vessels down the Delaware River. In an action defending the convoy, Barney captured HMS *General Monk*, a larger vessel, and brought her back to Philadelphia to much rejoicing. Naval historian and novelist James Fenimore Cooper called this action "one of the most brilliant that ever occurred under the American Flag."

After the Peace of Paris that ended the War for Independence in 1783, Barney engaged in business ventures and became a staunch Federalist. He was one of the first recipients of the medal of the Society of Cincinnati, a hereditary order formed to honor officers who had served in the Revolutionary War.

Seeking a new opportunity for command at sea, Barney sailed to France where the National Assembly welcomed him. With the encouragement of the U.S. minister to France, James Monroe, he offered his services to that nation in its struggle against Great Britain and the other counterrevolutionary powers. He received command of a frigate and served in the Caribbean to protect the trade between the French colonies and Europe. He left French naval service with the rank of commodore in 1802. During the ensuing years, leading up to the War of 1812, Barney engaged in commerce and managed a farm in Maryland.

With Congress's declaration of war against Great Britain in 1812, Barney was the first to receive a privateer's commission. He fitted out the schooner *Rossie* and made two successful cruises in the summer and fall of that year, capturing eighteen vessels collectively valued at one and a half million dollars. Remaining ashore for the next year, he fretted at seeing the British navy's tightening blockade and the enemy's pillaging of Chesapeake farms and villages. The U.S. Navy was challenged to come up with an adequate response in these interior coastal waters. Its ships were either at sea in search of enemy convoys or blockaded on the New England coast.

He proposed to Secretary of the Navy William Jones the building of a flotilla of gunboats and barges armed with long guns to annoy the enemy and protect the shores of the Chesapeake. Barney predicted that unless something could be done to confront the British, there was the danger of an amphibious attack on both Washington and Baltimore. Being of shallow draft and manned by Sailors from Baltimore, these vessels could employ a hit-and-run strategy that would lure the British into shallow waters where they would be at a disadvantage. The vessels would be particularly effective during the calms that frequented the bay. At fifty-three years of age, Barney realized that as commander, his seniority would pose a problem for William Jones. He proposed that his flotilla be under the secretary's control but separate from the regular

Navy. Jones eagerly accepted this plan and promised to provide Barney with ordnance and other materials to enable the outfitting of the vessels. In August 1813, he appointed Barney an acting master commandant in charge of the "Chesapeake Flotilla," and in the spring of 1814, Jones commissioned Barney as captain and named two local Sailors as his lieutenants.

Learning that the British were active in the southern portion of the bay, Barney got his flotilla under way in early April, heading for Tangier Sound. His strength was then thirteen vessels and included the sloop-rigged gunboat *Scorpion*, Gunboats 137 and 138, and ten barges. Although failing to make contact with the enemy, this foray served as a shakedown cruise. Barney returned to Baltimore complaining of low freeboard and faulty rudders. He made a second sortie in May, this time with fifteen vessels, and again missed contact. On the third attempt, Barney had a favorable wind and advanced toward a British barge unit off Smith Point at the mouth of the Potomac. With a change of wind, a British seventy-four-gun ship, three schooners, and seven barges attacked. Barney retreated to Cedar Point at the mouth of the Patuxent River and there engaged the enemy. In the ensuing days, the enemy diverted several small frigates to bolster their force at the Patuxent.

Seeking a better defensive position, Barney sailed his flotilla up the Patuxent to St. Leonard's Creek where the British sent boats to attack him. He responded in kind, chasing them out, despite their return of fire with Congreve rockets. On 9–10 June, Barney's flotilla was again attacked. His counterattack caused a British retreat. Upon retreat, one of the enemy schooners, HMS *St. Lawrence*, ran aground and was subsequently destroyed by fire from Barney's vessels.

Barney then asked Secretary Jones to send a battery to be set up on the right bank of St. Leonard's Creek. Soon, Lieutenant Samuel Miller and 110 Marines arrived with three light twelve-pounder carriage guns from the Marine barracks at Washington. The army also sent a battery that set up to provide covering fire from a bluff above St. Leonard's Creek. On 26 June,

Barney sortied, attacking the British boats that blockaded his position in the creek, and by careful coordination, gained the opportunity to sail his squadron and supply ships out of the creek and up the Patuxent River as far as navigation permitted. He had received orders from Secretary Jones to destroy the flotilla if the British landed, saving all the equipment that he could in the process.

On 19 August, learning that the British had landed troops at Benedict on the west bank of the Patuxent River, Barney scuttled his boats and marched his Sailors and Marines toward the Washington Navy Yard. He rendezvoused with General William Winder and his militia troops. On 23 August, Winder, anticipating the British would attack Washington, ordered the entire force to Bladensburg, a port on the eastern branch of the Potomac River and the location of the nearest bridge crossing capable of supporting the body of troops approaching Washington. This was the best defensive position from which to confront the British, whose troops numbered about forty-five hundred effectives. Barney and his naval troops, including four hundred flotilla Sailors, over one hundred

Naval Historical Center

Marines, and five carriage guns brought up the rear of an extended line of march. He deployed his men and guns across the Washington Road.

The militia provided initial resistance but ultimately retreated in the face of the tough British campaigners. But Barney and his men stoutly held their ground. With Marines serving the batteries and the flotilla men acting as infantry, Barney's men soon became the target of the British advance. As the British flanked and surrounded this hard fighting group, Barney and Captain Miller fell wounded, and with many others killed and wounded, Barney ordered the remainder to retreat. As a credit to his steadfast leadership and sharp fighting, British General Robert Ross and his naval counterpart Rear Admiral Cockburn showed their respect, ordered Barney cared for, and gave him his parole. Although the Americans were defeated at Bladensburg, and the British invaded Washington briefly and burned the White House and other public buildings, Barney's unyielding attitude reflected quality leadership.

Always resourceful and outnumbered most of the time, Commodore Joshua Barney repeatedly made the most of an occasion to fight the enemy. Tested and proven at an early age, Barney's fighting spirit and naval skills brought him respect in the highest governing circles. He fought well in the Revolutionary War and sailed as a commander in the French navy against the British in the 1790s. In the War of 1812, he gained success commanding a privateer and as the innovative commodore of the Chesapeake Flotilla. Finally, he demonstrated strong leadership under adversity at the Battle of Bladensburg in 1814. He stands as a worthy example of patriotic naval virtue.

Suggested Reading

Barney, Mary. *A Biographical Memoir of the Late Commodore Joshua Barney*. Boston: Gray and Bowen, 1832.

Footner, Hulbert. *Sailor of Fortune: The Life and Adventures of Commodore Barney, U.S.N.* New York: Harper and Brothers, 1940.

Norton, Louis A. *Joshua Barney: Hero of the Revolution and 1812*. Annapolis, Md.: Naval Institute Press, 2000.

Paine, Ralph D. *Joshua Barney: A Forgotten Hero of Blue Water*. New York: Century, 1924.

Shomette, Donald G. *Battle for the Patuxent*. Solomons, Md.: Calvert Marine Museum Press, 1981.

About the Author

Dr. William S. Dudley has enjoyed a long tenure with the Naval Historical Center. From 1982 until 1990, he was head of the Early History Branch and editor of two multivolume series: *Naval Documents of the American Revolution* and *The Naval War of 1812: A Documentary History*. From 1990 to 1995 he served as senior historian, and since 1995 he has been proud to fulfill the duties of director.

He authored *Going South: U.S. Navy Officer Resignations and Dismissals on the Eve of the Civil War* (1981) and edited *The Naval War of 1812*, Vol. I (1985), Vol. II (1992), and Vol. III (2002). He authored the essay on the War of 1812 contained in *Encyclopedia of the American Military* (3 vols.), Vol. I (1994). Also the author of many articles and book reviews, Dr. Dudley is a member of the U.S. Naval Institute and the Society of Military History and is immediate past president of the North American Society for Oceanic History.

5

Oliver Hazard Perry

Perseverance in Adversity

Vice Admiral George W. Emery

U.S. Naval Institute Photo Archive

The first year of the War of 1812 did not go well for the United States. The enemy beat and humiliated the army at Mackinac Island, Detroit, Fort Dearborn, and the River Raisin. American Commodore Isaac Chauncey had failed to secure control of Lake Erie and Lake Ontario. The American people were questioning the competence of their military leaders. Few were hopeful of victory when a young officer, Oliver Hazard Perry, arrived on Lake Erie in the spring of 1813 and took charge of the small U.S. naval force there. Oliver Hazard Perry was a naval officer whose perseverance in building a fleet in the wilderness and leading that fleet to victory over British forces on Lake Erie in the War of 1812 marked him as an extraordinary leader in the history of the U.S. Navy.

Perry was appointed a midshipman in 1799 and went to sea onboard the sloop-of-war *General Green*, commanded by his father. During the Barbary Wars, Perry gained experience serving on frigates USS *Constellation*, USS *Essex*, and USS *Constitution*. In 1809, the young officer received command of the fourteen-gun schooner USS *Revenge*. Due to pilot error, Perry's ship ran aground. He was investigated, cleared of any blame, and assigned the duty of constructing a fleet of gunboats in Newport, Rhode Island. Before the end of 1812, discontented with command of a coastal gunboat flotilla, Perry requested a command at sea, where some of his contemporaries were winning glorious victories. Early in 1813, the U.S. Navy responded by posting him to Presque Isle (north of Erie, Pennsylvania) on Lake Erie where a small squadron was being constructed.

Before Perry arrived, Sailing Master Daniel Dobbins, under the direction of President James Madison, had struggled for six months to build a fleet. The harbor was an ideal site for a shipyard; its waters were shielded from severe storms and a bar at its entrance provided protection from the British flotilla. But transporting to Presque Isle the skilled artisans and materials he needed to build, mast, rig, and arm naval vessels proved especially difficult. Pittsburgh, the nearest industrial center, was only 130 miles to the south, but there was no usable road from that city to Presque Isle. Furthermore, carpenters ordered to the lake from East Coast cities were reluctant to make the dangerous journey through the wilderness.

American Commodore Isaac Chauncey, who was constructing a flotilla on Lake Ontario to the east, appropriated or delayed materials destined for Dobbins. Even though the Secretary of the Navy gave the Presque Isle effort a higher priority, Chauncey had few qualms about withholding resources intended for Presque Isle.

Once at Presque Isle, assisted by Dobbins and master shipbuilder Noah Brown, Perry redoubled efforts to strengthen the fleet. Critical to that force were the unfinished vessels on the building ways—the twenty-gun brigs *Lawrence* and *Niagara*, and four schooners. The young officer persuaded the naval agent at Pittsburgh to expedite the movement to Presque Isle of building materials and artisans. Perry even journeyed to Pittsburgh himself to emphasize the need for speed. He dispatched Sailors to Black Rock and Buffalo to obtain needed supplies and furiously set to work carpenters who had arrived from Philadelphia.

As July 1813 drew to a close, Perry prepared to float his ships over the bar at the head of the harbor, a difficult and risky task. The brigs drew nine feet of water, but the depth at the bar had fallen to five feet. If the lightened brigs got hung up on the bar, a waiting British flotilla under Robert Barclay would swoop in and destroy the American force. After several attempts, Perry guided *Lawrence* over the bar and into Lake Erie. Barclay mistakenly thought he saw the entire squadron free of the bay and under protective shore guns. As a result, he hastily withdrew to the lake's northern shore.

Now all Perry needed was more Sailors to man and fight his fleet. Emotional pleas to Chauncey and even the Secretary of the Navy fell on deaf ears; few additional Sailors found their way through the wilderness to Presque Isle. Undeterred, the energetic officer persuaded the army to place two hundred army regulars and militia volunteers under his command. During August, he whipped his entire 585-man force, Sailors and soldiers alike, into shape with frequent and intensive gunnery and seamanship training.

On 10 September 1813, now ready for action, Perry led his fleet of well-built ships crewed by trained and eager warriors out to battle Barclay's squadron. Perry sailed *Lawrence* directly at the enemy fleet. British guns raked the ship and killed or wounded 60 percent of her crew. Far from being beaten, Perry transferred his flag to *Niagara* and continued the three-hour naval battle. His perseverance paid off; when the British struck their colors, the Americans were masters of every British ship on the lake.

The Americans wasted no time consolidating control over Lake Erie. Army General William

Naval Historical Center

Henry Harrison, in close coordination with Perry, retook Detroit and soundly defeated the British army and its Indian allies at the Battle of the Thames. The British abandoned resistance and unceremoniously departed Lake Erie.

Perry's victory on the lake and Harrison's ashore restored the faith of Americans in their armed forces, forever freed the Old Northwest Territory of foreign occupation, and favorably influenced settlement of the War of 1812.

The stirring victory of the Battle of Lake Erie is a memorable event in American history. Even more remarkable is the manner in which Oliver Hazard Perry, through force of personality, drive, and ingenuity, persevered through adversity to build and man a fleet and lead it to victory.

Suggested Reading

Forester, C. F. *The Age of Fighting Sail: The Story of the Naval War of 1812.* Garden City, N.Y.: Doubleday, 1956.

Fowler, William M., Jr. *Jack Tars and Commodores: The American Navy, 1783–1815.* Boston: Houghton Mifflin, 1984.

Skaggs, David C., and Gerard T. Altoff. *A Signal Victory: The Lake Erie Campaign, 1812–1813.* Annapolis, Md.: Naval Institute Press, 1997.

About the Author

George W. Emery graduated from the U.S. Naval Academy in the class of 1959 and retired from the Navy in the rank of vice admiral. He served as Commander, United States and Allied Submarine Forces Atlantic. Following retirement, Vice Admiral Emery joined Raytheon Company as executive vice president, then president, of Raytheon Technical Services Company. Today he is an energy and defense consultant, a trustee of the USS *Constitution* Museum, and a member of the Secretary of the Navy's advisory subcommittee on naval history. He and his wife reside in Kennebunkport, Maine.

6

Matthew Fontaine Maury
Dynamic Intellect

Jan K. Herman

U.S. Naval Academy Museum

Every feature and lineament of his bright countenance bespoke intellect, kindliness, and force of character. His fine blue eyes beamed from under his broad forehead with thought and emotion, while his flexible mouth smiled with the pleasure of imparting to others the ideas which were ever welling up in his active brain.

Diana Maury Corbin

Maury Hall at the U.S. Naval Academy, four U.S. Navy vessels, a glacier in Antarctica, and a crater on the moon are all named for Matthew Fontaine Maury. This man is considered one of the most dynamic and controversial naval officers of the nineteenth century.

Matthew Fontaine Maury was born in 1806 in Spotsylvania County, Virginia. As a youngster he moved with his family to a farm near Franklin, Tennessee. In 1825, young Maury headed to Washington where he obtained a midshipman's warrant without his father's blessing.

The young midshipman began his training aboard USS *Brandywine* as that vessel escorted the Marquis de Lafayette back to France. This was followed by a circumnavigation of the globe aboard USS *Vincennes*. After another cruise as a sailing master, Maury took a leave of absence in 1834 to marry and to complete a book entitled *A New Theoretical and Practical Treatise on Navigation*. The work, clearly the best navigation textbook written up to that time, was an instant success.

Returning from leave in Tennessee, Maury was severely injured in a stagecoach accident that rendered him permanently lame. This unfortunate development was a turning point in his life.

During his convalescence, Maury wrote articles, many of which were critical of U.S. Navy inefficiency. Other articles called for legitimate and long overdue reforms. Although written with a pseudonym, there was no mistaking the real author. The brash, young lieutenant who dared was laying the foundation for a future clash with the naval establishment.

In 1841, Maury finally received orders for sea duty, but they were canceled, ostensibly because of his physical handicap. While awaiting another assignment, he continued to write about subjects ranging from geography and exploration to seaborne trade and education. In 1844, the U.S. Navy's Depot of Charts and Instruments moved into its new quarters on a hilltop overlooking the Potomac River in Washington, D.C., with Maury as its superintendent. The Depot's primary mission was to house the U.S. Navy's charts and navigational instruments, but Lieutenant Maury soon molded that institution into something much greater. As a result of Maury's changes, it was renamed the U.S. Naval Observatory and Hydrographical Office.

Selection of the young Virginian seemed completely wrong to members of the Washington scientific community. Maury was self-educated, had little astronomical experience, and lacked the scientific and intellectual credentials deemed necessary by these self-appointed professionals.

Despite the dire predictions, Maury began his tenure at the new observatory by practicing astronomy. He became an expert in using the astronomical instruments and proposed to the Secretary of the Navy a most ambitious project—the cataloging of "every star, cluster, nebula, or object that should pass through the field of view."

Maury's love affair with the heavens, however, was short-lived. His real interest was the study of the oceans—marine meteorology, tides, currents, the composition of seawater, the depth and makeup of the ocean bottom, and the feeding habits of marine mammals—now known as oceanography. Also, his personal experience at sea had revealed to him the lack of adequate information of the effects of wind and ocean currents on sailing efficiency. As a result, Maury shifted the Depot's and later the Observatory's mission to include the preparation of his own innovation—wind and current charts. The new charts made an immediate impact on ocean commerce. Clipper ship captains were able to shave an average of forty-seven days off the passage from New York to San Francisco, resulting in savings of millions of dollars annually.

In 1855, Maury published *The Physical Geography of the Sea and Its Meteorology*, the first textbook of oceanography, a science that had just come into its own. The young Navy lieutenant was soon universally acclaimed as the "Pathfinder of the Seas." Talk of a transatlantic cable intrigued him, and he prepared an undersea profile of the ocean bottom between Newfoundland and Ireland upon which that cable would be laid in 1858.

International appreciation for his work translated into countless medals and honors from much of Europe—honors that seemed excessive for a mere lieutenant. Or so said his principal detractors, Joseph Henry of the Smithsonian Institution and Dallas Bache of the Coast Survey, who attacked Maury's practical brand of science. For the lieutenant, science was not meant to be the exclusive domain of scientists.

Ill will and jealousy were not limited to Joseph Henry and his colleagues. The Navy hierarchy viewed the oceanographer as a maverick and self-promoter who often spoke out of turn. His superiors and peers made their disapproval obvious. For nearly thirty years, he remained a lieutenant, despite the honor and prestige he had brought to the U.S. Navy and the nation. Ironically, he became the victim of a reform he had urged—a review board to cut dead wood from the officer corps. The board met in July 1855 and, after deliberating for a month in secret and keeping no records, recommended that Maury be placed on the reserve list with leave of absence pay. However, he was to continue as superintendent of the observatory.

Characteristically, Maury used every resource at his command, including political connections and the press. Several officers who sat on the board suggested that the physical disability that rendered him unsuitable for sea duty also made him an undesirable naval officer. Maury demanded redress, insisting that he meet his accusers and defend himself. Succeeding in this, he was returned to active duty and promoted retroactively to commander. Attempts to silence the rebel had failed.

Maury's mental engagement and natural curiosity were his most obvious assets. Lack of a formal university education never deterred him from learning several languages, reading and memorizing scripture and the classics, and, of course, studying and promoting science. Although oceanography, geography, and meteorology were his favorites, he was also a reasonably competent astronomer.

His frenetic schedule and range of interests were as phenomenal as his publishing agenda. Articles and books poured from his pen. Working conditions seemed irrelevant. As a midshipman aboard *Brandywine* and *Vincennes*, he studied navigation and wrote part of his first book amidst the chaos of shipboard life. Years later at the observatory, he authored his most famous works in anything but solitude; the chaos generated by his large and ever-growing family had replaced the clamor of life at sea.

Maury was anything but apolitical. His support of the South during an era when sectional-ism was tearing the nation apart only aggravated his rift with those scientists of a unionist persuasion. Like his fellow Virginian, Colonel Robert E. Lee, Maury at first favored the Union, and disapproved of secession, but when his native state voted to leave the Union, Maury made the most wrenching decision of his life. He resigned on 20 April 1861, ending a thirty-six-year naval career.

He spent the Civil War in the Confederate service, at first devising and perfecting electrically detonated mines, an unhappy duty for a man who viewed science as a force to benefit mankind. The former superintendent of the U.S. Naval Observatory ended his service for the "lost cause" in Europe, working to enlist British aid for the South.

Maury returned to the United States in 1868 to accept a professorship of physics at the Virginia Military Institute. He also lectured extensively on another topic he had long promoted— land meteorology and its benefit to agriculture. This became his personal crusade, and he spoke out for the plan on a lecture tour throughout the country. During such a tour in late 1872, his deteriorating health forced him to quit. He died on 1 February 1873.

Naval Historical Center

His loss was felt in both the United States and Europe. Two days after his death, the *New York Herald* expressed the feeling of many: "As the founder and most successful prosecutor of the benign system of oceanic researches, which has illumined the perilous paths of the mariner and taught commerce how to make the winds and currents of the sea do its bidding, his labors will long be gratefully remembered."

Suggested Reading

Hearn, Chester G. *Tracks in the Sea: Matthew Fontaine Maury*. New York: International Marine/McGraw-Hill, 2002.

Maury, Matthew Fontaine. *The Physical Geography of the Sea and Its Meteorology*. Cambridge, Mass.: Harvard University Press, 1963.

Williams, Frances Leigh. *Matthew Fontaine Maury, Scientist of the Sea*. New Brunswick, N.J.: Rutgers University Press, 1963.

About the Author

Jan K. Herman is historian of the Navy Medical Department, editor of its journal, *Navy Medicine*, and curator of the old U.S. Naval Observatory, now the headquarters of the Bureau of Medicine and Surgery in the Foggy Bottom neighborhood of Washington, D.C. He received a master's degree in American history from the University of New Hampshire, where he was a Ford Foundation Teaching Fellow. He has written many articles for historical publications and is the author of *Battle Station Sick Bay: Navy Medicine in World War II* (Naval Institute Press, 1997).

7

Matthew Calbraith Perry

Military Bearing

Dr. Michael J. Crawford

U.S. Naval Institute Photo Archive

His military bearing and his countenance betokened his iron will and commanded attention, respect, and when necessary prompt obedience.

Rear Admiral John J. Almy

On 14 July 1853, when the dual governors of Uraga, Japan, accepted delivery of the letter from Millard Fillmore, president of the United States, proposing establishment of diplomatic relations, they did so in defiance of more than two hundred years of an official policy of isolation and in opposition to strictly enforced laws. Previously, Japan had allowed contact with foreign governments only through Dutch intermediaries at Nagasaki. The closely regulated trade with the Dutch was the only contact with the outside world that Japanese law permitted. The council advising the shogun, who ruled in the emperor's name, agreed to accept the letter at Uraga, rather than at Nagasaki.

They did so because Commodore Matthew C. Perry, U.S. Navy (1794–1858), left them no reasonable alternative. Perry took a carefully calculated series of steps to arrive at this result in strict conformity with, as he wrote, his orders to "do everything to impress [the Japanese] with a just sense of the power and greatness of this country, and to satisfy them that its past forbearance has been the result, not of timidity, but of a desire to be on friendly terms with them." As an essential element in his calculations, Perry included impressing the Japanese with his seriousness of purpose and with a sense of his dignity as a representative of the government of the United States.

Less than a week before the delivery, the American squadron, consisting of two steamships and two sailing vessels, entered Yedo Bay, the waterway leading to Tokyo, then called Edo, on 8 July 1853. Shortly thereafter, Perry communicated several important points to the Japanese.

No cordon of guard boats would be allowed to surround the American warships.

The squadron would not require local supplies, and thus would not depart if given supplies or because of a lack of them.

The Americans would not be deterred from surveying the harbor for the purpose of finding safe anchorage for the larger squadron Perry intended to bring on a return visit to receive an answer to the president's letter.

The squadron would not depart without delivering the letter.

Perry would deliver the letter near Edo, not at Nagasaki and not through a Dutch intermediary.

The commodore would deal only with a certified direct representative of the emperor.

Perry conducted all negotiations regarding delivery of the president's letter through subordinate officers. No Japanese caught even a glimpse of the American commodore until he made his appearance on 14 July to go from the flagship to the building constructed for receipt of the letter.

Perry made his appearance in a procession designed to create an aura of dignity. Landing from launches, Sailors in white blouses, blue trousers, and blue cloth caps filed off on the beach to the right, and Marines in blue jackets, white trousers, and plumed shakos, to the left. Each group, with a fife and drum corps, stood at attention with rifles at shoulder arms, lined up along the beach. Preceded by his officers, in blue dress uniform, Perry stepped onto his barge as the flagship fired a salute of thirteen guns. When the commodore came ashore, Marines presented arms, boat crews tossed oars, and a band played "Hail! Columbia." The procession then moved off to the meeting place: Marines; a band of musicians; Sailors; two ships boys carrying the box containing the president's letter and the commodore's letter of credence; a pair of large seamen bearing the ensign and the blue pendant; Commodore Perry, between two strikingly tall black seamen; more seamen; and a second band.

Seven months later, when Perry returned to Yedo Bay with his squadron, augmented to seven ships, the Japanese government was prepared to negotiate. The resulting Treaty of Kanagawa opened two Japanese ports for the resupply of American vessels; established procedures for repatriation of Americans shipwrecked on Japanese shores; provided that the United States would enjoy any privileges Japan granted any other nation; and permitted the appointment of an American consul. The door to Japan—which had been sealed shut for two centuries—stood open. Soon thereafter, Japan embraced foreign trade and transformed into a modern, industrialized nation.

Perry succeeded where predecessors had failed in no small measure because of the way he handled himself. As a witness observed, Perry's "firmness and persistence, his stalwart physical presence, his portly bearing, his dignity, his poise, his stately courtesy, were prime factors in his success." Perry was able to employ these qualities to good effect because they were characteristics cultivated through a lifetime as a naval officer.

His superior officers singled out Perry as a thoughtful and conscientious midshipman. Commodore John Rodgers, noting the youth's serious aspiration to become a good officer, appointed him his personal aide. Seeking the respect of the men, not their affection, Lieutenant Perry brooked no departure from rules and regulations; when on deck he always appeared serious and purposeful. Because of his gruff and intimidating presence and powerful voice, like that of a bear, the ratings called him "Old Bruin." By the time of his promotion to master commandant (equivalent of today's commander), he was known as a calm and deliberate officer. The solemn dignity with which he carried himself struck some people as stiff or stuffy but proved useful, especially in diplomatic dealings.

Matthew Calbraith Perry, a native of Newport, Rhode Island, son of a U.S. Navy captain, and younger brother of Oliver Hazard Perry, the victor of the Battle of Lake Erie, received his appointment as midshipman in 1809 and saw action in the War of 1812. His naval service included participation in anti-slave-trade patrols, the suppression of pirates in the West Indies, and the establishment of settlements in West Africa for African-Americans freed from slavery. He assumed diplomatic duties in the Mediterranean, which included contacts with both Greek revolutionaries and the Turkish navy. After a number of years of shore duty he commanded the African Squadron and, during the siege of Vera Cruz in the war with Mexico, the Gulf Squadron.

Throughout his career, Perry made the effectiveness of the U.S. Navy his principal pursuit. An advocate of steam propulsion and responsible for organizing the engineer corps, he has been called the father of the steam navy. He imposed stringent rules to preserve the health of his crews, especially on malarial coasts. He experimented with changes in naval ordinance. His arguments for changes in recruitment persuaded Congress to authorize a naval apprentice system. To promote professional education, he helped organize the Naval Lyceum (a society for public lectures and discussions on naval topics) and the *Naval Magazine* (which published articles on naval reforms) and supported establishment of a naval academy.

Perry's military bearing held a prominent place in any characterization by his contemporaries. Some criticized him for arrogance and inflexibility, but the following by an army officer who had frequent contact with him is a more judicious assessment: the commodore was "blunt, yet dignified . . . heavy and not graceful . . . held somewhat in awe by the junior officers and having little to do with them, seriously courteous to others. . . . The ship seemed to have a sense of importance because he was on board."

The first component of leadership is personal example. As Perry himself said, "Your subordinates will reflect your sincerity, enthusiasm, smart appearance, military behavior, technical competence, and coolness and courage under stress. To be an effective leader you must look and act like one." Matthew Calbraith Perry instinctively understood this principle. A subordinate who served under him in the Mexican War testified to Perry's leadership qualities, averring, "the impression he made on my mind and affections was such as to make me desirous of following him to the cannon's mouth, or wherever the fortunes of peace or war should appoint our steps."

Suggested Reading

Morison, Samuel Eliot. *"Old Bruin": Commodore Matthew C. Perry, 1794–1858.* Boston: Little, Brown, 1967.

Schroeder, John H. *Matthew Calbraith Perry: Antebellum Sailor and Diplomat.* Annapolis, Md.: Naval Institute Press, 2001.

About the Author

Dr. Michael J. Crawford is the head of the Early History Branch of the Naval Historical Center in Washington, D.C., where he is editor of two major, award-winning documentary publication series: *Naval Documents of the American Revolution* and *The Naval War of 1812: A Documentary History*. Dr. Crawford earned his PhD at Boston University, taught at Texas Tech University for two years, and served a year's fellowship in historical documentary editing with the Adams Papers at the Massachusetts Historical Society before coming to the Naval Historical Center in 1982.

8

David Glasgow Farragut
Inspiration

Mark L. Hayes

U.S. Naval Institute Photo Archive

By the summer of 1864, Lieutenant Commander George Hamilton Perkins had suffered the monotony of months on blockade duty off the Texas coast. He awaited relief from command of USS *Sciota*, desiring desperately to go home. He wrote his mother that it seemed like a "living death" to be on the blockade. But when he learned that Rear Admiral David Farragut would soon lead an attack on the Confederate defenses at Mobile Bay, in Alabama, the young officer experienced a resurgence of energy and successfully sought service in the squadron commanded by the man he so greatly admired. During the battle on 5 August, Surgeon James Palmer conveyed Farragut's order to Perkins to attack the Confederate ironclad CSS *Tennessee*. Palmer wrote in his diary, "Happy as my friend . . . habitually is, I thought he would turn a somersault overboard with joy when I told him."

Among the characteristics Karl von Clausewitz includes in the essence of military genius are those possessed by "men who are . . . like heat to a shower of sparks. These are the men who are best able to summon the titanic strength it takes to clear away the enormous burdens that obstruct activity in war. Their emotions move as great masses do—slowly but irresistibly." Overcoming the psychological as well as physical obstructions in battle demanded strong inspirational leadership. David Glasgow Farragut provided that leadership by making himself visible and approachable to the officers and men of his fleet and by encouraging them to share his enthusiasm.

Born near Knoxville, Tennessee, on 5 July 1801, Farragut and his family moved to New Orleans six years later where his father, George, accepted a position as a sailing master in the U.S. Navy. The elder Farragut developed a strong relationship with David Porter Sr., and in 1808, George rescued his friend when he collapsed from sunstroke while fishing. He brought the ailing Porter home and his wife, Elizabeth, tried to nurse him back to health. David never recovered, and Elizabeth herself fell ill with yellow fever. Both died on 22 June 1808. Grateful for the care the Farragut family gave his father, David Porter Jr. offered to care for one of the children. Young David Farragut, who had shown a strong interest in naval matters, accepted the offer.

Appointed a midshipman at the age of nine, Farragut served with David Porter Jr. onboard USS *Essex* during the War of 1812. Porter's frigate proved to be an ideal school for a young man seeking a navy life, and David Porter proved to be an excellent teacher and mentor.

After the war, Farragut spent five years in the Mediterranean Squadron, often serving as the aide to the flagship's captain. Over the next four decades, Farragut benefited from a variety of appointments and experiences, which prepared him well for the great trials of the American Civil War.

During the summer of 1861, the U.S. Navy embarked on a strategy whose goal was to strangle the Confederacy's ability to move supplies and troops on internal waterways and to interdict overseas trade. A naval blockade was not enough; the Union Navy needed to control the South's major ports and rivers. The task called for bold leadership. Recognizing this quality in Farragut, Secretary of the Navy Gideon Welles placed the naval officer in command of the West Gulf Blockading Squadron.

The South's largest port, New Orleans, became Farragut's primary objective. The new commodore carefully planned his operations and vigorously trained his subordinates. During the early morning hours of 24 April 1862, Farragut audaciously ran his warships past the Confederate guns of Fort Jackson and Fort St. Philip, which guarded the Mississippi River. The Union force also destroyed southern naval vessels barring the way. New Orleans fell the next day. Cut off, the two forts surrendered on 28 April. Recognizing this great victory, Congress promoted Farragut, making him the first admiral in the

U.S. Navy. He remained in command of the West Gulf Blockading Squadron, which interdicted trade and provided support for the Union Army in the West.

In March 1863, he once again demonstrated inspired leadership. He directed naval forces that bypassed the guns at Port Hudson and shut down Confederate river traffic on the Mississippi and the lower reaches of the Red River. In August the following year, Farragut confirmed his status as the greatest naval hero of the Civil War when his forces won the Battle of Mobile Bay. With his health spent in service to the Union cause, Farragut then turned over command to trusted subordinates. Congress, reflecting the nation's gratitude for Farragut's successful battle leadership, promoted him initially to vice admiral, and after the war to full admiral.

Secretary Welles spoke of the admiral's leadership qualities: "Farragut has prompt, energetic, excellent qualities, but no fondness for written details or self-laudation. Does but one thing at a time, but does that strong and well. Is better fitted to lead an expedition through danger and difficulty than to command an extensive blockade; is a good officer in a great emergency, will more willingly take great risks in order to obtain great results than any officer in high position in either Navy or Army, and, unlike most of them, prefers that others should tell the story of his well-doing rather than relate it himself."

Farragut made an especially strong impression on young men who were new to war. John Russell Bartlett, a midshipman in 1862, recalled, "I was much impressed with his energy and activity and his promptness of decision and action. He had a winning smile and a most charming manner and was jovial and talkative. . . . The officers who had the good fortune to be immediately associated with him seemed to worship him."

The future hero of the Battle of Manila Bay, George Dewey, was a twenty-four-year-old lieutenant on board USS *Mississippi* during the New Orleans campaign. Late in life he summed up his view of his old squadron commander. "Farragut has always been my ideal of the naval officer, urbane, decisive, indomitable. Whenever I have been in a difficult situation, or in the midst of such a confusion of details that the simple and right thing to do seemed hazy, I have often asked myself, 'What would Farragut do?'"

Farragut's men grew accustomed to their commander's presence. He seemed almost ubiquitous, giving the impression that he had his men always under his watchful eye. Bartlett remembered, "Farragut was about the fleet from early dawn until dark, and if any officers or men had not spontaneous enthusiasm he certainly infused it into them. I have been on the morning watch, from 4 to 8, when he would row alongside the ship at 6 o'clock, either hailing to ask how we were getting along, or, perhaps, climbing over the side

to see for himself." Dewey confirmed this assessment. "Farragut was always on the move, overseeing everything in person, breathing an air of confidence and imparting a spirit of efficiency."

During the nineteenth century, generals in command of armies had opportunities in battle to ride to the point of danger, encourage their men, and clarify commands. These opportunities were not available to flag officers in command of several ships. Farragut compensated for this by making himself visible to the officers and men of his fleet. He shared with them his ideas, infected them with his enthusiasm, and encouraged them with his determination. Then during the chaos of battle his officers could often find solutions to their problems by simply asking themselves, "What would Farragut do?"

U.S. Naval Institute Photo Archive

Suggested Reading

Friend, Jack. *West Wind, Flood Tide: The Battle of Mobile Bay*. Annapolis, Md.: Naval Institute Press, 2004.

Hayes, Mark. "The Battle of New Orleans." In *Great American Naval Battles*, edited by Jack Sweetman. Annapolis, Md.: Naval Institute Press, 1998.

Lewis, Charles Lee. *David Glasgow Farragut*. 2 vols. Annapolis, Md.: Naval Institute Press, 1941–43.

Schneller, Robert J., Jr. *Farragut: America's First Admiral*. Washington, D.C.: Brassey's, 2003.

About the Author

Mark L. Hayes served in the 1980s as an officer in the U.S. Navy and is now a historian in the Early History Branch at the Naval Historical Center, Washington, D.C. He is an assistant editor of *Naval Documents of the American Revolution* and is coauthor of *The Spanish-American War: Historical Overview and Select Bibliography* and *Sea Raiders of the American Revolution: The Continental Navy in European Waters*. Mr. Hayes has published two essays on Civil War naval actions: "The Battle of Port Royal Sound" in *Forgotten History: Hilton Head Island during the Civil War* and "The Battle of New Orleans" in *Great American Naval Battles*, edited by Jack Sweetman.

9

William B. Cushing
Daring

Captain Robert Schoultz

Midshipman First Class Nicholas Pinkston

National Archives

"I deem it my duty to leave for the point of danger at once," Lieutenant William Cushing once wrote to Rear Admiral Samuel Lee, the North Atlantic Blockading Squadron commander, upon learning of a Confederate Navy ironclad threat to Union Navy ships. Because of Cushing's successful record, the Secretary of the Navy instructed that Cushing be given the men and resources to find and destroy the Confederate vessel.

Cushing, while never the epitome of decorum, indeed displayed persistence, fearlessness, and intrepidity in the face of danger. He faced challenges directly and endured. Cushing was uniquely self-confident and resolute in his focus on the offensive and his desire to take the battle to the enemy. Though he was accused of being reckless, he clearly possessed the good judgment to suspend the attack and withdraw when necessary to permit later engagement. His aggressiveness and impatience did not always serve him well, and his impulsive behavior outside of battle presented numerous setbacks for him. Regardless, his courageous leadership and penchant for success became legendary in the Union Navy, and he never lacked for volunteers to accompany him on his most daring missions.

William Barker Cushing was born in Wisconsin on 4 November 1842 but spent most of his youth in Fredonia, New York, where his family moved after the death of his father in 1847. He stood out as a leader of the young men in his school and community but sometimes got into trouble by leading his mates on missions of which authorities did not always approve. Wanting nothing more than to be a military officer, he sought an appointment to the U.S. Naval Academy with the class of 1861. On 25 September 1857, he was sworn in as a midshipman in the U.S. Navy, before his fifteenth birthday—not unusual at that time.

The structure and regimentation of the Naval Academy challenged Cushing's independent spirit. He was frequently in trouble with the staff and faculty, though he was well respected among his peers. For the first time in his young life, Cushing found himself in an environment that existed to serve something larger than his own personal ambitions. Even though he never committed any egregious conduct offenses, he was a renowned rabble-rouser and accrued many demerits. Ultimately, his failure on a Spanish exam and a distasteful cartoon he made about the professor in February of his senior year finally led to his separation from the academy. He was ordered to leave on 23 March 1861.

The separation initially shocked Cushing. After several days of melancholy and self-assessment, he refused to accept the decision as final. While conducting his termination processing from the U.S. Navy, he looked up a former mentor from the Naval Academy, Lieutenant Charles W. Flusser, who had since moved to the Navy Department, and asked for help.[1] Flusser provided Cushing with a book entitled *Naval Enterprise, Illustrative of Heroism, Courage and Duty*, which further motivated Cushing's desire to serve.

Cushing begged to serve in the U.S. Navy in any capacity. After Lieutenant Flusser and others spoke to Cushing's potential, Secretary of the Navy Gideon Welles appointed him acting masters mate in the U.S. Volunteer Navy and assigned him to the USS *Minnesota*, flagship of the North Atlantic Blockading Squadron, on 1 April 1861. Even though he slept in a hammock with the Sailors as the lowest of junior officer positions, he was elated to be a member of the crew of a great ship going off to war.

The North Atlantic Blockading Squadron was responsible for preventing rebel ships from establishing commerce routes and supply lines to the Confederacy. Cushing excelled in his duties as a masters mate, and consequently when the squadron captured their first blockade runners, Cushing took the first sailing vessel and its crew to Philadelphia. Shortly thereafter, he volunteered for and participated in foraging and raiding parties ashore, activities that he thoroughly enjoyed and in which he would later excel.

While on the *Minnesota*, Cushing's spirited behavior eventually got him into trouble with his superior officers. Cushing believed that a particular lieutenant was overly arrogant in his dealings with subordinates. As a matter of honor, Cushing felt obligated to resign from the naval service in order to challenge him to a duel. He submitted his resignation, and Cushing was separated again, this time at his own request. But during the processing of his request, Cushing had a change of heart about leaving the U.S. Navy, and when to his disappointment he received his discharge, he sought to return. He requested letters of reference for his application to the Secretary of the Navy. In responding to this request for reinstatement, one of his former superiors wrote, "His visionary and speculative frame of mind makes him unfit for naval service." While Gideon Welles later wrote that at the time he believed Cushing to be "too full of levity, too fond of fun and frolic to make a valuable officer," Welles also received more commendatory recommendations. Based on Cushing's otherwise strong record, Welles decided to give Cushing another chance. Welles reinstated Cushing as a midshipman. The credibility of Cushing's performance and his persistence paid off in overcoming his mistake in judgment. Cushing was assigned to an admiral's staff where at one point he was suspended for going on leave without permission. Cushing later recalled that because "a midshipman is hardly considered a responsible being" he was forgiven and assigned to the small gunboat *Cambridge*. On *Cambridge*, he took advantage of opportunities to lead boarding parties and to continue to develop naval officership at war.

Eventually Cushing requested and was assigned duty under his old mentor, Flusser, now a lieutenant commander and commanding officer of the gunboat *Commodore Perry*. Cushing was made executive officer. After an intense battle in which the *Commodore Perry* was surrounded by rebel forces on a narrow river in North Carolina, Flusser gave Cushing high marks for his gallantry and cool performance under fire. Based on his outstanding performance aboard *Commodore Perry*, and the U.S. Navy's need for intrepid junior officers, Cushing soon received command of his own small gunboat with a twenty-eight-man crew, the *Ellis*. He was nineteen years of age.

Ellis had the mission of intercepting blockade-running ships trying to enter or leave Bogue inlet west of Cape Hatteras. After a period, Cushing grew bored patrolling the waters and looking for enemy ships. He began seeking vessels outside his area of responsibility and began conducting raids ashore. His innovative missions and the creative means by which he used a small military force to apply pressure to the Confederacy in his area of operations convinced his superiors to overlook their discomfort at his "somewhat exceeding the letter of his instructions by leaving his station." They rewarded him with what Cushing later called a "roving commission" to conduct operations in accordance with his own best judgment.

Cushing then proceeded to initiate a series of remarkable reconnaissance, harassment, and interdiction missions ashore. Once, after capturing two rebel schooners, he misread the channel while departing the inlet to escape, and *Ellis* ran aground. When discovered by the rebels, Cushing sent most of his crew ahead on one of the schooners and remained with *Ellis* to try to extract her. With the extraction unsuccessful and rebel fire increasing, Cushing had no option but to torch his own ship and row with his men under fire to the schooner waiting a mile and a half away (surrender was *not* an option). They escaped, but Cushing in his report of the incident requested an investigation to determine if "the honor of the flag has suffered in [his] hands." Yet again, his superiors, to include Rear Admiral Lee, were impressed and lauded his "coolness, courage, and conduct."

Rear Admiral Lee wanted to encourage and reward Cushing's bold initiative and thus gave him command of a larger vessel, *Commodore Barney*. Cushing soon found himself again in harm's way. As the leader of a small flotilla of gunboats supporting a Union Army mission ashore, Cushing again showed great courage and leadership in battle, maneuvering his ships up and down the western branch river, constantly under fire. He also led several raids ashore to obtain supplies for his ships and to retaliate against Confederate forces. One raid in particular resulted in a letter from Secretary Welles, which noted that his conduct added "additional luster to the character [he] had already established for valor in the face of the enemy." Cushing's performance under fire was helping him to overcome his reputation as a troublemaker.

Eventually Cushing received command of the *Monticello*, the fastest, largest, and most seaworthy of the ships he had commanded to that point; the ship was also one of the fastest in the North Atlantic Blockading Squadron. Unwilling to assume risk or take responsibility for Cushing's innovative and daring proposals, Cushing's commander restricted the proposed missions. On several occasions, Cushing chose to run missions without permission. When they were reported after the fact and their success acknowledged, he was praised by his commander's superiors. Once he even went over his commander's head with a mission request. In addition to receiving permission to conduct the requested mission, he received permission to conduct missions at his own discretion.

Time after time, Cushing proved his courage and initiative in his operations against the enemy, but he did not fulfill his potential until the fate of the North Atlantic Blockading Squadron was threatened. In the spring of 1864, the Confederate Navy sent its newly built ironclad *Albemarle* and seven thousand soldiers to take the Union fort in Plymouth, North Carolina, from which the Union Navy had controlled the Albemarle Sound. The Confederates successfully seized the fort.[2] With control of Plymouth and the presence of the virtually invulnerable iron-clad, the Confederates displaced the Union, establishing naval dominance in the Albemarle Sound.

Rear Admiral Lee desperately sought a way to neutralize the *Albemarle* and regain control of Albemarle Sound and the North Carolina waters. Sending his own ironclads into Albe-marle Sound was impossible because they drew too much water. He turned to Cushing to pre-pare options for a small boat raid. Cushing and Rear Admiral Lee together developed a small boat option that they believed had the greatest likelihood of success, but the mission was so risky that Rear Admiral Lee felt he needed authority from Washington. He sent Cushing to see Secretary Welles, who approved the plan. He believed it to be a suicide mission, but he could not leave the *Albemarle* to dominate the North Carolina waterways.

Meanwhile, Cushing received written repri-mands expressing the ire of his sponsor, Secre-tary Welles, for activities outside the stress of combat. On one occasion, he insulted a British officer whom he believed to have been rude and insufficiently deferential when Cushing's forces stopped and boarded his ship for inspection. This indiscretion resulted in an official com-plaint by the British to the American govern-ment. On another occasion, Secretary Welles expressed his extreme displeasure when he learned that Cushing had not provided close supervision over the transporting of picket boats that had been designed and built specifically for the mission against the *Albemarle*. Cushing had thought it a routine mission and had taken leave. One of the boats was captured by the rebels and was therefore not available for the mission. However, Cushing was the only officer Welles or Rear Admiral David Dixon Porter (Rear Admiral Lee's successor as North Atlantic Blockading Squadron commander) believed capable of destroying the *Albemarle*, so they per-mitted him to stay and gave him the support he requested.

Cushing planned to approach the *Albemarle* under the cover of darkness and detonate a tor-pedo (now called a mine) under the hull of the ironclad to sink it. Though this was considered an extremely risky operation, Cushing had no shortage of volunteers. On 27 October 1864, the weather was perfect—raining and cool—air tem-peratures in the sixties, water temperatures around fifty-five degrees Fahrenheit. Cushing set out in one small picket boat with fifteen men, towing a cutter with another thirteen men in it. They reached the mouth of the Roanoke at 2330, where they left the cutter to await their return and proceeded up the river.

The *Albemarle* was berthed at Plymouth, North Carolina, a town eight miles farther up the river. About a mile before reaching the *Albe-marle*, Cushing and his volunteers approached a rebel group guarding the approaches to Ply-mouth in two boats. The Union men held their breath as they anxiously maneuvered around the rebels with a muffled engine, oarsmen ready to start paddling if the rebel shout were made. The bad weather and inattention of the rebel guards allowed Cushing to slip by. Had it not been for a dog barking as they closed in on the *Albemarle*, they would have achieved complete surprise. Upon realizing that their presence had been noticed, the men began paddling furiously toward the ironclad. Rebel pickets aboard the *Albemarle* spotted Cushing's boat and sounded the alarm. A rebel voice cried out, "Who's there? Who's there?" and got no response. Cushing and his men remained steadfast until abreast of the *Albemarle*. Cushing then answered the rebel shout, "What boat is that?" with, "We'll soon let you know!"

Once about ten yards away, Cushing tugged on the lanyard to his howitzer. A double dose of shots fired onto the hull of the ironclad and ric-ocheted into a crowd of scurrying rebels on the shore. Right after the shots, Cushing's launch hit the *Albemarle* and came to a grinding halt. The torpedo could now be put into position. But so could an eight-inch rebel cannon. Only ten feet away at this point, Cushing and his men heard every order being given by the rebel skipper aboard the *Albemarle*. In about twenty seconds, the cannon pointed directly at Cushing's head would fire. With complete disregard for his personal safety, Cushing carefully maneuvered the torpedo into place. As this was happening, one of the many rebel bullets fired at Cushing connected with the collar of his coat, and the cannon fired just missing Cushing's head, neither one causing him to lose his focus. The rebel captain then yelled, "Surrender!" only to have Cushing boldly reply, "Never! I'll be damned first!" Cushing was then shot in the hand as he detonated the torpedo. With the loud explosion that followed, Cushing yelled, "Men, save yourselves!" He then ripped off his sword belt, jacket, and shoes and jumped into the frigid water.

A strong swimmer, Cushing evaded the rebel patrol boats for the ninety minutes that it took him to get to an isolated part of the shore. Rebel soldiers passed within feet of where he lay without seeing him in the mud. Carefully avoiding the patrols, he eventually found a fishing boat along the shore. He paddled continuously for ten hours to the Union blockade ships where he was picked up by a Union Navy ship and given medical attention. Of the fourteen men who accompanied Cushing on this mission, two drowned, eleven were captured, and one escaped. Without the *Albemarle*, the Confederate Navy could no longer defend Plymouth, North Carolina. The Union forces retook the city within a week and once again controlled the Albemarle Sound.

With the success of his attack on the *Albemarle* and his unlikely return to Union lines, Cushing instantly became a national hero. Rear Admiral David Dixon Porter had a statement read to the officers and men of his fleet, stating that "Lt. William B. Cushing [had] displayed a heroic enterprise seldom equaled and never excelled. . . . The gallant exploits of Lt. Cushing previous to this affair [formed] a bright page in the history of the war, but they [were] all eclipsed by the destruction of the *Albemarle*." For the physical courage he demonstrated in the sinking of the *Albemarle*, President Abraham Lincoln recommended Cushing for a Vote of Thanks, which Congress granted on 20 December 20.[3]

In the ensuing years, he received several more ship commands and was promoted to commander on 31 January 1872, becoming the youngest commander in the U.S. Navy. He suffered from recurring back and hip pain throughout the war, and his health continued to plague him after it ended. He caught pneumonia frequently, which aggravated his chronic hip and back ailments. His condition had deteriorated badly enough to cause him to take a winter off in Fredonia, New York. In April 1874, after several successful overseas deployments, he returned home with constant back and hip pain. The U.S. Navy assigned him to the Washington Navy Yard as the executive officer, where it was hoped he could recover his health. He served at the Navy Yard until his pain finally drove him from work and into the hospital, where morphine was able to dull but not kill his pain. He died in a government hospital on 17 December 1874 at the age of thirty-two.[4]

While active, William Cushing loved the challenge and thrill of combat. Though some considered him reckless, he was no fool—his missions were well planned and remarkably successful. He was ahead of his time in creatively employing naval power against an enemy's infrastructure; he initiated riverine operations, punitive operations, reconnaissance missions, and harassment and interdiction operations; he conducted small unit amphibious raids well behind enemy lines. While he accepted the need for authority, he had difficulty following those he did not respect. His personal pride and his impatience with officers and leaders who did not share his readiness to take daring action often got him into trouble. But he persisted, and with the help of leaders such as Rear Admiral Lee and Secretary Welles, who recognized the value of

Naval Historical Center

his energy and fighting spirit and were willing to overlook his indiscretions and occasional poor judgment in garrison, he was able to overcome his shortcomings and to have a great impact on the Union Navy and the war.

Notes

1. Cushing and Lieutenant Flusser had a relationship of mutual respect while the two were at the academy.
2. Lieutenant Commander Flusser was killed in the battle.
3. This was a higher tribute than the Medal of Honor at that time.
4. He died while reciting the Lord's Prayer with his wife.

Suggested Reading

Schneller, Robert J., Jr. *Cushing: Civil War SEAL.* Washington, D.C.: Brassey's, 2004.

Van Dorn, Charles. *Lincoln's Commando: The Biography of Cdr. William B. Cushing.* Annapolis, Md.: Naval Institute Press, 1995.

About the Authors

Captain Robert Schoultz, a Navy SEAL, is the Director, Officer Development, at the U.S. Naval Academy. Midshipman First Class Nicholas Pinkston, rugby player and midshipman Battalion Commander, has service selected SEALs.

10

Stephen B. Luce
Scholarship

Dr. John B. Hattendorf

NWC Museum

For his generation of American naval officers, Stephen Bleeker Luce was the U.S. Navy's most capable seaman and its leading figure in professional education and training. His achievements in the second half of the nineteenth century were innovative ones, a number of which have endured and adapted for the twenty-first century. Three destroyers have been named for Luce (DD-99, DD-522, and DLG-7), and his name is memorialized in buildings at the U.S. Naval Academy, the Naval War College, and the State University of New York Maritime College at Fort Schuyler. In addition, a small park is named for him in Newport, Rhode Island.

Luce was born in Albany, New York, on 25 March 1827. President Martin van Buren appointed Luce as a midshipman in 1841. Luce reported to a series of ships over the next seven years, serving in the Mediterranean, South America, and the Far East. In 1848, Luce was ordered to the three-year-old Naval Academy at Annapolis for a year-and-a-half course of study. At Annapolis, he was falsely implicated in a disturbance and reduced in seniority by seventy-two places. This injustice slowed his early career and was not rectified until 1862, despite the fact that he had passed all his examinations at the top of his class. Leaving the academy as a passed midshipman, Luce returned to sea duty in the eastern Pacific and then served on special duty in Washington, D.C., calculating the results of astronomical observations to determine solar parallax. In 1853, he served briefly with the Home Squadron at Pensacola in a steamer. He then received orders to the U.S. Coast Survey for duty along the North and South Carolina coast as well as in the James and Savannah Rivers.

Promoted to lieutenant in September 1855, Luce served in the Home Squadron in the West Indies and off the coast of Central America. In May 1860, Luce returned to Annapolis, where he took up his first assignment as an instructor in seamanship and gunnery. This shore duty also afforded him his first opportunity to write for publication. He revised a short gunnery manual: *Instruction for Naval Light Artillery, Afloat and Ashore.* Upon completing that work in February 1861, Luce began to compile a textbook on seamanship for the academy, drawing from various previously published materials. In May 1861, Luce left this project incomplete when the Navy Department ordered him to report to the screw frigate USS *Wabash*, flagship of the Atlantic Blockading Squadron. In this period, Luce's ship saw much action and participated in both the attack at Hatteras Inlet and the Battle of Port Royal, South Carolina.

In January 1862, Luce returned to the staff of the Naval Academy, now relocated for the duration of the war to Newport, Rhode Island. There, he took up work on his unfinished seamanship textbook and quickly published the first of the nine editions that would appear over the next forty years. It became the standard manual until superseded by *Knight's Modern Seamanship* in 1901. In the summer of 1863, Luce took his first command, the academy practice ship *Macedonian*, to Europe. On his return Luce submitted a report on European naval training, later using this information in a series of articles in the *Army and Navy Journal* recommending an innovative training system for the U.S. Navy.

On his return, Luce took command of the monitor USS *Nantucket* of the North Atlantic Blockading Squadron, then commanded USS *Sonoma* and USS *Pontiac* before returning to the Naval Academy in Annapolis, where he became commandant of midshipmen. After three years, he took command of USS *Mohongo* on the Pacific Station for ten months in 1868, followed by USS *Juniata* on the Mediterranean Station from 1869 to 1872. During this assignment in European waters, Luce was ordered to Heligoland to observe French blockade operations during the Franco-Prussian War. While visiting London on this deployment, he made his first contact with Professor John Knox Laughton of the Royal Navy, who was just beginning his pioneering work in the field of naval history.

In 1872, while assigned to the Boston Navy Yard, Luce became increasingly interested in naval training. A year later, he lectured to the newly established U.S. Naval Institute on "The Manning of the Navy and the Mercantile Marine." This lecture became the first article in the first issue of what would become the Naval Institute's *Proceedings*. The New York City Board of Education consulted Luce on the establishment of a nautical school, and Luce helped to draft a congressional bill that authorized the U.S. Navy to loan vessels for use as state training ships. In late 1874, he supervised the outfitting of the sloop-of-war *St. Mary's* for the New York State Maritime School, the predecessor of the State University of New York Maritime College at Fort Schuyler. For use by this school and others that followed it, Luce prepared a textbook, *The Young Seaman's Manual.*

In November 1875, Luce received command of USS *Hartford*, flagship of the North Atlantic Station. Then in August 1877, he served for a brief period as inspector of training ships before taking command of the training ship USS *Minnesota*. For this assignment, Luce initiated a system of annual awards, medals, and prizes for proficiency in training. In April 1881, he was promoted to commodore and appointed commander of the Naval Training Squadron. After successfully helping to secure for the U.S. Navy the permanent acquisition of Coaster's Harbor Island in Narragansett Bay, Rhode Island, Luce recommended to Secretary of the Navy William Chandler that he establish a school for the education of naval officers in professional subjects: diplomacy, strategy, tactics, international law, and logistics. As a result of Luce's initiative, Chandler approved establishment of the Naval War College on 6 October 1884.

The college's first course opened a year later for a month-long series of lectures in September 1885. Luce recruited Army Lieutenant Tasker Bliss, a future army chief of staff, and international law specialist Professor James Soley as the college's first faculty members. Captain Alfred Thayer Mahan took the first year to research lectures that linked naval history to international affairs. Repeated and developed over the next few years with Luce's encouragement, Mahan published them in 1890 as *The Influence of Sea Power Upon History, 1660–1783*. At the same time, Luce engaged Lieutenant William McCarty Little to develop innovative ideas on naval war gaming at the college.

In June 1886, Luce left the Naval War College to resume command of the North Atlantic Squadron, the U.S. Navy's most senior flag assignment afloat. In September 1888, he dramatically demonstrated the usefulness of the intercoastal waterway system by taking his flagship's Herreshoff steam launch *Vixen* from New York to Norfolk. While the senior active duty flag officer, Luce was also the president of the Naval Institute from 1887 to 1889.

He retired from active duty on 1 February 1889 and settled at Newport, Rhode Island, where he remained active in the life of the Naval War College, frequently lecturing and writing.

Naval Historical Center, courtesy of Chaplain C. M. Drury

In 1892, he served as commissioner general of the U.S. Commission for the Columbian Historical Exposition at Madrid, Spain. In 1901, the Navy Department ordered him to return to active duty at the Naval War College, where he remained a member of the staff until 1910. During this period, President Theodore Roosevelt appointed him to the commission headed by Secretary of the Navy Dwight Moody to consider how to reorganize the Navy Department in a way that best reflected its military character.

On 28 July 1917, Luce died at his home in Newport at the age of ninety. Both on active duty and in retirement, Stephen B. Luce was the foremost leader and catalyst for the development of professional education and training in the U.S. Navy from the 1860s to about 1910, during a period of general innovation, reform, and revitalization.

Suggested Reading

Gleaves, Albert. *The Life and Letters of Stephen B. Luce.* New York: Putnam, 1925.

Hattendorf, John B. *Naval History and Maritime Strategy: Collected Essays*, pp. 17–28. Malabar, Fla.: Robert Krieger, 2000.

Hattendorf, John B., B. Mitchell Simpson III, and John R. Wadleigh. *Sailors and Scholars: The Centennial History of the Naval War College*, chapters 1–4. Newport, R.I.: Naval War College Press, 1984.

Hayes, John D., and John B. Hattendorf, eds. *The Writings of Stephen B. Luce.* Newport, R.I.: Naval War College Press, 1975.

Nordhoff, Charles. *Man of War Life: A Boy's Experience in the United States Navy, During a Voyage Around the World in a Ship-of-the-Line.* With an introduction and notes by John B. Hattendorf. Annapolis, Md.: Naval Institute Press, 1985.

About the Author

John B. Hattendorf is the Ernest J. King Professor of Maritime History and chairman of the Maritime History Department at the U.S. Naval War College. He is the author of many books and articles on naval history, including being coauthor of *Sailors and Scholars: The Centennial History of the United States Naval War College* and *America and the Sea: A Maritime History*. A former naval officer, he holds degrees in history from Kenyon College, Brown University, and the University of Oxford.

11

Theodorus Bailey Myers Mason
Commitment

Ensign Christian M. Weber

In most history books, even those on American naval history, Lieutenant Commander Theodorus B. M. Mason appears, if at all, in little more than a footnote. Despite the paucity of written material on Mason, his leadership was crucial in the shaping of American naval power, and his influence is still widely felt today at the Naval War College, the U.S. Naval Academy, and throughout the naval intelligence community. Perhaps more than any other officer of his day, Mason exemplified that at the core of every great U.S. Navy officer is the dedication to mastery of the discipline of naval science. His particular commitment to naval science brought about a renaissance in American naval thought and resulted in the exploration of new strategies and theories by subsequent generations of naval leaders.

The years following the close of the Civil War saw the rise of a great debate within Congress and the naval community over the future role of the U.S. Navy. Massive cuts in appropriations reduced the size of the U.S. Navy by over 90 percent as isolationists in Congress focused upon the reconstruction of the South and the westward expansion of the country. The nation's maritime strategy, as it was during the Civil War, was relegated to little more than coastal defense and commerce raiding.

Like his contemporaries Captain Alfred Thayer Mahan and Commodore Stephen B. Luce, Mason believed prevailing American naval doctrine was obsolete in an increasingly sophisticated and dangerous world. He saw the need to not only build more capital ships and maintain a powerful peacetime U.S. Navy, but also to aggressively gather information on the technology and tactics of other prominent navies.

He was an ardent believer that U.S. Navy officers needed to be more than just great seaman and strategists; they needed to embrace the science of naval warfare in its totality. To Mason, being a naval officer meant being an astute observer of not just naval warfare, but also the scientific and technical subjects that were inherently relevant to the maritime service.

His early naval career was one of distinction. Shortly after graduating from the U.S. Naval Academy in 1868, Mason received the Order of the Rose from the emperor of Brazil in recognition of his bravery while serving aboard the USS *Guerriere* for rescuing two crewmen from the shark-infested waters of the harbor of Rio de Janeiro.[1]

In addition to several sea tours in Europe and South America, Mason went on to work in the Hydrographic Office, teach at the U.S. Naval Academy, serve as an aide to the Secretary of the Navy, and later serve as a special aide to President Ulysses S. Grant. In February 1873, he volunteered to join the U.S. expeditionary forces in the Columbian state of Panama to protect American interests.[2] In December 1873, Mason was awarded the silver naval medal from the King of Italy for saving the Italian bark *Detaide*, laden with gunpowder and railroad supplies, from fire in the harbor of Callao, Peru.

Mason's initiative and dogged determination to demonstrate the value and necessity of information on foreign advances in naval science was what left a lasting imprint upon the American naval community. Advocates of a strong U.S. Navy had a major obstacle in bringing their argument to Congress. Reports from various overseas observers accumulated in the various U.S. Navy bureaus with little or no coordination among the bureaus. This prevented unanimity of opinion among bureau chiefs as to which developments in Europe were important to the future needs of the U.S. Navy and conflicting views and theories on specifications for new ships.

On his own initiative, Mason took an extended leave of absence in November 1878 to travel Europe to gather and compile information on the latest technological advances in naval warfare. An experienced naval observer, Mason was able to accumulate a wealth of information on the widespread naval development in Europe.

Upon his return, Mason returned to the U.S. Naval Academy as an ordnance instructor and began discretely advancing his views among select naval strategists on the need to assign naval attachés to embassies and legations for the purpose of collecting information on advances in naval science abroad. He also advocated that a special section be created in the Secretary of the Navy's office for the purpose of converting the information (including the translation of foreign manuscripts) into intelligence and preparing intelligence products in support of known or anticipated dissemination needs.

Mason's ideas greatly impressed Secretary of the Navy William H. Hunt, who issued General Order No. 292 on 23 March 1882. Order 292 established the Office of Naval Intelligence (ONI); on 15 June 1882, Hunt appointed Mason as the chief intelligence officer.

The new office was almost immediately beset with seemingly insurmountable challenges. As the United States began to move definitively in the direction of rebuilding the U.S. Navy, the need for intelligence to guide the effort was extensive. The demand on ONI's limited resources was further exacerbated by the Navy bureau's unwillingness to provide access to their foreign information, and what data they did provide the office was a mass of uncorrelated facts. Moreover, because ONI was created by general order and not congressional mandate, it was not eligible to receive direct funding. Without congressional funding, ONI could not employ civilian clerks or linguists. Not until fiscal year 1900 would Congress pass an appropriations bill with funding specifically allocated to ONI.

Mason, however, realized ONI's potential integral role in the reconstruction of the U.S. Navy and was unbowed by the adversity facing his fledgling office. He located his staff—three officers temporarily assigned to the Bureau of Navigation on special duty—in whatever office space was vacant at the state, U.S. Navy, and war departments and borrowed clerks, as needed and as available, from other offices.

Mason immediately initiated the creation of an intelligence collection capability specifically targeted to meet the needs of his primary customers, the Secretary of the Navy and the Navy bureaus. Naval attachés were dispatched abroad to begin systematic collection of technical information concerning foreign governments and their naval advances.

Stateside, Mason directed his staff to translate and process the wealth of data already available in foreign books and publications in the stacks of the Navy Department Library. Mason was an accomplished linguist, but his staff would often have to translate foreign documents word for word using foreign language dictionaries.

To further enhance the collection and processing capabilities of the office, Mason organized ONI along functional rather than geographic lines in order to facilitate the correlation of intelligence material according to its usefulness to the Secretary of the Navy and the Navy bureaus. He diligently studied the filing systems used by the various government departments to incorporate the practices most suitable to his purpose and indexed the subjects parallel to the intelligence requirements of each bureau. Desks were set up by subject according to the interests of each bureau and researchers at each desk maintained files on each subject.

In order to meet the vast intelligence needs of the Navy bureaus with limited manpower, Mason enlisted the resources of the Navy Department Library and the Naval War College to produce intelligence products. The first publication produced by ONI was called *Information from Abroad* (part of the four-volume Naval Warfare Publication Series), which covered naval advances by French, British, and South American navies.

As Mason's reports of foreign advances in technology and naval science began to circulate amongst the Navy bureaus, ONI's problems gradually subsided as the bureaus found the work of ONI of value to their planning and design work. Moreover, the quality and value of ONI products provided convincing justification to Congress for the need for appropriations for the reconstruction and expansion of the U.S. Navy.

Mason continued to ardently advocate that ONI, in partnership with the U.S. Naval Institute and Naval War College, should be used as a conduit to stimulate an interest in naval science within the naval officer corps. Already an active participant in the U.S. Naval Institute and a contributor to its periodical *Proceedings*, Mason believed that ONI's products would be of value and interest to all naval officers in their professional advancement and duties. Under his direction, ONI produced the unclassified General Information Series, including the highly regarded and much-used annual *Notes on Naval Progress*, which provided practical information on the fleets of the major powers for the purpose of discussion and debate.

Today, few physical reminders of Lieutenant Commander T. B. M. Mason remain. Among them is a memorial stained glass window in the U.S. Naval Academy chapel[3] and the sword he wore during his thirty years of active service, which is on display at the U.S. Naval Academy Museum in Annapolis, Maryland. But the effect of Mason's reform, initiative, and guidance on the naval community and in advance of naval science cannot be overstated. Under Mason's leadership, what began as a small office of borrowed officers grew to assume the role of war planning for the U.S. Navy and paved the way for American victories in every subsequent naval conflict.

Notes

1. He was allowed to accept only by a special act of Congress.
2. He returned again in 1885 to command a battery of light artillery on the Isthmus of Panama.
3. The window was designed by Frederick Wilson and manufactured by Louis Comfort Tiffany.

Suggested Reading

Hammersley, Lewis Randolph. *The Records of Living Officers*. Philadelphia, Pa.: L. R. Hammersley, 1894.

Office of Naval Intelligence. "About ONI: Our History." http://www.nmic.navy.mil/history.htm/

Packard, Wyman. *A Century of Naval Intelligence.* Washington, D.C.: Naval Historical Center, 1996.

About the Author

Ensign Christian M. Weber is pursuing a master's degree in unconventional warfare at American Military University.

12

George Dewey
Foresight

Mark L. Hayes

Library of Congress

On the night of 30 April 1898, the U.S. Asiatic Squadron successfully passed the underwater mines and the modern Spanish guns guarding the entrance to Manila Bay. The American commander, Commodore George Dewey, knew he was taking a calculated risk, but it was one based on intelligence gathered specifically for this mission. The following morning, Dewey engaged and defeated the Spanish squadron commanded by Rear Admiral Patricio Montojo y Pasaron. American gunfire destroyed the enemy squadron, which suffered 371 casualties; the United States suffered nine wounded. When official word on the magnitude of the U.S. Navy's victory reached the United States nearly a week later, the American public heaped enthusiastic praise on Dewey, and the country erupted in wild celebration. This previously unknown naval officer soon became the most widely recognized name in America.

Although it is popular to view naval history in terms of extraordinary figures, heroic actions, and revolutionary change, Dewey won the Battle of Manila Bay because of the planning and administrative decisions he initiated during the months prior to engaging the enemy. These actions demonstrated his foresightedness, a characteristic that all naval officers should strive to develop throughout their careers.

George Dewey was born on the day after Christmas in 1837 in Montpelier, Vermont. He lost his mother to tuberculosis when he was only five years old. The tragedy drew him close to his father, whom Dewey remembered with great respect and affection. He credited his father with his own "vigorous constitution and active temperament."

Dewey received an appointment to the relatively new Naval Academy in 1854, and four years later he graduated fifth out of a class of fifteen. He joined the new steam frigate USS *Wabash* just before she embarked on a seventeen-month cruise as flagship of the Mediterranean Squadron. Dewey took and passed his lieutenant's examination early in 1861. During the American Civil War, he served as executive officer on six ships, most of which were in the squadron of David Glasgow Farragut, perhaps the most skilled and influential officer in the U.S. Navy. "Valuable as the training at Annapolis was," wrote Dewey, "it was poor schooling beside that of serving under Farragut in time of war."

For the next three decades, service as an officer in the downsized and technologically stagnant U.S. Navy was often a frustrating experience. Dewey chose to labor in obscurity, perfecting his own organizational skills and contributing to the greater efficiency of the service. Beginning in 1889, he was in charge of three successive administrative offices, during which time he became familiar with the technology of the "New Steel Navy" and earned a reputation as a friend of innovation.

In the fall of 1897, Dewey approached what he thought was the end of his naval career. With the assistance of Assistant Secretary of the Navy Theodore Roosevelt, he obtained his last command at sea, the Asiatic Squadron in the Western Pacific. Dewey prepared for his new command by studying all the charts and descriptions of the Philippine Islands that he could lay his hands on and by reading selected books during his journey across the continent and the Pacific.

At the time, war with Spain seemed remote to most Americans, but Dewey took seriously his duty to prepare his squadron for any crises. While examining records in Washington, he found that his ships were far below their allowance of ammunition. The commodore cut through the red tape holding up new shipments and ordered USS *Concord*, then fitting out at San Francisco, to transport as much ammunition as she could carry. He arranged for the old sloop USS *Mohican* to carry more to Honolulu where it would be transferred to the cruiser USS *Baltimore*, sent to reinforce Dewey the following March.

The commodore knew that the latest Navy Department war plan called for the U.S. Asiatic Squadron to tie down or divert Spanish ships in the Philippines and give the United States a stronger bargaining position at the peace settlement. As tensions heated up between Spain and the United States, Dewey decided to concentrate his squadron only six hundred miles from Manila at British-controlled Hong Kong.

In 1898, there were essentially three sources of fuel for naval squadrons: coaling stations at friendly bases, neutral ports (which were unreliable sources), and other ships (usually colliers). From Hong Kong, the nearest American base was seven thousand miles away. Most major warships of the U.S. fleet had an operational range in the neighborhood of four thousand nautical miles, or just over two weeks of continuous steaming at ten knots. Naturally, ships' commanding officers were reluctant to allow their bunkers to get anywhere near empty, and they availed themselves of nearly every opportunity to add to their supply of coal.

The war appeared imminent following the destruction of USS *Maine* in Havana harbor on 15 February. Dewey needed a vessel to act as a collier along with plenty of extra coal, and he needed to purchase it before war was declared. The commodore found a suitable vessel in the British steamer *Nanshan*, and he contracted to bring five thousand tons of coal to the American squadron. The Navy Department approved Dewey's request to purchase the steamer. The department also approved the commodore's request to purchase the supply ship *Zafiro*, and the two were registered as American merchant steamers. But his efforts did not end there. Taking advantage of China's weak national government at the time, Dewey arranged through his paymaster to get coal and provisions from a Chinese source at an isolated locality. Thinking ahead, Dewey cabled the Navy Department on 11 March to make certain that preparations to transport additional coal and ammunition from the United States were moving forward.

During the weeks at Hong Kong prior to the outbreak of war, Dewey had his vessels overhauled and docked and kept full of coal and provisions. He ensured that his ships' machinery was in prime condition and that the crews were thoroughly drilled. He also oversaw plans to remove woodwork and other material that could easily catch fire in battle.

Dewey kept in contact with the American consul at Manila, Oscar Williams, by telegraph, asking him for information on Spanish ordnance and preparations. When forced to leave Hong Kong on 23 April by the outbreak of war, the commodore moved his ships thirty miles up the coast, partly to wait for Williams to provide him with the latest intelligence before Dewey set a course for the Philippines. From the information Williams supplied, Dewey realized that the Spanish were in some confusion. After consulting with his officers, Dewey judged that any mines at the entrance to Manila Bay would probably not have been laid with the care necessary to make them effective in the deep waters of the channel. The dire warnings regarding mines reminded Dewey of the bluffs made by the Egyptian rebels in 1882,

who claimed to have mined the Suez Canal in an effort to prevent passage. An Italian torpedo expert called their bluff because he believed the mines to be ineffective, considering the length of time they had been in the warm salt water. The Italians then safely transited the canal.

Dewey's historic victory on 1 May 1898 was the result of foresightedness and months of hard work. He gathered all available information and analyzed it in consultations with others. In short, he practiced the skills taught to every naval officer and exercised them well. Dewey understood these virtues when he summarized the reason for his victory: "It was the ceaseless routine of hard work and preparation in time of peace that won Manila. . . . Valor there must be, but it is a secondary factor in comparison with strength of material and efficiency of administration."

Suggested Reading

Barrett, John. *Admiral George Dewey: A Sketch of the Man.* New York: Harper and Brothers, 1899.

Dewey, George. *The Autobiography of George Dewey.* Classics of Naval Literature. Annapolis, Md.: Naval Institute Press, 1987. First published in 1913 in New York.

Spector, Ronald. *Admiral of the New Empire: The Life and Career of George Dewey.* Baton Rouge: Louisiana State University Press, 1974.

Williams, Vernon L. "George Dewey." In *Admirals of the New Steel Navy: Makers of the American Naval Tradition, 1880–1930*, edited by James C. Bradford. Annapolis, Md.: Naval Institute Press, 1990.

About the Author

Mark L. Hayes served in the 1980s as an officer in the U.S. Navy and is now a historian in the Early History Branch at the Naval Historical Center, Washington, D.C. He is an assistant editor of *Naval Documents of the American Revolution* and is coauthor of *The Spanish-American*

U.S. Naval Institute Photo Archive

War: Historical Overview and Select Bibliography and *Sea Raiders of the American Revolution: The Continental Navy in European Waters.* Mr. Hayes has published two essays on Civil War naval actions: "The Battle of Port Royal Sound" in *Forgotten History: Hilton Head Island during the Civil War* and "The Battle of New Orleans" in *Great American Naval Battles,* edited by Jack Sweetman.

13

Theodore Roosevelt
Knowledge

Commander Henry J. Hendrix

U.S. Naval Institute Photo Archive

Henry Adams, the grandson and great-grandson of American presidents, once described Theodore Roosevelt as a creature of "pure act," but, in retrospect, this characterization seems more like snobbish petulance from a man who considered the White House somewhat as a family inheritance than an accurate assessment of Roosevelt's life. Although the native New Yorker did possess and expend prodigious amounts of energy in his daily activities, this description tends to patronize and diminish one of the great intellects to occupy the presidency. Roosevelt's incessant acquisition and use of knowledge set his life apart from others.

Theodore Roosevelt's genius could not be doubted. His memory was photographic; he read in six languages (at a pace of a book a day) and spoke four. His expertise in the natural sciences led officials of the Smithsonian to consult him regularly on North American birds and mammals. His inexhaustible stores of energy and tremendous powers of concentration allowed him to master whatever interested him, including the U.S. Navy and the application of sea power.

Roosevelt had long been fascinated by stories of naval combat. His maternal uncles fought in the Civil War (albeit, from his perspective, on the wrong side), and the young Roosevelt admired them. During his college years, a new book published in Great Britain that slighted the role of the American Navy in the War of 1812 enraged Roosevelt. Forsaking his opportunity to graduate from Harvard with honors, Roosevelt took up the unauthorized topic of the naval War of 1812, and over the next three years, he mastered the technicalities of early nineteenth-century sailing ships and sea combat. A friend later recounted arriving at Roosevelt's home for a planned evening on the town only to find Theodore hovering over a collection of deck logs, diagrams, and ship models; he was lost in the act of recreating long past battles. His final product, *The Naval War of 1812*, remains the classic treatment of the subject. Shortly after its appearance, Rear Admiral Stephen B. Luce selected it as a textbook for his newly formed Naval War College and invited the young author to address its students.

Over the ensuing years, Theodore Roosevelt continued to ponder and write about the U.S. Navy, becoming one of the nation's recognized proponents of naval power. He formed close associations with Captain Alfred T. Mahan and Senator Henry Cabot Lodge of Massachusetts. When Mahan published his seminal book, *The Influence of Sea Power Upon History*, Roosevelt devoured it in one night and then pronounced it an instant classic in the pages of the *Atlantic Monthly*. Recognizing Roosevelt's prominence in naval matters, Mahan had commissioned him to review the book.

Lodge's influence led Theodore Roosevelt to his big opportunity. In 1896, the Republican William McKinley of Ohio was elected to the presidency. Lodge lobbied the new president successfully to appoint Roosevelt to the position of Assistant Secretary of the Navy. At the time, the position was one of the most influential foreign policy positions in Washington.

Ensconced in his new office in the Executive Office Building at the age of thirty-five, Roosevelt began learning the intricacies of his new appointment. Over the next two years, he systematically applied himself to the task of mastering the numerous administrative, logistical, and technical challenges facing the rapidly modernizing U.S. Navy. He personally chaired numerous committees, considering, among other things, the composition and thickness of naval armor, the promotion system of officers and enlisted men, and new approaches to gun manufacturing. Roosevelt reviewed and modified summer war games planned for the fleet and then went to sea to watch them unfold. By the time he resigned his post in the Navy Department to don the uniform of a Rough Rider in the Spanish-American War, Roosevelt's quest for knowledge had left him a master of sea power.

Returning from Cuba as a national hero after the Spanish-American War, Roosevelt's next step took him to the governor's mansion in Albany, New York. Then in 1901, he assumed the vice presidency. Along the way, Roosevelt applied his knowledge of the U.S. Navy and a traditional balance of power politics and American strategic interests to create a strategic construct that later became know as "The Large Policy." This policy called for the rapid enlargement of the U.S. Navy and the establishment of virtual U.S. hegemony in the Western Hemisphere. When the tragic assassination of McKinley elevated Theodore Roosevelt to the White House, he arrived as one of the most knowledgeable commanders in chief to occupy the office.

Particularly as the chief executive, his quest for knowledge continued. He still read a book a day, even as he wrote two books and over twenty-six thousand pages of correspondence while in office. Roosevelt also maintained his ties to the U.S. Navy; his interests in the technical aspects of naval warfare continued throughout his presidency. He championed the all-big-gun battleship two years before the appearance of Britain's HMS *Dreadnought*. He mentored and protected Commander William S. Simms in his drive to revolutionize American naval gunnery techniques. He was the first president to go down in a submarine and, upon surfacing, signed an order authorizing hazardous duty pay for submariners. He also clearly saw the potential of aviation; he funded additional research and became the first president to fly in an airplane.

Roosevelt's mastery of the technical U.S. Navy became increasingly important as the fleet took its place at the center of his diplomacy. Due to his understanding of naval power, he formulated a sophisticated and nuanced foreign policy through the practical application of naval presence. In the case of Venezuela's default on loans to Britain and Germany in the winter of 1902–3, Roosevelt committed the entire Atlantic Fleet under the command of Admiral George Dewey to successfully convince the two imperial powers of his commitment to upholding the Monroe

U.S. Naval Institute Photo Archive

Doctrine. In Panama, a year later, he introduced the force necessary to guarantee the success of the Panamanian revolution in order to gain the coveted canal. In 1904, Roosevelt selected the composition of the naval force dispatched to Morocco to peacefully gain the release of an American citizen who had been taken hostage. He also dispatched the Great White Fleet on its cruise around the world, formally announcing the United States' emergence as a great power. No president before or since was so involved in the day-to-day activities of the U.S. Navy.

Roosevelt left office in March of 1905, retiring to a life of hunting, exploring, and writing. His inexhaustible curiosity led him to Africa and the unexplored regions of South America. In 1909, he collected the Nobel Peace Prize that had been awarded to him for his role in negotiating the end of the Russo-Japanese War in 1905. Theodore Roosevelt died of heart failure in January 1919.

Suggested Reading

Beale, Howard K. *Theodore Roosevelt and the Rise of America to World Power.* Baltimore: Johns Hopkins University Press, 1956.

Morris, Edmund. *Theodore Rex.* New York: Random House, 2001.

Wimmel, Kenneth. *Theodore Roosevelt and the Great White Fleet.* Washington, D.C.: Brassey's, 1998.

About the Author

Commander Henry J. Hendrix is an associate of the Weatherhead Center for International Affairs at Harvard University and a naval flight officer who has screened for command. A two-time recipient of the Naval Historical Center's Samuel Eliot Morison Scholarship, he has a master's degree in national security affairs from the Naval Postgraduate School and is finishing a master's degree in history from Harvard. Commander Hendrix has authored numerous articles on various strategic and historical subjects. He currently serves on the executive board of the Theodore Roosevelt Association and on the board of directors of the U.S. Naval Institute.

14
Alfred Thayer Mahan
Professionalism

Dr. John B. Hattendorf

U.S. Naval Institute Photo Archive

Alfred Mahan is known throughout the world for his intellectual achievements and leadership in the area of naval history and naval strategy. His twenty books and 161 journal articles, along with other pamphlets and newspapers articles that he published during his writing career, laid the foundation for the modern approach to naval strategy at the end of the nineteenth century and in the opening years of the twentieth century. His work focused on the U.S. Navy's role in national grand strategy and on the art and science of naval command in war. Mahan's ideas influenced navies and naval policy around the world and, for a time, dominated naval thought. Four destroyers have been named for him (DD-102, DD-364, DLG-11, and DDG-72) and buildings at the U.S. Naval Academy and the Naval War College bear his name.

Born on 27 September 1840 at the U.S. Military Academy, West Point, Alfred was the eldest son of Professor Dennis Hart Mahan, who became the principal instructor in the art and science of warfare at the Military Academy. The boy was given the middle name of Thayer in honor of Brigadier General Sylvanus Thayer, "the father of West Point."

The influence of his family played a role in the boy's future development. His father initially hoped that Alfred would have a civilian career. Beginning in this direction, Mahan studied for two years at St. James School in Hagerstown, Maryland, and then spent a year at Columbia University in New York, where his uncle, Milo Mahan, was nearby as professor of ecclesiastical history at the General Theological Seminary. On his own initiative in 1856, young Mahan obtained the assistance of Secretary of War Jefferson Davis and President Charles King of Columbia to obtain an appointment to the Naval Academy through his local congressman. Entering the academy in 1856, Mahan graduated three years later in 1859, second in his class with high achievement in the practical aspects of seamanship and gunnery.

Mahan's early naval career was typical for a junior officer in his era. His first assignment was to the frigate USS *Congress* on the Brazil Station. Promoted to lieutenant, his next duty was in USS *Pocahontas* on the South Atlantic Blockading Squadron during the first phase of operations in the Civil War. In 1862–63, he was assigned to the Naval Academy, then temporarily located for the duration of the war in Newport, Rhode Island, as an instructor in seamanship and executive officer of the academy's practice ship, USS *Macedonian*. Mahan's department head and commanding officer onboard *Macedonian* in these dual assignments, Lieutenant Commander Stephen B. Luce, became critical to the development of his long-term career more than twenty years later.

In 1863–65, Mahan returned to combat assignments in USS *Seminole* on the West Gulf Blockading Squadron and on USS *James Adger* in the South Atlantic Blockading Squadron. Following the Civil War, he served on USS *Muscotta* to observe French operations off the Mexican coast. In 1866, he was assigned temporarily to ordnance duty at the Washington Navy Yard before becoming the executive officer of USS *Iroquois* bound for duty on the Asiatic Station. Remaining two years in the Far East, Mahan finished his tour in 1869 by taking temporary command of USS *Iroquois* and then of the gunboat USS *Aroostock*. When he returned home to West Point in May 1871, Mahan had served continuously at sea for twelve years, except for his brief eight months ashore in 1862–63, teaching seamanship to the midshipmen at Newport. After a brief period at the New York Navy Yard, Mahan was assigned to USS *Worcester* carrying relief supplies to France in 1871. Next, newly married and promoted to commander, he took command of the iron-hulled, side-wheel steamer USS *Wasp* in 1873–74, protecting American interests and carrying American diplomats on the South American coast and in the waters of the Rio de la Plata and the Uruguay River.

For the following nine years, he served ashore at the Boston Navy Yard, the Naval Academy, and the New York Navy Yard. While these years proved frustrating to Mahan's wish for a return to sea duty, they laid the foundation for his future writing career. While serving as head of the Ordnance Department at the Naval Academy, Mahan won third prize with honorable mention in the U.S. Naval Institute's 1878 Prize Essay competition on the subject, "Naval Education for Officers and Men." This essay was his first published piece of writing, and it appeared in the U.S. Naval Institute's *Proceedings*. This period at the academy allowed him to read widely in American, British, and French professional military journals and in military history. At this time, he was particularly influenced by reading the six volumes of Sir William Napier's *History of the War in the Peninsula and in the South of France: From the Year 1807 to the Year 1814*. In the summer of 1880, Mahan was transferred to the navigation department at the New York Navy Yard, and while there in 1882 Charles Scribner's Sons, the New York publishing house, commissioned Mahan to write the final volume of its narrative series on "The Navy in the Civil War," entitled *The Gulf and Inland Waters*. Already recognized as someone who was well read in history and having served in the Gulf of Mexico during the war, Mahan produced the manuscript in his off-duty hours within five months. Published in 1883, it was Mahan's first book.

In August 1883, Mahan received orders to command the screw sloop-of-war USS *Wachusett* on the Pacific coast of South America. Just a year later, Rear Admiral Stephen B. Luce wrote to Mahan, offering him the position of lecturer in naval history and tactics at the Naval War College, which would be established in October 1884. Luce outlined for Mahan a wide study that linked the history of naval operations to international affairs in a way that had never previously been done to produce a theory of naval strategy. In replying positively to the offer, Mahan thought of his father when he said, "I believe I have the capacity and some inherited aptitude," but admitted that he needed time and a good library to gather the wide historical knowledge required. It would take another year to be relieved of command and to report to the Naval War College as a newly promoted captain. Luce placed him on study leave in New York City to undertake the work of writing his series of lectures. Mahan returned to the college in August 1886, relieving Luce as president of the Naval War College.

Subsequently, Mahan served as president of the commission that selected the Bremerton Navy Yard site, served again as president of the Naval War College (1892–93), commanded the cruiser USS *Chicago* (1893–95), and returned to special duty at the Naval War College until he retired in 1896 after forty years of service. He was recalled to duty on the Naval War Board during the Spanish-American War in 1898 and promoted to rear admiral on the retired list in 1906, serving again on special duty at the Naval War College (1908–10 and 1911–12). He died in Washington, D.C., on 1 December 1914.

Two of Mahan's books, *The Influence of Sea Power Upon History, 1660–1783* (1890) and *The Influence of Sea Power Upon the French Revolution and Empire, 1793–1812* (1892), were the basis for

Naval Historical Center

his Naval War College lectures. A study of the War of 1812 and a biography of Nelson completed his sea power series. Another volume, *Naval Strategy* (1911), comprised a variety of other Naval War College lectures given over the years. Throughout his works, Mahan showed that the critical study of history should be the primary agent for advanced professional military education.

Suggested Reading

Hattendorf, John B., ed. *Mahan on Naval Strategy: Selections from the Writings of Rear Admiral Alfred Thayer Mahan*. Annapolis, Md.: Naval Institute Press, 1991.

Hattendorf, John B., and Lynn C. Hattendorf [Westney], comps. *A Bibliography of the Works of Alfred Thayer Mahan*. Newport, R.I.: Naval War College Press, 1986.

Seager, Robert, II. *Alfred Thayer Mahan: The Man and His Letters*. Annapolis, Md.: Naval Institute Press, 1977.

Seager, Robert, II, and Doris Maguire, eds. *The Letters and Papers of Alfred Thayer Mahan*. Annapolis, Md.: Naval Institute Press, 1977.

Sumida, Jon Tetsuro. *Inventing Grand Strategy and Teaching Command: The Classic Works of Alfred Thayer Mahan Reconsidered*. Washington, D.C.: Woodrow Wilson Center Press; Baltimore, Md.: Johns Hopkins University Press, 1997.

Turk, Richard W. *The Ambiguous Relationship: Theodore Roosevelt and Alfred Thayer Mahan*. Contributions in Military Studies, No. 63. New York: Greenwood, 1987.

About the Author

John B. Hattendorf is the Ernest J. King Professor of Maritime History and chairman of the Maritime History Department at the U.S. Naval War College. He is the author of many books and articles on naval history, including being coauthor of *Sailors and Scholars: The Centennial History of the United States Naval War College* and *America and the Sea: A Maritime History*. A former naval officer, he holds degrees in history from Kenyon College, Brown University, and the University of Oxford.

15

John A. Lejeune
Pedagogy

Midshipman First Class
William J. Moran

Major John Hatala

Defense Department Photo (Marine Corps)

The eleven Marine Corps leadership principles currently taught to all Marines were heavily influenced by John A. Lejeune. One of those principles is, "set the example," a favorite theme of Lejeune's teachings. Through numerous speeches, letters, and ultimately the Marine Corps Manual of 1921, Lejeune expressed his theory of leadership that was intended to serve as the guideline for every officer. Lejeune emphasized that the behavior of the Corps' officers set the standards for the entire Marine Corps: "You should never forget the power of example. The young men serving as enlisted men take their cue from you. If you conduct yourselves at all times as officers and gentlemen should conduct themselves, the moral tone of the whole Corps will be raised, its reputation, which is most precious to all of us, will be enhanced, and the esteem and affection in which the Corps is held by the American people will be increased."

Lieutenant General John Archer Lejeune, often described as "the greatest of all Leathernecks," served more than forty years in the U.S. Marine Corps, including two terms as the thirteenth Commandant of the Marine Corps. Born in Louisiana in 1867, Lejeune attended Louisiana State University prior to his appointment to the U.S. Naval Academy, from which he graduated in 1888. After serving two years as a midshipman aboard various naval vessels, he earned his commission as a second lieutenant in the U.S. Marine Corps. After service in the Spanish-American War, Panama, the Philippine Islands, Cuba, Mexico, and various assignments in the United States, Lejeune embarked on a most significant deployment to war-torn Europe during World War I.

Lejeune became the first Marine officer to command an army division when he assumed command of the 2nd Division of the American Expeditionary Force in Europe in 1918. The 2nd Division, which included the 4th Marine Brigade, gained widespread recognition for its decisive victories against the Germans during the Saint-Mihiel Offensive and the Champagne Offensive at Mont Blanc. Among the many honors bestowed upon him, Lejeune earned the Army and Navy Distinguished Service Medals, the French Legion of Honor, and the Croix de Guerre for his stalwart command of the 2nd Division during the campaigns that precipitated the German defeat.

Shortly after his return from the war, General Lejeune was appointed Commandant of the Marine Corps in 1920, where his vision was instrumental in the development of the modern Marine Corps. As Commandant, Lejeune emphasized the importance of education for officers, the need for increased numbers of Marines, and the expansion of the role of Marines as an expeditionary and amphibious force. In addition to his impressive service record and enhancement of the Marine Corps' future roles and missions, Lejeune's remarkable legacy is highlighted by his exceptional leadership. Lejeune imparted the principles of officer leadership through a twofold method: by exemplifying the ideal qualities of a leader himself and by relentlessly teaching officers how to be fit examples of leaders.

Lejeune's insight with regard to a Marine officer's personal accountability encompassed a total person, to include intellect, morals, conduct, appearance, and demeanor. While many of his remarks focused on military performance, Lejeune was keenly aware that officers should act responsibly in *every* environment. Additionally, Lejeune reminded officers that special trust and confidence is a privilege unique to the officer corps—a privilege that must be guarded, maintained, and polished by the superior example of that corps. In the Marine Corps Manual, Lejeune addressed the special trust and confidence, noting: "As a concomitant, commanders will impress upon all subordinate officers the fact that the presumption of integrity, good manners, sound judgment, and discretion, which is the basis for the special trust and confidence reposed in each officer, is jeopardized by the slightest transgression on the part of any member of the

officer corps." What is so powerful about those words is the mention of *presumed* character of officers. The basis for the presumption of good character was the outstanding efforts, sacrifices, and honor of officers throughout history.

Although the number of Marine officers is few relative to the overall strength of the Marine Corps, the influence of the officer is substantial. Lejeune taught officers that "the efficiency, the good name, and the *esprit* of the Corps are in [their] hands. [They] can make or mar it." Further, one of the implied duties of an officer is to ensure that every other officer knows and understands the responsibilities they each share. The trust of each and every officer is intertwined; a single person can discredit the others. Lejeune maintained that the preservation of special trust and confidence "is an obligation to the officer corps as a whole, and transcends the bonds of personal friendship."

Officers should not be hypocrites; they should never ask their subordinates to do something that they would not do themselves. Officers lead their subordinates primarily through their own personal example. This is not done solely to avoid hypocrisy, which will certainly alienate an officer from his assigned men and women, but leading by example contributes to a sense of teamwork hewn from the shared experiences of officers and their subordinates. Lejeune believed strongly that the periods of interpersonal interaction between officers and enlisted lay at the core of leadership. He specifically addressed how an officer should behave in establishing a positive leadership example for enlisted Marines: "Young Marines respond quickly and readily to the exhibition of qualities of leadership on the part of their officers. Each officer must endeavor by all means in his power to develop within himself those qualities of leadership, including industry, justice, self-control, unselfishness, honor, and courage, which will fit him to be a real leader of men and which will aid in establishing the relationship described [between officers and their enlisted]."

The relationship between officers and their enlisted subordinates involves caring, trust, and respect. Unlike most civilian work-related relationships, an officer is often entrusted with the very lives and physical well-being of the young men and women whom he commands. Lejeune recognized this unique relationship and offered ample guidance on how an officer could set the example in the treatment and caring of subordinates. Lejeune held that an officer should appreciate that young enlisted men and women "are in the formative period of their lives and officers owe it to them, to their parents, and to the Nation, that when discharged from the service they should be far better men [and women] physically, mentally, and morally than they were when they enlisted." Accordingly, an officer must be an unwavering moral compass, a role model able to demonstrate by personal example the highest standards of character.

Officers must be thoroughly cognizant of the destructive impact that an individual lapse in judgment has on all other officers. Negative perceptions can seriously undermine the presumed sound character earned by officers in the past. These negative perceptions are lasting and quite difficult to repair.

General Lejeune further instructed officers that training their enlisted men and women should resemble the teaching techniques of "teacher and scholar," or "father and son." To be sure, officers should never be arrogant and believe that they are better than their subordinates. Rather, they should recognize their duty to humbly serve the enlisted and care for them, through firm but fair leadership. Although in a position of authority, a father or teacher does not humiliate, brutalize, or downplay the worth of

Defense Department Photo (Marine Corps)

his child or student. Similarly, good officers place more importance on the well-being, success, and recognition of their subordinates than on their own.

The Commandant himself, while addressing his officers, spoke precisely and firmly, yet always kindly. In the clearest example of his humble leadership, General Lejeune expressed, "wishes for your success and happiness," in notes to his officers, and even signed letters with, "Your sincere friend." Lejeune was adamant in professing that officers should balance discipline and rigorous military training with patience and encouragement. He saw patience and encouragement as virtues that contribute to appropriate interpersonal relations among Marines and essentially demanded that officers set the example in this realm.

The principles of sound leadership that General John Lejeune professed are enduring and will certainly guide leaders for years to come. Leading by example is especially enduring, as it calls to the fore a wide range of characteristics that have a significant impact on an officer's ability to lead. These characteristics, as identified by Lejeune, include industry, justice, self-control, unselfishness, honor, and courage. Whether a recent graduate of the U.S. Naval Academy or a seasoned senior officer, the principle of setting the example should be the cornerstone of officership.

Suggested Reading

Bartlett, Merrill L. *Lejeune: A Marine's Life, 1867–1942*. Annapolis, Md.: Naval Institute Press, 1996.

Brown, Ronald J. *A Few Good Men: A History of the Fighting Fifth Marines*. New York: Random House Ballantine, 2001.

Lejeune, John A. *The Reminiscences of a Marine*. Philadelphia: Dorrance, 1930.

———. "Letters of John A. Lejeune," 1920–22. http://hqinet001.hqmc.usmc.mil/HD/Historical/speeches.htm/.

About the Authors

Midshipman First Class William J. Moran service selected Marine Corps. Major John Hatala, USMC, serves as a Company Officer at the U.S. Naval Academy.

16

Earl H. Ellis
Insight

Captain Jeffrey M. Harrington

Defense Department Photo (Marine Corps)

Victory smiles upon those who anticipate the changes in the character of war, not upon those who wait to adapt themselves after the changes occur.

Giulio Douhet, 1921

Military history is replete with testaments of praise and adulation for conventional military strategists and leaders whose contributions were bold, audacious, and successful—Rommel, Eisenhower, Patton, Nimitz, Montgomery, Halsey, and Puller are just a few that come to mind from the twentieth century. To be sure, each of these distinguished gentlemen is due every accolade penned in their honor.

Far fewer military thinkers have defied the conventional wisdom of the time. As a result, their importance was not recognized until decades later. These visionaries are less prominent and far fewer in number than well-known military leaders because of their eccentric personalities, unconventional methodology, and arrogant attitude toward the establishment. In fact, these same traits kept them from a reputation equal to their more conventional counterparts. Such visionaries were so fueled by an extreme passion, conviction, and commitment to their ideas and innovations that they were willing to sacrifice their reputations, livelihoods, and even their lives.

In the history of the U.S. Marine Corps, Lieutenant Colonel Earl H. "Pete" Ellis is perhaps one of the most prominent and mythical figures whose character can only be described as enigmatic and eccentric. Scholars now acknowledge him as one of the most visionary strategists in twentieth-century military history. Ellis's brilliance and vision were demonstrated through his prediction that the colonialism of the Empire of Japan after World War I would eventually lead to a conflict between the United States and Japan. More specifically, he indicated that the Japanese would be so bold as to launch a surprise attack and destroy the American Pacific Fleet, and he did this twenty-one years before it came to fruition.

In 1921, Lieutenant Colonel Ellis wrote "Advanced Base Operations in Micronesia," which later became known as War Plan Orange. This comprehensive document outlined a probable war with Japan, predicted the problems that troops would encounter, and recommended the seizure of a number of fleet bases that would require an assault across well-defended beaches during daylight. Lieutenant Colonel Ellis predicted with astonishing exactness the manpower, training, and equipment required to execute these operations, the crux of which were advanced base operations conducted by the Marine Corps. Lieutenant Colonel Ellis's ideas about amphibious operations were based primarily on his involvement in an operation involving the movement of a three-inch gun across the reef at Orote Point in Guam in 1915. While commanding a small detachment, Ellis proved that artillery could be moved from ship to shore. This was the genesis of successful amphibious operations.

His service on General John A. Lejeune's staff in France during World War I, where he was involved in planning, guiding, and assisting the execution of an operation on the Hindenburg Line along Mont Blanc Ridge, developed his operational expertise and vision. Following World War I, Lieutenant Colonel Ellis participated in an intelligence-gathering mission to Santo Domingo and was later assigned to an intelligence section at the newly created Division of Operations and Training in Quantico, Virginia. While there, he completed the aforementioned "Advanced Base Operations in Micronesia."

Lieutenant Colonel Ellis postulated the proposition that the Marine Corps would be tasked with seizing and holding advanced bases for the U.S. Navy. According to "Advanced Base Operations in Micronesia," these assaults would be made against heavily fortified islands in remote parts of the Pacific. Such vision was innovative for two reasons. First, the bungled operation of the British at Gallipoli clearly indi-cated that an amphibious assault against a defended beachhead was absurd. Using the doctrine of the time, the British had failed miserably in their attempt to seize a foothold into Turkey at Gallipoli in 1915–16. "Advanced Base Operations in Micronesia" challenged that doctrine by suggesting such an operation would indeed succeed with proper advanced planning and application of naval gunfire. Second, the Marine Corps conventionally provided defense of bases for the U.S. Navy. Lieutenant Colonel Ellis's vision transformed conventional doctrine by proposing the Marine Corps would not just defend, but seize and hold advanced bases for the U.S. Navy. After reviewing "Advanced Base Operations in Micronesia," General Lejeune wrote that it was vital to have "a mobile Marine Corps force adequate to conduct offensive land operations against hostile Naval bases," a sweeping doctrinal and cultural change for the Marine Corps influenced by Ellis.

Later in 1921, Ellis was granted permission to visit Japanese mandates in the Central Pacific to verify and gather information in support of "Advanced Base Operations in Micronesia." This is perhaps the last known official Marine Corps sanction of his activities. Following his departure from Quantico for the Central Pacific, Lieutenant Colonel Ellis's journey was marked with bouts of nephritis, binge drinking, hospitalization for alcoholism, erratic behavior, disregard for direct orders from superiors, and absence without leave.[1] Lieutenant Colonel Ellis's intelligence-collection journey ended on Koror, where the Japanese and native police force surveillance on him was increased. According to oral accounts of native Palauans, Lieutenant Colonel Ellis was found dead on 12 May 1923. The Japanese confiscated his belongings, including maps, charts, notes, and confidential codebook.

After the news of Lieutenant Colonel Ellis's death was dispatched to Washington, there was wide speculation that the Japanese had poisoned him. Recently, scholars have suggested that he died of complications due to alcoholism. Both theories are plausible, but the mystery of Ellis's death will likely remain unsolved due to insufficient evidence. When the United States initially requested permission to retrieve Ellis's body, the Japanese refused. Eventually they allowed Lawrence Zembsch, an American chief pharmacist with seventeen years of experience, to retrieve the remains. Once there, Zembsch exhumed, photographed, and cremated the corpse that the Japanese delivered. Unfortunately, before he arrived, the remains had been interred according to the local custom for over sixty days. While Zembsch was experienced in the field of pharmacy, he was neither a forensic anthropologist nor a medical examiner. Complicating matters, Zembsch was killed and all his records destroyed in an earthquake shortly after he left Koror. The only version of the facts that has been published with any scholarly veracity are oral statements given by eyewitnesses forty-five years after Ellis's death. Because the remains were cremated, further scientific study cannot identify the remains or determine a cause of death with any degree of certainty.

Regardless, Lieutenant Colonel Ellis had the vision and passion that allowed him to see the future differently and thereby provide solutions to problems in decades to come.

Note

1. Lieutenant Colonel Ellis had been treated previously for neurasthenia exacerbated by alcohol consumption. This diagnosis is no longer in use, but at the time, it was a psychological disorder characterized by chronic fatigue and weakness, memory loss, and generalized aches and pains formerly thought to result from exhaustion of the nervous system. Ellis had a known history of alcoholism.

Suggested Reading

Ballendorf, Dirk A. "Earl Hancock Ellis: The Man and His Mission." U.S. Naval Institute *Proceedings* 109, no. 11 (November 1983): 53–60.

Ballendorf, Dirk A., and Merrill L. Bartlett. *Pete Ellis: An Amphibious Warfare Prophet, 1880–1923*. Annapolis, Md.: Naval Institute Press, 1996.

Montross, Lynn. "The Mystery of Pete Ellis." *Marine Corps Gazette* 38 (July 1954): 30–33.

Pierce, P. N. "The Unsolved Mystery of Pete Ellis." *Marine Corps Gazette* 46 (February 1962): 34–40.

Reber, John J. "Pete Ellis: Amphibious Warfare Prophet." U.S. Naval Institute *Proceedings* 103, no. 11 (November 1977): 53–64.

About the Author

Captain Jeffrey M. Harrington, USMC, EdD, currently serves as an Education Officer, Ground Training Branch, Marine Corps Training and Education Command, Quantico, Virginia.

17

William A. Moffett
Vision

M. Hill Goodspeed

Naval Historical Center

Conventional wisdom dictates that most naval officers thrive in one of two distinct arenas. There are warriors, whose personal courage combines with a keen tactical mind to succeed in the demanding environment of combat, and there are diplomats, whose skills enable successful maneuverings within the military and government bureaucracy. Rare is the officer who possesses the personal attributes to succeed in both endeavors. William A. Moffett was such a person. His blend of personality, conviction, character, and military bearing made him a central figure in shaping the way the U.S. Navy would fight at sea.

A native of Charleston, South Carolina, William A. Moffett was born on 31 October 1869, the son of a Confederate Army officer commended for bravery as a member of General Robert E. Lee's Army of Northern Virginia. The death of his father when he was five years old forced Moffett to grow up quickly. The guiding force in his life was his mother, who instilled strength of character in him that would shine forth during her son's naval career. Moffett entered the U.S. Naval Academy in 1886 and graduated thirty-first out of thirty-four midshipmen in the class of 1890. The U.S. Navy of the era rested on the tradition that the only proper education for a Sailor was time at sea, so Moffett spent the next two decades serving on ships ranging from wooden sloops to modern battleships and cruisers. Captain Alfred Thayer Mahan, author of the treatise *The Influence of Sea Power Upon History*, was among his commanding officers.

After promotion to commander, Moffett became the skipper of the cruiser *Chester* in November 1913. Within a matter of months, he honed the crew of the ship, which had spent the previous two years in inactive reserve, into an effective fighting force. Their skills would be put to the test in April 1914, when *Chester* joined other ships of the Atlantic Fleet to support a landing at Veracruz, Mexico. Skillfully maneuvering his ship into position off the Mexican city during the evening of 21 April, Moffett landed a party of Sailors and Marines the following morning. Throughout the day, *Chester* provided gunfire support while under nearly constant small arms fire. He had not hesitated to place his ship in the thick of the action, and his bravery and leadership was recognized with an award of the Medal of Honor.

During Moffett's tenure as commanding officer of *Chester*, he developed an interest in the new instrument of warfare that shaped his subsequent career. His first exposure to the U.S. Navy's fledgling air arm had occurred the previous year during winter maneuvers at Guantánamo Bay, Cuba. He initially regarded flying as something for the crazy or foolish. When *Chester* entered overhaul at the Boston Navy Yard following Veracruz, Moffett was assigned command of the armored cruiser *North Carolina*. During this time, he met with Lieutenant Commander Henry C. Mustin, a pioneer of naval aviation. Mustin helped change Moffett's opinion about the use of aircraft in the U.S. Navy.

In the fall of 1914, Moffett took command of the Great Lakes Naval Training Station outside Chicago, a post he would hold throughout World War I. At the burgeoning training base, he learned the importance of public relations and the value of cultivating influential individuals to support a cause. He also received firsthand experience working with the U.S. Navy's bureaucracy as he obtained the necessary tools for his projects at Great Lakes, which included establishment of flight training and the opening of schools for aviation mechanics, quartermasters, and armorers.

Just after the end of World War I, Moffett received the plum assignment of his career with orders to command the battleship *Mississippi*. The ship's first extended cruise under her new skipper occurred early in 1919 during exercises at Guantánamo Bay. It was also a pivotal moment for aviation in the U.S. Navy. Having

observed operations of the Royal Navy during the Great War, American aviators were pressing to operate aircraft at sea with the fleet. The battleship *Texas* was fitted with wooden decks to evaluate the operation of spotting aircraft from ships of the fleet. Moffett did the same for *Mississippi*, and he discovered during exercises in 1920 off the coast of California that spotting aircraft helped improve the accuracy of his ship's guns.

That December, Moffett was assigned to Washington as director of aviation in the office of the Chief of Naval Operations. One of his first challenges was to respond to the efforts of the army air corps, led by air power enthusiast Brigadier General William "Billy" Mitchell, to denigrate the fleet's survivability against airplanes and to get control of all military aviation. Mitchell grabbed headlines by orchestrating bombing tests against old, stationary American and German warships off the Virginia Capes.

Partly through Moffett's advocacy, in July 1921 the U.S. Navy established the Bureau of Aeronautics, which accorded naval aviation a more prominent place in the U.S. Navy's bureaucracy. Moffett was promoted to rear admiral and named the bureau's first director. Moffett realized that he needed to establish a strong aviation organization within the U.S. Navy to counter Mitchell's actions. Moffett espoused the view that naval aviation and the fleet it supported would only be successful if the airplane were fully integrated into operations at sea. He wrote that "naval aviation cannot take the offensive from the shore; it must go to sea on the back of the fleet. . . . The fleet and naval aviation are one and inseparable."

With Moffett's support, the U.S. Navy commissioned three aircraft carriers, USS *Langley*, USS *Lexington*, and USS *Saratoga*, which entered the fleet in the 1920s. Moffett, however, also understood that the keys to an effective naval air arm would be its aircraft and aircrews. Perhaps his greatest achievement was securing funding support from Congress for the development of modern aircraft and engines. The Naval Aircraft Expansion Act of 1926, which he championed, provided the U.S. Navy with one thousand operational aircraft by 1931. His bureau worked closely with Boeing, Grumman, Consolidated, and other aircraft manufacturers to employ the latest technologies and supported development of shipboard catapults and seaplanes. Moffett also waged a spirited battle with the Bureau of Navigation, then responsible for managing U.S. Navy personnel, to have more say in the assignment of aviation officers and enlisted men.

Moffett supported the U.S. Navy's rigid airship program. He believed that lighter-than-air ships could serve as platforms for operating long-range scouting planes in support of fleets. The U.S. Navy's dirigible program, however, proved to be a failure. Heavy weather caused the crash of two huge airships, the *Macon* and the *Akron*, and the loss of many officers and men. William A. Moffett was among the Sailors who perished aboard *Akron* on 4 April 1933.

It is perhaps odd that William A. Moffett became the "Father of Naval Aviation." After all, he was a nineteenth-century graduate of the U.S. Naval Academy taught to consider the big gun as the deciding factor in naval warfare. He was also a middle-aged man in a distinctly young man's

endeavor. But he was convinced that naval aviation was the wave of the future and was prepared to fight for it. As Admiral John H. Towers recalled years later, Moffett was "[a] man who loved a fight and who could think of more ways to win one." His unprecedented twelve-year tenure as chief of the Bureau of Aeronautics enabled him to use all the skills he had acquired during his career—political acumen, public relations savvy, bureaucratic management, and command presence—to create an organization that would change the face of naval warfare.

Suggested Reading

Arpee, Edward. *From Frigates to Flat-tops: The Story of the Life and Achievements of Rear Admiral William Adger Moffett, U.S.N.* Chicago: Lakeside, 1953.

Reynolds, Clark G. "William A. Moffett: Steward of the Air Revolution." In *Admirals of the New Steel Navy: Makers of the American Naval Tradition, 1880–1930*, edited by James C. Bradford. Annapolis, Md.: Naval Institute Press, 1990.

Trimble, William F. *Admiral William A. Moffett: Architect of Naval Aviation.* Smithsonian History of Aviation Series. Annapolis, Md.: Naval Institute Press, 1994.

U.S. Naval Institute Photo Archive

About the Author

M. Hill Goodspeed is a historian at the National Museum of Naval Aviation on board historic Naval Air Station Pensacola, Florida. A graduate of Washington and Lee University and the University of West Florida, he has authored or edited three books, including *U.S. Naval Aviation*, which was named by the U.S. Naval Institute as one of the notable books of 2001, and *U.S. Navy: A Complete History*. He is also an adjunct professor in the College of Continuing Education at the Naval War College and serves as a public affairs officer in the U.S. Naval Reserve.

18

Lewis B. Puller
Drive

Midshipman First Class Eric A. Scherrer

U.S. Naval Institute Photo Archive

To many, Lieutenant General Lewis B. "Chesty" Puller is *the* Marine Corps. But he was not a man set apart for greatness. He was gifted neither with natural athletic ability nor a refined sense of leadership. He was simply a man who loved his nation, believed in the ideals with which she was founded, and worked persistently to serve his nation well. Lieutenant General Puller, who occupied nearly every rank within the Corps, was a man of unorthodox training; no formula could explain his advancement in command. The respect his Marines held for him was genuine and grew out of what they heard him say as well as what he had to offer them from his experience. Puller set a standard for leadership and expectation for decisive leadership that continucs to affect the U.S. Marine Corps.

Puller grew up on his family's farm in Virginia. Deeply affected by the Civil War, the Puller family was still working to reestablish themselves. Unfortunately, his father passed away when Puller was eleven years old. The death of his father profoundly saddened Puller. The loss also forced him to become the man of the house for the rest of the time that he lived at home. With the ever-present reminder of being the eldest male in the household, Puller developed a strong sense of responsibility at an early age. This sense of responsibility remained with Puller throughout his life and was apparent to every Marine who served with him.

As a young man, Puller lacked a desire for academic study. He tended to be rather apathetic toward his schoolwork, a reality he detested and regretted later in life. However, Puller's apathy did not extend to his personal reading. He was a voracious reader who poured over nearly every military book he could get his hands on. Puller relished the historical novels of G. A. Henty and studied Caesar's *Gallic Wars* in his free time.

His interest in military history led Puller to military service following high school. He enrolled at Virginia Military Institute (VMI) on

1 September 1917 as a state cadet. Upon graduation, he would owe the government two years of duty in the National Guard. During his summer training, American armed forces fought the Battle of Belleau Wood in France. Knowing that American soldiers and Marines were fighting in France, Puller could no longer stand the reality of sitting in a classroom. He resigned from VMI and enlisted in the U.S. Marine Corps.

Puller reported to Parris Island in 1918 and did well enough to secure a position as a noncommissioned officer (NCO), used to train new groups of Marines as they entered Parris Island. Puller then prepared to deploy to Europe, but the Armistice ended the war before he could participate.

Determined to become an officer of Marines, Puller applied and was accepted to Officer's

U.S. Naval Institute Photo Archive

Training Camp (OTC). One observer noted, "He did not possess any special athletic ability or a superior intellect. His final standing after [OTC] left him just below the middle of his class. Though his class standing certainly did not indicate any outstanding military aptitude, he had his mind set on a military career and would persevere with relentless resolution in pursuit of his dream."

Upon Puller's graduation, the Marines had an abundance of officers. Thus, Puller was given the option of leaving the Marine Corps or resigning his commission and traveling to Haiti as an NCO acting in a lieutenant billet. The choice was an easy one for Puller. He accepted the NCO position and headed to Haiti, where he would finally get his first taste of combat leadership.

Puller believed in leadership by example. The natural aggressiveness that Puller had demonstrated in other aspects of his life proved advantageous in this new phase of his career. While involved in the Haitian conflict, he participated in numerous small skirmishes, setting the standard that the young Marine would follow for the rest of his career: aggressive action and leadership from the front. As a result Puller's men gave him their complete loyalty.

After his service in Haiti, Puller went to Officer Candidates School, hoping to receive a commission this time. He started off strong and was given a very high military efficiency grade, no doubt attributed to his action in Haiti. Although Puller struggled academically, he did pass his exams. Upon completion, Puller was ranked fifth out of ten officer candidates. Puller was heard remarking to a friend, "I may not have much else to go on, but I have some perseverance." At last, he had achieved a dream that began seven years prior.

Puller's career went on to span numerous small engagements, World War II, and the Korean War. His reputation for being a man of action and courage preceded him everywhere he went. Puller's daring tactics earned him nicknames like "El Tigre," which added to his legendary reputation within the Corps. Though he developed his talents as a leader in action, nothing came easily for Puller. Knowing his own weaknesses, he pushed himself harder than his peers, desiring to lead his Marines by personal example.

Suggested Reading

Hoffman, Jon T. *Chesty: The Life of LtGen Lewis B. Puller.* New York: Random House, 2001.

About the Author

Midshipman First Class Eric A. Scherrer is the Brigade Executive Officer at the U.S. Naval Academy. He has service selected Marine Corps.

19

William F. Halsey
Adaptation

John F. Wukovits

U.S. Naval Institute Photo Archive

Among human endeavors, leading armies and navies into battle demands great organization. Operational plans for major campaigns easily reach into the hundreds of pages. Despite the involved strategy, success or failure in battle often depends less on following the design and more upon adapting to circumstances. No one can foresee every eventuality; unexpected occurrences frequently disrupt timetables and negate months of planning. In those situations, victory goes to the individual who adapts more quickly, who improvises, who makes use of what is available to him or her at that precise time.

Admiral William F. Halsey, born 30 October 1882 in Elizabeth, New Jersey, personifies the trait of adaptation. Frequent moves—Halsey never spent two successive years at the same school until he was thirteen years old—dominated Halsey's youth. While this constant uprooting impeded his intellectual development, it strengthened Halsey's flexibility. He learned that he either had to adjust to adversity and employ the tools at hand or be overcome.

His performance in World War II illustrated the benefits of adaptability. On three occasions during the war's first two years, Halsey adapted to circumstances, rallied his forces, and boosted the nation's morale through the sheer force of his powerful, outrageous utterances.

As early as the war's first week following the disastrous 7 December assault at Pearl Harbor, the nation knew of Halsey as a warrior, not so much for what he did, but because of what he said. The pugnacious leader had few weapons at his disposal—much of the Pacific Fleet lay on Pearl Harbor's bottom—so he turned to what he had available at the time: his words.

He started on 8 December 1941. When he steamed into Pearl Harbor and witnessed the smoking ruins of what remained of the fleet, the admiral muttered through clenched teeth the first of many declarations that endeared him to his men and rocketed him to public prominence.

"Before we're through with 'em," he swore, "the Japanese language will be spoken only in hell!" He vowed to "lead that scoundrel [Yamamoto] up Pennsylvania Avenue in chains." After learning that three American pilots had been executed by the Japanese following their capture, in a near rage Halsey promised, "We'll make the bastards pay! We'll make 'em pay!" His men and the people back home rallied behind his statements, in part because they had little else behind which to coalesce. To a nation that felt militarily impotent, these were just the words needed to vent America's rage and to restore morale that had been devastated by the enemy's triumphs.

Finally, the nation had a hero, someone who gave reason for Americans to walk with pride. In the war's first weeks, Halsey was the belligerent, cussing antagonist to Yamamoto who would gain satisfaction for the dead at Pearl Harbor and lead the nation to victory. A naval aviator later wrote after listening to Halsey, "Those Japs had better look out for that man."

Halsey became the face of the U.S. Navy and its most attractive public relations phenomenon. *Time* magazine and every other major news publication featured him on their covers and in profiles. Reporter Clark Lee wrote at the time that Halsey "was all the United States Navy needed." Neither Halsey's peer, Admiral Raymond A. Spruance, nor his superior, Admiral Chester W. Nimitz, enjoyed the attention Halsey grabbed with his bold tactics and quotable wit. Europe had Patton; the Pacific had a man the American press dubbed the "Bull."

Halsey then assumed command of the South Pacific Area in October 1942. The war in that region, which centered on the brutal land and sea combat around Guadalcanal, fared poorly. His presence breathed life into the beleaguered Marines ashore and into the nation at home. His appointment brought cheers from the weary Marines previously cringing in Guadalcanal's dugouts. "One minute we were too limp with malaria to crawl from our foxholes," said one Marine, "the next we were whooping it up like

kids." Two Marines discussed Halsey's value to the fight. As one officer recalled, "One of them was arguing that getting the Old Man was like getting two battleships and two carriers, and the other was swearing he was worth two battleships and three carriers. If morale had been enough, we'd have won the war right there."

Halsey waged the campaign for Guadalcanal on two fronts. Before the week ended, Halsey transmitted the order to his captains, "Attack-repeat-attack!" While his officers and men fought the Japanese on land and at sea, holding on with scant resources until America's factories could produce the first of what would become a torrent of ships, planes, and weapons, Halsey garnered the attention of the press and of the American public with his words. He monopolized the public spotlight and occupied headlines, realizing that he had to instill hope not only at Guadalcanal, but in the United States as well, and that the most effective tool he had at his disposal at this time were again his words.

His opening verbal salvo minced no words. He boasted to the press that his formula for fighting the war was to, "Kill Japs, kill Japs, and keep on killing Japs." *Time* magazine placed Halsey on its 30 November 1942 cover and titled the profile of the admiral, "Hit Hard, Hit Fast, Hit Often." A torrent of words and promises followed. "As long as I have one plane and one pilot," vowed Halsey, "I will stay on the offensive." Almost single-handedly, Halsey willed his forces to victory in the waters off Guadalcanal. "Until then he [the Japanese] had been advancing at his will," he later wrote. "From then on he retreated at ours."

Halsey also turned to words a few months later. On New Year's Eve 1942 he predicted to the press that the war would end in 1943. Halsey later admitted that he had not believed his words, but he had felt they would help raise the morale of nations and men still numbed from Japanese offensives and inject optimism for the future. The ploy worked. Even a New Zealand editorial praised Halsey for his statement and added, "We shall certainly not conquer in 1943 unless we believe we can, and plan and work to do it. The willing must precede the doing, and the action will be fortified by faith." Halsey verbalized what factory workers and homemakers and police officers wanted to hear. Halsey's exuberant command style also persuaded his men to believe that no other outcome except victory was possible. Later in the war an American prisoner, liberated by forces dispatched by Halsey, shouted, "I knew it! I told those Japanese bastards that one day Admiral Halsey would come for us!" The optimism Halsey evoked helped attain the complete victory that marked the end of World War II.

Following the war, the U.S. Navy retained Halsey on active duty until 1 April 1947. On 16

U.S. Naval Institute Photo Archives

August 1959, Halsey succumbed to a heart attack near Mystic, Connecticut. An airplane transported Halsey's body to Washington, D.C., where he was placed in the National Cathedral. On 20 August, a horse-drawn caisson took his casket through Washington to Arlington National Cemetery, where a nineteen-gun salute honored him in a brief graveside ceremony.

Suggested Reading

Frank, Richard B. *Guadalcanal: The Definitive Account of the Landmark Battle.* New York: Random House, 1990.

Halsey, Fleet Admiral William F., and J. Bryan III. *Admiral Halsey's Story.* New York: McGraw-Hill, 1947.

Morison, Samuel Eliot. *History of the United States Naval Operations in World War II.* Vol. 5, *The Struggle for Guadalcanal, August 1942–February 1943.* Boston: Little, Brown, 1960.

Potter, E. B. *Bull Halsey.* Annapolis, Md.: Naval Institute Press, 1985.

About the Author

John F. Wukovits has written about World War II for the last two decades. He has published numerous articles in different magazines, including *Naval History* and *WWII History*, and has authored biographical essays on Admiral George Dewey, Raymond Spruance, and William Halsey. He has published two books: *Devotion to Duty: A Biography of Admiral Clifton A. F. Sprague* in 1995, and *Pacific Alamo: The Battle for Wake Island* in 2003. A graduate of the University of Notre Dame, Wukovits is the father of three daughters: Amy, Julie, and Karen. He is currently at work on a biography of Admiral Halsey and on a book about the Battle of Tarawa.

20

Slade D. Cutter
Teamwork

Ensign Joel I. Holwitt

Naval Historical Center

Slade D. Cutter started life as a farm boy in Illinois, but he was destined for greater things. A man of many talents, athletic ability, unprepossessing modesty, and strong determination, Cutter became a national champion flautist, a Naval Academy boxing legend, an all-American football star, one of the top U.S. submarine aces of World War II, and an inspiration to scores of naval officers and midshipmen during his thirty-year naval career.

Although Cutter was a big man even as a growing boy, his father forbade him to play contact sports throughout his childhood. Cutter turned to music instead. After a stint on the piano, he found his niche as a flautist. He even earned money by giving flute lessons. Cutter later attended Elmhurst College in Elmhurst, Illinois, on a music scholarship. Cutter may never have entered the U.S. Navy at all had a family friend not asked him to join her son at the Severn School, Severna Park, Maryland. For the first time in his life, Cutter began to play football, and he made adequate grades to be appointed to the U.S. Naval Academy's Class of 1935. Although some midshipmen did not enjoy their time at the academy, Cutter loved every minute. While not an ace student, Cutter excelled at athletics, lettering all four years in boxing and football. As a boxer, Cutter caught the attention of legendary boxing coach Spike Webb, who ranked him up with national boxing champions Max Baer and Primo Carnera. In fact, one boxing manager offered Cutter fifty thousand dollars, a princely sum in 1935, to leave the U.S. Navy and become a professional boxer. It was an offer Cutter never regretted refusing. Cutter also showed he was a natural leader, earning a billet as a company commander during his first-class year.

Cutter launched his way into legend as a football player. Playing for coaching legend Rip Miller, Cutter alternated between playing fullback, center, and eventually tackle. Cutter's finest gridiron moment came at the 1934 Army-Navy game. Navy had not won the Army-Navy game for thirteen years, and the alumni and the midshipmen were hungering for a win. Despite heavy mud, which made aggressive play almost impossible, Cutter succeeded in scoring the only points of the game—a first quarter field goal. At the time, neither Cutter nor the other players felt it was very important, because they were confident that they would rack up the score later in the game, but even so, Cutter had the presence of mind to change his mud cleats to regular cleats in order to get a solid kick. Although Cutter's actions that day became legendary, he preferred to be remembered for his subsequent accomplishments.

Cutter was not selected for the Marine Corps, and he was too big for naval aviation, so he was assigned his third choice of service assignment: submarines. After two years onboard the battleship USS *Idaho*, Cutter served as an assistant coach at the Naval Academy before attending submarine school in New London. Upon graduation from submarine school, he was assigned to submarines *S-30* and *Pompano*. Onboard *Pompano* Cutter learned the skills that made him one of the legends of the submarine service.

Cutter's commander onboard *Pompano* was Lewis Parks, a 1925 Naval Academy graduate who relentlessly worked his officers and crew into one of the finest submarine crews in the fleet. Although normal practice was for submarine officers to be qualified in one year, Parks chose to delay his officers' qualification boards for over two years, until he felt ready for an impressive demonstration. One by one, Parks ran his three unqualified officers through a practice approach in front of their division commander. Each officer, including Cutter, scored a direct torpedo hit on their target, and showed themselves to not only be fully qualified as submarine officers, but also fully qualified for command. As a result, Cutter was one of very few officers to simultaneously qualify both for submarines and command in one day.

On 7 December 1941, *Pompano* was sailing on the surface toward Hawaii when they were attacked by Japanese planes that were taking part in the Pearl Harbor attack. With this abrupt and rude realization that the United States was at war, Cutter, Parks, and *Pompano* took the war to the Japanese. Despite being bedeviled by poor torpedoes and equipment, *Pompano* aggressively attacked Japanese shipping, and Cutter learned valuable lessons regarding torpedo approaches and submarine tactics. By the time he was detached in the fall of 1942 to a new construction, USS *Seahorse*, Cutter was a hardened submarine veteran.

Unfortunately, Cutter's new commanding officer was not aggressive; during *Seahorse*'s first war patrol, he allowed numerous contacts to go by without attacking them. Always a man to speak his mind, Cutter and his new captain clashed throughout the patrol, and Cutter ended the patrol in hack and restricted to his stateroom. However, Cutter's former officer representative from the football team, Captain J. H. Brown, was also the Pacific Fleet's submarine force training officer. Brown realized what had happened on *Seahorse*'s first patrol; he instantly relieved *Seahorse*'s captain and fleeted Cutter up to command. Finally in command, and with a well-trained crew and a brand-new submarine, Cutter departed on his first war patrol in October 1943. When he returned, *Seahorse* was credited with the most successful patrol thus far in the war. In the course of three more patrols, Cutter continued to prove he was one of the top submarine warriors in the U.S. Navy, aggressively pursuing and destroying any shipping that crossed his path. At the end of the war, Cutter was credited with nineteen confirmed sinkings, becoming the second-top U.S. submarine ace of World War II. After four war patrols in *Seahorse*, Cutter was sent back to New London to command another submarine, USS *Requin*, which arrived in the Pacific just in time for the war to end.

After the war, Cutter continued to show his versatility and talents by taking on assignments such as director of the Public Information Division in the Office of Public Information, director of athletics at the Naval Academy, commanding officer of USS *Neosho* and USS *Northampton*, commander of the Naval Training Center, Great Lakes, and finally the director of the Navy Memorial Museum at the Washington Navy Yard.

Throughout his life, Cutter showed that he prized not his own accomplishments, but rather his contributions to a greater whole or a greater purpose. As a teenager in 1928, Cutter won a national flute championship. Even then, he characteristically credited his victory to his talented accompanist.

Cutter's time on the Naval Academy football team helped reinforce his focus on the importance of a team—not an individual—to victory. Cutter directly correlated football to his experience as a submarine officer, stating, "It is a team effort; if one guy falls down the whole team suffers. . . . That is exactly what happens in a submarine. . . . All these things have to be done and you have to count on the people doing them in the proper sequence. It's teamwork."

Despite heroic achievements, such as a dogged and successful eighty-two hour attack on a heavily escorted convoy, Cutter believed that the most important achievement he made during the war was to find the Japanese fleet before the Battle of the Philippine Sea. Although he was unable to attack the Japanese, who remained out of range, Cutter persistently maintained contact with the enemy fleet, running *Seahorse*'s engines well past their limits in order to continuously relay information to headquarters. As a result of *Seahorse*'s efforts, other U.S. submarines and Admiral Spruance's Fifth Fleet intercepted the Japanese, resulting in the Battle of the Philippine Sea and the Marianas Turkey Shoot. Although he did not sink any ships, Cutter characteristically labeled *Seahorse*'s successful tracking of the Japanese fleet as "the best contribution we made to the war." Once again, Cutter highlighted not his own personal accomplishments, but rather his contribution as a part of a team.

After thirty years of service to the U.S. Navy, Slade Cutter retired as a captain in June 1965. He had earned four Navy Crosses, two Silver Stars, the Bronze Star with a Combat "V," and the Presidential Unit Citation Ribbon, among numerous other decorations. Even decades after his retirement, however, he remained a loyal team player to his alma mater and his service, flipping the coin at the beginning of the Naval Academy's successful 2003 football season and continuing to inspire and motivate young midshipmen at the U.S. Naval Academy with his modest but amazing tales of heroism and perseverance.

Naval Historical Center, courtesy of D. M. McPherson

Suggested Reading

Blair, Clay, Jr. *Silent Victory: The U.S. Submarine War against Japan.* Philadelphia: J. B. Lippincott, 1975.

Cutter, Slade. Oral History. Annapolis, Md.: U.S. Naval Institute, 1979.

Cutter, Captain Slade D. Interview by Paul Stillwell. *The Reminiscences of Captain Slade D. Cutter, U.S. Navy (Retired).* 2 vols. Annapolis, Md.: U.S. Naval Institute, 1985.

LaVO, Carl. *Slade Cutter: Submarine Warrior.* Annapolis, Md.: Naval Institute Press, 2003.

About the Author

Ensign Joel I. Holwitt graduated with honors and distinction from the U.S. Naval Academy in May 2003. He is currently studying military history at the Ohio State University before beginning the nuclear submarine officer pipeline.

21

Joseph J. Rochefort
Dedication

Dr. John R. Schindler

Naval Historical Center, courtesy of Capt. R. Pineau, USNR

Joe Rochefort never rose to flag rank, never saw combat, and performed his war-winning work as a commander. A modest man devoted to duty over self, his remarkable achievements were known to but a few. Only after his death did Rochefort receive the attention from historians he deserved. Like so many Sailors engaged in secret work, Joe Rochefort had served in silence. Yet his brilliance, determination, innovation, and, above all, his selfless dedication to the U.S. Navy and the nation remains a benchmark of excellence and a model for his successors.

His early years offered few clues of the greatness to come. Of modest background, Rochefort enlisted in the Naval Reserve Force in 1918, hoping to become an aviator. As he was neither a Naval Academy man nor a college graduate, he stood little chance of earning his wings of gold. Yet he stayed in the U.S. Navy after World War 1 and was commissioned an ensign after graduation from the Stevens Institute of Technology.

Thus began a conventional line officer's career, with service in engineering and deck duties in the fleet. And so it might have continued but for a chance observation in 1925 when the junior officer was serving on the battleship *Arizona*. The executive officer discovered that Rochefort liked crossword puzzles—a fact that moved the executive officer to recommend Rochefort to Lieutenant Laurence Safford, then serving in Washington, D.C., in a secret job.

Lieutenant Safford was looking for promising naval officers who excelled at crossword puzzles—a sign of aptitude in code breaking. Safford was the newly appointed head of the euphemistically termed "Research Desk" of the Code and Signal Section in the Navy Department building on the Mall in Washington, D.C. This fledgling outfit—the whole complement could sit at a small table and leave chairs empty—was devoted to studying, and breaking, foreign naval codes. They called themselves cryptologists, what are popularly termed code breakers, speaking to no one about what they did.

Lieutenant junior grade Rochefort reported for duty in October 1925 and quickly became the shining star of the program, displaying a remarkable aptitude for cryptanalysis, the cracking of codes. He excelled in the unit's informal training, and when Safford returned to line duty at sea in early 1926—there was no career path in intelligence—Rochefort found himself head of the Research Desk, which was soon renamed OP-20-G.

In three years, Rochefort honed OP-20-G's attack on the codes of the main enemy, the Imperial Japanese Navy. Thanks to the theft of a Japanese codebook, Rochefort and his tiny team made significant breakthroughs in exploiting sensitive Japanese naval communications. But heading the team pushed the workaholic Rochefort to the breaking point.

He was sent to Japan in 1929 for a three-year stint to learn the language, a needed rest. Rochefort healed his ulcer and insomnia and acquired excellent Japanese. The tight-lipped officer was a model student. A fellow officer in the program recalled that, in three years together, Rochefort never once mentioned his OP-20-G assignment. On the eve of World War II, Rochefort was the only officer in the U.S. Navy who was both a cryptanalyst and a Japanese linguist.

In early 1941, with a Pacific war looking increasingly likely, Safford, again the chief of naval cryptology, dispatched now-Commander Rochefort to Hawaii to head up the code-breaking effort against the Japanese navy. Rochefort's team was known officially as the Combat Intelligence Unit, unofficially as Station Hypo, and he selected the best officers and men he could find to tackle the vexing problem of breaking into the enemy's fleet ciphers. Hypo's work was starved of funds—most of OP-20-G's resources were devoted to the German U-boat threat in the Atlantic—but as was his custom, the quiet and studious Rochefort drove his Sailors hard and himself harder, according to his com-mand philosophy, prominently displayed above his desk: "We can accomplish anything provided no one cares who gets the credit."

In what they called "the dungeon," a dark and windowless room in the Pearl Harbor administration building, behind the supply office, to which almost nobody had access, Rochefort's team put in long hours doing mysterious work. They were striving for breaks in JN-25, which was the primary Japanese naval system, an exceptionally difficult code to exploit. On the eve of the attack on Pearl Harbor, Rochefort's efforts had begun to pay off—Hypo was breaking into and translating three to four percent of JN-25 traffic—but it was not enough. Shortages of men, funds, and equipment, plus a strong effort against the Japanese Flag Officers' Code, a rival system, meant that JN-25 was barely being broken.

Rochefort took the 7 December attack hard, swearing to never fail again. There had been no actionable warning. His response was trademark: "I can offer a lot of excuses, but we failed in our job. An intelligence officer has one job, one task, one mission—to tell his commander, his superior, today what the Japanese are going to do tomorrow." And so he did.

Determined to give the Pacific Fleet's new commander, Admiral Chester Nimitz, the intelligence he needed to defeat the Japanese, Rochefort descended into Hypo's dungeon on the morning of the Pearl Harbor attack and hardly left for the next half year.

A demon for work, Rochefort led the all-out assault on JN-25. Finally he had the resources he needed to get the job done. New equipment appeared. Sailors were no longer in short supply. Rochefort took all the help he could get, even pressing into service the band of the sunken battleship *California;* the shipless musicians proved to be surprisingly adept code breakers.

Twenty-hour days became Rochefort's norm in the winter of 1942. He rarely left his office, even to sleep; he personally translated much of the intercepted traffic. Life in the dank dungeon was difficult, but the cryptologists admired

Rochefort for his determination to win. His ardent desire to do the impossible was infectious, and he saved the hardest tasks for himself.

Insanity jokes abounded. Rochefort's line, "You don't have to be crazy to work here, but it helps," became a mantra. The commander was not a stickler for discipline—he was known to wear a smoking jacket and slippers in his too-air-conditioned office—but he cared a great deal about performance. His performance concern was particularly apparent beginning in the third week of March 1942. Hypo had won the battle with JN-25, and Rochefort's team commenced "current decryption": they were reading Japanese fleet communications as fast as the intended recipients were.

Rochefort had developed a seamless partnership with Commander Edwin Layton, an old friend and Nimitz's intelligence officer. Together, they assembled a detailed picture of the Japanese fleet and its operations that wasn't encouraging. The Japanese had more—and in most categories better—ships and aircraft, plus they held the strategic initiative. Admiral Nimitz faced ominous choices; one significant misstep could cost the U.S. Navy what had not been sunk at Pearl Harbor.

The only advantage the Pacific Fleet held over the enemy was in intelligence—an advantage that was later termed "priceless" by Nimitz. By the spring, thanks to Rochefort's efforts, which were producing 140 decrypted JN-25 messages each day, it was evident that the Japanese were planning a major naval offensive soon. But where?

Rochefort confidently predicted a drive in the central Pacific, aimed at Hawaii via Midway Island. Others, including Nimitz's staff and OP-20-G headquarters in Washington, disagreed, believing the offensive was directed at

U.S. Naval Institute Photo Archive

the Aleutians. To prove his point, Rochefort devised a clever deception operation using faked U.S. traffic that convinced Layton and Nimitz that Midway was indeed the target. This gamble led directly to the Battle of Midway, the incredible victory of 4–6 June 1942, the greatest triumph in the history of the U.S. Navy, and thereby turned the tide in the war with Japan. Had it not been for Rochefort, Nimitz's carriers would have been in the wrong place when Admiral Nagumo's fleet appeared off Midway. The courage and skill of America's Sailors, particularly of naval aircrews, won the battle, but Rochefort's code-breaking triumph made the victory possible.

His rewards for this epic feat were few. Higher-ranking rivals in Washington, who had bet against the Midway gamble, exacted their revenge. Over Nimitz's objection, Rochefort was recalled to the Pentagon and forbidden to take the ship command he wanted—he knew far too many secrets to be allowed to go to sea—and instead wound up commanding a dry dock. Rochefort never received a decoration for his war-winning work and never worked on codes again. He peacefully remained silent about his war service.

In 1986, a decade after his death, Joe Rochefort received the President's National Defense Service Medal, the highest military award during peacetime, for his support to the Battle of Midway. As long as there are cryptologists in the U.S. Navy, the name Joe Rochefort will be spoken with reverence.

Suggested Reading

Holmes, W. J. *Double-Edged Secrets: U.S. Naval Intelligence Operations in the Pacific during World War II*. Annapolis, Md.: Naval Institute Press, 1979.

Layton, Edwin T., Roger Pineau, and John Costello. *"And I Was There": Pearl Harbor and Midway—Breaking the Secrets*. New York: William Morrow, 1985.

Parker, Frederick D. *Pearl Harbor Revisited: United States Navy Communications Intelligence 1924–1941*. Ft. Meade, Md.: National Security Agency, 1994.

———. *A Priceless Advantage: U.S. Navy Communications Intelligence and the Battles of the Coral Sea, Midway, and the Aleutians*. Ft. Meade, Md.: National Security Agency, 1993.

About the Author

Dr. John R. Schindler is the Naval Security Group's command historian. He previously served as a senior intelligence analyst with the National Security Agency. A historian by background (PhD, McMaster University, 1995), he has taught at three universities and sits on the faculty of the Joint Military Intelligence College and the National Cryptologic School. He is the author of *Isonzo: The Forgotten Sacrifice of the Great War* (2001) as well as numerous articles on military and naval history and intelligence studies. He is a cryptologic officer in the Naval Reserve.

22

Clarence W. McClusky
Intuition

Captain Chris Johnson

Naval Historical Center, courtesy of Mrs. C. Wade McClusky Jr.

The facts about Wade McClusky tell a story that is both intriguing and inspirational. His brief moment in history on a June day in 1942 just north of Midway Island provides an indispensable and informative lesson in true leadership. Lieutenant Commander C. Wade McClusky—in the heat of battle, engulfed in the fog of war, and at the tip of a spear that had to find its mark if the United States were to win the War in the Pacific—made an absolutely perfect tactical decision that changed the entire course of World War II. One man, one decisive action, and thirty minutes of flying time resulted in three quarters of the Japanese carrier striking force set ablaze and sinking.

During the winter of 1941–42, the Pacific theater was bleak. The Japanese juggernaut, propelled by a magnificent fleet that included more than half a dozen fleet carriers and the super-battleships *Yamato* and *Musashi*, was emboldened by a succession of crushing victories, including Pearl Harbor, and was dominating the war. Jimmy Doolittle, flying from *Hornet*, bombed Japan, producing temporary elation for the United States, some paranoia in Japan, but not much actual damage. Coral Sea produced a much-needed moral victory in the form of a stalemate, but *Lexington* was lost and *Yorktown* badly damaged. Fortunately, two Japanese carriers were damaged as well and had to return to Japan for repairs. They were not available for the Midway operation.

At this crucial moment, courage, commitment, and inspiration begin to emerge from many quarters, including some entirely unlikely places. Admiral Nimitz's eccentric, smoking jacket–clad cryptologist Joe Rochefort and his men were reading the Japanese Naval Code JN-25. Using sly tactics, Rochefort enticed the Japanese into making communications that confirmed their next target to be Midway Island. If Japan took Midway, Hawaii would become indefensible, the fleet would have to retire to the West Coast, and peace on Japan's terms would become a distinct possibility.

Immediately, Nimitz recalled *Hornet* and *Enterprise* from the southwest Pacific, and apparently through sheer force of will, he got *Yorktown* back from Coral Sea and partially repaired in just three days. The three carriers sailed undetected to positions northeast of Midway, officially under Frank Jack Fletcher's command, but with Admiral Spruance functionally in command of *Hornet* and *Enterprise*, which operated together, separate from *Yorktown*.

At 0534 local on 4 June 1942, a PBY sighted the Japanese carriers northwest of Midway, and the first Japanese bombs dropped on Midway an hour later. Spruance, armed with these reports and knowing that the Japanese air wing was returning to its carriers, ordered *Hornet* and *Enterprise* to launch their aircraft at maximum range, hoping to catch the Japanese as they rearmed and refueled their planes. It was a quick, decisive, and aggressive order that resulted in the first carrier planes being airborne at 0702.

Although a coordinated attack against the Japanese—combining torpedo planes, fighters, and dive-bombers—was planned, the various squadrons became separated. McClusky's group of thirty-two dive-bombers flew to the calculated intercept point but found nothing except ocean. The torpedo planes did find the Japanese but were slaughtered by the faster, more maneuverable Zeros. A snapshot of this moment seemed to indicate that the stage was irretrievably set for defeat and disaster: the torpedo planes were ineffective; McClusky had no fix on the enemy and his planes were running low on fuel (in fact several of his aircraft would run out of fuel and be forced to ditch; McClusky himself ultimately landed with less than two gallons in his tank); and *Yorktown* had been located by a Japanese scout plane.

But in truth, the scene was actually set for the most improbable reversal of fortunes in modern naval warfare. McClusky's bombers were at altitude, still undetected, and they were close to the enemy—although McClusky was unaware of that fact. The defending Zeros were on the deck finishing off the torpedo plane attack and were ill

positioned to contest McClusky's dive-bombers. Vice Admiral Nagumo, the Japanese carrier strike force commander, was engaged in a sequence of oscillating decisions and vacillating appreciations of the tactical situation that resulted in having his flight decks covered with high explosive ordnance and packed with refueled or refueling aircraft.

At this moment in his career, Clarence Wade McClusky, U.S. Naval Academy Class of 1926, was forty years old and a distinguished naval aviator. He had been assigned to *Enterprise* for two years, moving up from command of Fighter Squadron 6 to command of the entire *Enterprise* air group in April 1942. A week before Midway, McClusky received the Distinguished Flying Cross from Admiral Nimitz for his actions at Coral Sea. Although he led a group of Dauntless dive-bombers, he was barely qualified in the aircraft. In fact, he had never practiced dropping a bomb from a Dauntless. But, as Gordon Prange observed: "What he brought to his job was a gift for command, composed in equal parts of personal fearlessness and the ability to feed unexpected data into his brain cells and click out a prompt, intelligent response."

McClusky was at twenty thousand feet, leading two squadrons of bombers. He arrived at his calculated intercept point, about 150 miles southwest of *Enterprise*, but saw no Japanese carriers. He reasoned that it was not possible for the carriers to be between his position and Midway Island because he had already projected them moving toward Midway at maximum speed when he calculated the intercept point. He headed west thirty-five miles, then turned northwest to retrace the Japanese track. At 0955 McClusky knew that he had only five minutes before he had to turn around and return to *Enterprise*. McClusky described the situation with the following words:

Call it fate, luck or what you may, because . . . I spied a lone Jap cruiser [actually the destroyer *Arashi*] scurrying under full power to the northeast. Concluding that she possibly was a liaison ship between the occupation forces and the striking force, I altered my Group's course to that of the cruiser. At 1205 (1005 local time) that decision paid dividends.

Peering through my binoculars, which were practically glued to my eyes, I saw dead ahead about 35 miles distant the welcome sight of the Jap carrier striking force. They were in what appeared to be a circular disposition with four carriers in the center, well spaced, and an outer screen of six to eight destroyers and inner support ships composed of two battleships and either four or six cruisers.

At 1022 McClusky's group, joined by bombers from *Yorktown*, attacked. *Kaga*, *Akagi* (Nagumo's flagship), and *Soryu* erupted into infernos and sunk or were scuttled within twenty-four hours. That afternoon, aircraft from *Enterprise* attacked *Hiryu*, the lone surviving carrier of the strike group, and she was lost as well. The Japanese offensive was crushed, Japanese naval domination of the Pacific was ended, and Japanese naval power would endure defeat after defeat, with only small exceptions, until the end of the war. Nimitz later said that McClusky "decided the fate of our carrier task force and our forces at Midway."

Zeros attacked McClusky's Dauntless as he tried to depart after the attack. He was hit four times in the shoulder but successfully evaded and escaped, returning to *Enterprise*. Upon landing, he discovered that his plane had taken fifty-five hits.

Many historians followed McClusky's lead and attributed the victory at Midway to luck, fortune, or fate. The U.S. Navy's unofficial historian, Samuel Eliot Morison, used the word *luck* to describe parts of the battle, and Nimitz himself dubbed the carrier rendezvous point for the operation "Point Luck." A recently published professional article even called Midway a "crapshoot."

Some might claim that the evidence of "good luck" is too compelling: Nimitz could read the Japanese naval code; the Japanese split their force unwisely; the U.S. carriers moved into

position just before the Japanese submarine picket line formed; the *Arashi*, which had been delayed while it attacked USS *Nautilus*, was just where McClusky could see it at just the right juncture of the battle; the Japanese carriers were unusually vulnerable because of the planes and ordnance on deck; the picket plane that discovered *Yorktown* was late launching and therefore late in giving the Japanese critical intelligence on the presence of U.S. carriers, and so on. This was all tantamount to asserting that McClusky was simply a surrogate hero, and that any experienced aviator, aided by such overwhelmingly good fortune, would have fared just as well.

In military operations, the mental environment created by the leaders of the force shapes the vision, anticipation, and actions of individuals. The mental environment that surrounded McClusky was not a chain of "good luck"; it was, instead, a chain of courage and commitment that shaped McClusky personally and influenced the battle at large. It began with Rochefort, who would not be denied in his effort to understand the meaning of the Japanese intercepts. It included Nimitz, who was willing to trust Rochefort and act aggressively in response to that information. Nimitz's willingness to trust Spruance, a cruiser Sailor, in command of the *Hornet-Enterprise* task force also played a role. Finally, Spruance was willing to launch his aircraft early and at long range in order to surprise the Japanese and catch their carriers in the reload-refuel cycle. In the end, this chain of courage and commitment came to rest with Wade McClusky.

There is another element to consider. Those who have gone to sea know that there is an inner voice, an intuition, that springs to life when reason alone cannot provide a definitive answer to a problem. Some commanders are attuned to that voice; some are so calculus-bound that they ignore it.

On 4 June 1942, McClusky managed all the logical things superbly. He plotted an intercept course; when no contact was achieved, he reasoned correctly that the Japanese force had to be away, not toward, Midway. He searched west, then northwest, to cover the possibility that the

Japanese had retraced their track. He did not begin an expanding square search; that would have used too much fuel and endangered his formation's ability to return safely to the ship. Then the clue came: a destroyer was running at full speed to the northeast. It was an ambiguous clue at best; destroyers drove through the ocean in many directions and for many reasons. At this supreme moment of decision, he acted decisively. He interpreted the clue correctly, committed to the northeast without hesitation, and the Pacific War changed in minutes.

McClusky never talked about intuition. He did what all do when faced with an improbable and stunning victory. He pointed to vague forces beyond himself as the cause of success. But at a moment where another, like Nagumo, might fumble or consider returning to the carrier, or split the force for separate search patterns, or do nothing but fly in circles, McClusky acted perfectly. McClusky's counterpart, who led the dive-bombers from *Hornet* that day, came up empty, like McClusky, at the intercept point. But Commander Stanhope C. Ring turned his attack to the southeast, toward Midway, and never engaged the enemy that day.

At the moment of decision, something in McClusky said imperatively, "damn the low fuel state, go this way!" This was a decision that began with shreds of logic, but ultimately was propelled and validated by intuition, courage, determination, and character. He focused on duty rather than on simply avoiding mistakes. He represented that essence of leadership under fire that every officer earnestly seeks to emulate.

After Midway, McClusky appeared to fade into the relative obscurity from which he emerged meteorically on 4 June. He commanded the escort carrier *Corregidor* (CVE-58) later in the war and served as chief of staff to two fleet commanders during Korea. He later commanded various unremarkable shore facilities, including the Boston Group of the Atlantic Reserve Fleet. He was never selected for flag officer while on active duty. Perhaps he was like others for whom the art of war comes naturally,

Naval Historical Center, courtesy of Mrs. C. Wade McClusky Jr.

but the science of peacetime politics never comes. He retired at thirty years of service, at which time he was symbolically promoted to rear admiral, a rank derisively termed "tombstone admiral." Wade McClusky passed on in 1976. But when the nation desperately needed heroes and victories, a man of courage, commitment, and intuition, leading his flight of bombers into battle, answered that call superbly. His name was Wade McClusky.

Suggested Reading

Department of the Navy, Naval Historical Center. "Rear Admiral Clarence Wade McClusky, Jr., USN (1902–1976)." http://www.history.navy.mil/photos/pers-us/uspers-m/c-mcclsk.htm/.

Gaillard, L. "The Great Midway Crapshoot." U.S. Naval Institute *Proceedings* 130, no. 6 (June 2004): 126–32.

Morison, Samuel Eliot. *History of the United States Naval Operations in World War II.* Vol. 4, *Coral Sea, Midway, and Submarine Actions, May 1942– August 1942.* Boston: Little, Brown, 1949.

Prange, Gordon W. *Miracle at Midway.* New York: McGraw-Hill, 1982.

USS *Enterprise,* "LCDR C. Wade McClusky: Battle of Midway." http://www.CV6.org/ company/accounts/wmcclusky/.

About the Author

Chris Johnson is a retired Navy captain (SWO) whose career specialization in tactics and tactical thinking made Wade McClusky, and the battle of Midway, a longtime focus of reading and thinking. Captain Johnson now works in industry and resides with his family in Northern Virginia.

23

Joseph J. Foss
Focus

Major Kevin Brooks

U.S. Naval Institute Photo Archives

An examination of the successful life and Marine Corps aviation career of Brigadier General Joe Foss provides an excellent character study of focus. Joe Foss epitomizes the military leader with the crucial ability to focus intensely on the immediate task at hand and achieve superb results. His service provides numerous examples of noteworthy determination, focus, and concentration, worthy of emulation by future officers.

Joseph Jacob "Joe" Foss was born in 1915 to Norwegian-American parents in South Dakota. Although he had a modest childhood on a family farm, he took an early interest in aviation. Like many young people in the 1920s, he was impressed with Charles Lindbergh. At the age of sixteen, Joe Foss watched an aerial demonstration by a Marine squadron and became excited about the idea of service in a military aviation unit.

Joe Foss demonstrated an innate ability to focus as a young man. He began his college education in 1934, but he was forced to quit school in order to assist with managing the family farm. Undaunted by life's events, Foss returned to his education and graduated from college in 1940. In the same year, he completed a civilian pilot training program using his own savings and earned his civilian wings, showing his ability to focus on two major goals simultaneously. In 1940, Foss enlisted in the Marine Corps Reserves as an aviation cadet, subsequently earning his commission as a second lieutenant and his Marine aviator wings. Although considered "old" for an aviator at twenty-seven years of age, Foss lobbied doggedly for assignment to a fighter squadron. He received his wish and, after training in the F4F Wildcat, he joined VMF-121 and headed for the Pacific theater.

One incident from Joe Foss's early days as a junior officer particularly demonstrates his ability to focus. Foss was the officer of the day at Pensacola, Florida, on 7 December during the Japanese attack on Pearl Harbor. Convinced that enemy forces could attack the air station at Pensacola, Foss focused his energy and action on proper defense of the base. He rode a bicycle around the base numerous times, acting as a roving patrol and also checking the base defenses. Although his actions may seem comical today, Foss was determined to adequately defend the base and to remain focused on the task at hand for the duration of his duty.

In October 1942, Foss landed at Henderson Field on Guadalcanal as the executive officer of VMF-121. Immediately, Foss puts his energy and focus toward the destruction of Japanese aircraft. His superior determination and concentration made him an ace in only nine days! Although Japanese fighters and bombers usually outnumbered the American fighters, Foss and his squadron mates were able to defend Henderson Field and Guadalcanal successfully against the daily onslaught from the Japanese. Foss used his intense focus during aerial attacks, getting extremely close to enemy aircraft before firing. His concentration was so complete that he routinely shot down enemy aircraft while performing complicated aerobatic maneuvers. Foss's wingmen reported watching him shoot Japanese fighters while he was inverted, straight up, straight down, rolling—in any imaginable position. Perhaps Joe Foss himself expressed this necessity of focus the best when he stated, "Dogfights are normally over in a matter of seconds. If you blink, you could miss the fight. If you blink during the fight, you could die."

Possibly the greatest combat day in the life of Joe Foss was 25 October 1942. The Japanese forces intended to occupy Henderson Field, and Foss played an instrumental role in defeating their attack and denying their plan. Notably, Foss downed five Japanese aircraft during multiple missions on 25 October to become the first "ace in a day" for the Marine Corps. Again, his ability to focus in the face of overwhelming enemy numbers contributed directly to his success and the overall success of the American forces.

Foss displayed the same determination and focus on other types of aviation missions. He was cited for exemplary skill while escorting bombers and reconnaissance aircraft. His squadron participated in numerous attack missions, performing difficult and dangerous strafing runs against enemy ships. In order to have reasonable accuracy while strafing, Foss and his fellow aviators needed to penetrate thick curtains of antiaircraft fire and fly perilously close to the Japanese ships. The pilots required intense focus to avoid the antiaircraft fire and track their targets. Even more astonishing, sometimes they required intense focus to avoid crashing into the enemy ships! In a March 2000 interview, Foss said, "We're flying just five, ten feet off the water, strafing these ships and . . . just like it started snowing, those [Zeros] were behind us. And so I got on the tail of another [Zero], and almost ran into a ship, concentrating on the airplane."

Perhaps most impressive was Foss's ability to concentrate and focus when his own aircraft was badly damaged. Within the first month of his arrival on Guadalcanal, Joe Foss shot down enemy aircraft after his plane was damaged by enemy fire, landed his damaged aircraft safely numerous times, and even survived a deliberate ditching of his own aircraft. On 7 November 1942, when Foss shot down a Japanese float plane, Foss's airplane was severely damaged by the Japanese tail gunner. Foss attempted to limp home, but he was forced to ditch his plane before reaching Henderson Field. Foss focused on the long, slow, shallow dive into the ocean and survived the impact. He nearly drowned while attempting to evacuate the sinking airplane, but managed to successfully inflate his life vest and surface. Avoiding the circling sharks, Foss was rescued by Catholic missionaries. Two days later, he received the Distinguished Flying Cross for his aerial kills and his heroic survival of the ocean ditching.

Shortly thereafter, Foss contracted malaria and spent six weeks recuperating in New Caledonia and Australia. However, his focus was always on the war and how quickly he could return to fight on Guadalcanal, not how quickly he could return home. On 1 January 1943, Joe Foss returned to Henderson Field and resumed flying combat missions against the Japanese. He shot down three planes in January, bringing his total aerial victories to twenty-six kills—a Marine Corps record. Even when he was not shooting down Japanese Zeros or bombers, his intense focus benefited his wingmen and other aviators. On one of his last missions, Foss "led his eight F4F Marine planes and four Army P-38s into action and, undaunted by tremendously superior numbers, intercepted and struck with such force that four Japanese fighters were shot down and the bombers were turned back without releasing a single bomb." Foss did not shoot down a single plane on this mission, but

his focus in coordinating the attack led directly to its success. Upon his return to the United States in May 1943, Foss was awarded the Congressional Medal of Honor for his aerial prowess and inspirational leadership at Guadalcanal.

After the war, Joe Foss led a highly successful life. He demonstrated the same level of intense focus in his civilian work, and it paid huge dividends for him. He was twice elected the governor of South Dakota, served as the first commissioner of the American Football League, and served as the president of the National Rifle Association. Additionally, he contributed directly to the organization of the South Dakota Air National Guard. His success in combat and his accomplishments in civilian life stem directly from his ability to focus. Joe Foss is a true Amer-

U.S. Naval Institute Photo Archive

ican hero and his attributes are worthy of emulation by future military leaders.

Suggested Reading

Foss, Joseph. *A Proud American: The Autobiography of Joe Foss.* Novato, Calif.: Presidio, 2002.
Frank, Richard B. *Guadalcanal: The Definitive Account of the Landmark Battle.* New York: Random House, 1990.

About the Author

Major Kevin Brooks is a Marine Corps F/A-18 pilot and is currently an English instructor at the U.S. Naval Academy.

24

Archer A. Vandegrift
Moral Courage

Richard B. Frank

Department of Defense Photo (Marine Corps)

In the third week of September 1942, Major General Archer Alexander Vandegrift confronted what loomed as the most intense test yet of his leadership of the 1st Marine Division on Guadalcanal. Just four months prior, he had arrived in New Zealand swaddled in comforting assurances that his novice division would not enter combat before the New Year. But Admiral Ernest King seized radio intelligence evidence of Japanese designs for an airfield on this obscure South Pacific island as a warrant to launch a countermove. Despite the shock of this sudden about-face, Vandegrift and his staff acted swiftly and shrewdly to forge key elements of the plan.

No sooner had the Marines seized what became Henderson Airfield on Guadalcanal than the Imperial Navy drove off the naval covering force with a humiliating thrashing that left the Marines besieged. The Imperial Army mounted monthly punches to destroy the American lodgment. In August 1942, Colonel Kiyoano Ichiki recklessly steered his reinforced battalion in a frontal attack into one of the few places where the Marines waited behind prepared defenses. Ichiki was virtually annihilated.

In September, a reinforced brigade under the infinitely more astute Major General Kiyotaki Kawaguchi surged to within a hairbreadth of success. Kawaguchi aimed to strike at what he believed would be the undefended jungled southern rim of the American enclave. But Vandegrift's staff persuaded him to rearrange his dispositions just in time to place Lieutenant Colonel Merritt Edson's combined 1st Raider and 1st Parachute Battalions athwart the exact axis of Kawaguchi's thrust along an elevation in the jungle known thereafter as Edson's Ridge. The Marines just held.

While the U.S. Navy followed up this triumph by landing the 7th Marines, it had not broken the siege. Vandegrift and his staff then began preparing to parry the next Japanese onslaught. He now fielded ten infantry, one raider, four field artillery, and a small tank battalion plus support units. His new scheme established for the first time a complete perimeter defense around the airfield. The eastern anchor was Alligator Creek. The inland edge of the defense formed a rough hemisphere south and west into the jungle across Edson's Ridge before curving back to the commanding ground west of the Lunga River and then the beach. Of the ten subsectors of the perimeter, support units manned the three fronting the beach. Each infantry regiment (1st, 5th, and 7th) manned two inland sectors; the division controlled the seventh sector.

It is not the pedestrian facts but the thought process behind the scheme that glitters. Vandegrift and his staff frankly admitted that the new layout exemplified a "cordon defense of the worst type." Since Napoleon's days, staff colleges had excoriated such long, thinly held lines for their vulnerability to any enemy who simply massed his infantry and artillery for a thrust at one point. For generations, the "school solution" for Vandegrift's dilemma dictated a set of fortified "horseshoe" defense positions along likely avenues of approach backed by reserves for "defense in depth."

According to his operations officer, Lieutenant Colonel William Twinning, Vandegrift "had that rare faculty of deciding every case on its own merits." Thus, Vandegrift and his staff discarded sacrosanct principles because of their thoroughly pragmatic appraisal of the enemy, the terrain, and their own capabilities. They reasoned that Henderson Field flyers would preclude an amphibious attack. Besides, the Japanese had already twice displayed a penchant for unopposed landings followed by overland assaults. That meant the enemy thrust must come from the east, south, or west. Vandegrift aimed to meet an enemy approach proximate to the coast from the east and west not at the perimeter, but at crossing points on the Tenaru or Matanikau rivers where there was scope for the favored Marine tactics of inland flanking

movements or amphibious hooks. The incredibly dense jungle terrain to the south, however, not only made detection of the enemy approach by air or ground reconnaissance problematic; it precluded active defense. A jungle march, however, would handcuff the Japanese into a bargain where they would trade concealment and surprise for exhaustion, supply nightmares, and breakdowns of command and control.

The critical issue in defensive arrangements is usually reserves, and here the plan favored pragmatism over theoretical elegance. The cordon defense yielded a degree of economy of force as it permitted unusually long frontages. It also allowed the Marine command to thin to the bone unthreatened sectors or even contract the line in places to gather more reserves. The new scheme further recognized that in night jungle combat, the practical difficulty of movement and deployment could negate the timely intervention of large conventional reserves. Experience against Ichiki and Kawaguchi fortified Vandegrift's confidence that, even heavily outnumbered, resolute and confident Marine rifle units in well-prepared positions behind barbed-wire obstacles and stiffened by the terrific firepower of supporting mortars and artillery could defeat Japanese attacks. Each sector held small local reserves ready in covered positions for immediate reinforcement or counterattack. Finally, this arrangement denied the Japanese their favored infiltration tactics.

Simultaneous with adoption of this radical defense scheme, Vandegrift performed a painful duty. Six weeks of active combat campaigning had conducted a rigorous audit of the professional competence of the division's officers. It exposed failures at every level. Conspicuous among them was the division's chief of staff, Colonel Casper James. Another was one of Vandegrift's closest personal friends and an outstanding Marine hero of World War I, Colonel LeRoy Hunt, the leader of 5th Marines. Easing Vandegrift's task was an 8 September directive from Commandant of the Marine Corps Thomas

Holcomb, requesting the release of excess senior officers created by a spate of recent promotions for duties stateside within the rapidly expanding corps. Besides citing this directive to assuage the pain these reliefs caused, Vandegrift also seized the ploy of announcing that he would use the criterion of seniority in length of service with the division for reasons of "fairness." These standards covered the relief of James, Hunt, and a number of others. At the same time, Vandegrift shuffled a group of aggressive field grade officers into battalion commands.

An eventful month passed before the Japanese administered the fierce final examination of Vandegrift's decisions. By then, Vandegrift dared further by establishing a dangling defensive position west of the main positions to block the crossings of the Matanikau for Japanese artillery and vehicles. Meanwhile his Japanese counterparts had discarded approaches from the east or west as inviting inevitable firepower contests they could not win. They instead elected a bold strategy to feint along the Matanikau while the main force of the 2nd ("Sendai") Infantry Division conducted a deep envelopment south through the Guadalcanal rain forest to pierce the lightly defended southern stretch of the American perimeter. While Vandegrift's picture of Japanese aims in October proved out of focus, the fundamental set of calculations proved correct. The jungle march exhausted and disordered the Sendai Division. The slender cordon of Marine riflemen, backed by mortars and artillery, checked the Japanese thrust, and reserves hurled it back with enormous loss. Any other form of defense likely would have granted the Japanese victory.

Navy Department Photo in the National Archives

The essential quality that linked Vandegrift's September 1942 decisions was moral courage. In this instance, moral courage involved both the fortitude to do what he believed was right in the face of not just failure, but disgrace, and the willingness to set aside profound personal considerations. Military education emphasizes and rewards "boldness": taking calculated risks to win. But that same education inculcates limits on acceptable risks. Many officers could have conducted the same pragmatic analysis of the situation. But when that analysis pointed to the solution of a cordon defense, the prospect of savage professional ridicule for resorting to what had been reviled as tactical imbecility for generations would have dissuaded all but a very select few. What those few possess is properly labeled not boldness, but moral courage. Likewise, the tough leadership changes Vandegrift wrought demanded that he set aside long personal friendship—and even an institutional hero—and act in the best interests of his command. This also was moral courage. Junior officers at the beginning of service typically envision physical courage as at or near the pinnacle of martial virtues and are apt to overlook or diminish moral courage. Those who go on to extended careers discover that physical courage is commonplace in American armed forces, but that a depth of moral courage is an indispensable quality for higher command and that it is rarer than physical courage—or boldness.

Suggested Reading

Frank, Richard B. *Guadalcanal: The Definitive Account of the Landmark Battle*. New York: Random House, 1990.

Twinning, Merrill B. *No Bended Knee: The Battle for Guadalcanal*. Novato, Calif.: Presidio, 1996.

About the Author

Richard B. Frank, a nationally recognized authority on U.S. Marine Corps operations in World War II, is retired from the Marine Corps Historical Center.

25

Mary Sears
Intellectual Analysis

Dr. Kathleen Broome Williams

Courtesy of the Denton family

Who would have thought that a shy, arthritic, middle-aged woman, a professor of biology specializing in a species of minute plankton, would in a two-and-a-half-year active duty career rise to head the U.S. Navy's oceanographic effort? Yet that is exactly where Mary Sears's encyclopedic mind and formidable organizational powers took her.

It is much easier to think of leadership qualities, particularly in the military, in terms of courage, physical ability, and charisma. Less noted, but equally important, are the quiet arts of judgment and tact. Mary Sears had judgment and tact in abundance and they were essential to her successful U.S. Navy career. Even more important, though, was her remarkable facility for analysis and synthesis. Those qualities enabled her to oversee production of oceanographic intelligence reports vital to the prosecution of America's World War II Pacific campaign.

Mary Sears was born in 1905 in a country town not far from Boston. She and her siblings grew up in a comfortable middle-class home with a Unitarian minister father and a devoted stepmother. Nothing in her background predisposed Sears toward the U.S. Navy or to anything military. In fact, she had always been interested in animals, and her schoolmates thought she would become a farmer and raise cows. But traipsing through the boggy pools and brooks near home sparked a lifelong fascination with marine invertebrates. Later, at nearby Radcliffe College, Sears majored in zoology, and though the field was generally inhospitable to women, she persisted, earning a doctorate from Harvard in 1933. She spent the next ten years in the conventional academic environment of Harvard, Wellesley College, and the Woods Hole Oceanographic Institute in Massachusetts. Because women were barred from Woods Hole research vessels, the only time Sears was on the water during those years was on a six-month research trip to study plankton off the coast of Peru.

When the United States entered World War II in December 1941, there were no women in the U.S. Navy (apart from nurses). Wartime naval expansion soon caused critical personnel shortages, however, requiring the admission—for the duration only—of women, known as WAVES (Women Accepted for Volunteer Emergency Service). Sears tried to join the WAVES in 1942 but was rejected because of an earlier bout with arthritis.

By this time, the U.S. Navy's awareness of the significance of military oceanography was developing rapidly. Planning future amphibious operations required good marine intelligence, and with the escalating war against Japan, the U.S. Navy's need for oceanographic information far outstripped its ability to deliver. The shortage of trained oceanographers propelled Sears into the U.S. Navy. Her previous medical disability overlooked, Sears was recruited in February 1943, commissioned a lieutenant junior grade in March, and immediately posted to the Hydrographic Office in Washington. There this shore-bound marine biologist ran Hydro's oceanographic effort, directing twelve women and three men, most of them academics like herself, in the application of oceanography to war.

As the head of the Oceanographic Unit, Sears's most critical task was to provide intelligence reports for both long-range strategic and immediate tactical planning for amphibious operations in the Pacific. Responding to specific queries, her reports were required to demonstrate the main oceanographic factors affecting the location and timing of such operations. Often, under the pressure of war, forecasts were demanded on extremely short notice. The strictest standards of secrecy had to be maintained at all times because revealing specific areas under investigation could jeopardize operations, cost lives, and perhaps affect the course of the war itself.

Sears's day-to-day activities involved pouring over all sorts of empirical research data obtained from oceanographic centers around the country.

Reports came in from the Scripps Institution of Oceanography in California on the latest methods for predicting sea, swell, and surf conditions. The Naval Research Laboratory sent studies of the salinity of seawater affecting the radio acoustic ranging used for coastal hydrographic surveys. Woods Hole sent data on water temperature and pressure obtained by submarines deployed to forward areas.

To accurately forecast the effect of waves on amphibious operations, the Oceanographic Unit requested reports from a variety of beachhead intelligence-gathering groups such as underwater demolition teams, Marine Corps reconnaissance companies, and meteorologists working with the fleets and task forces. Sears also made use of observations collected by the Office of Naval Intelligence from merchant ship captains, and she studied reports produced by the Coast and Geodetic Survey. She and her staff were handicapped by the paucity of charts of the Pacific although eventually captured Japanese charts and tide tables made their way to her desk. Even the Office of Strategic Services supplied intelligence culled from the reports of its agents overseas.

Sears's task was to analyze and evaluate the information pouring in from this wide variety of sources. It was up to her to supervise her team, sifting through the masses of data, identifying and selecting what was pertinent. She then transformed her synthesis into a report that provided a readily comprehensible picture of the factors at play when selecting a suitable location for an amphibious assault. As a scientist, she understood the highly technical data she received, but what made her an effective leader was her ability to convey the essence of what she learned in concise terms transparent to the nonscientists who made the command decisions. Her reports were created for decision makers right up to the level of the Joint Chiefs of Staff.

If successful leadership is measured by outcomes, Sears was a successful leader. In the speculative field of forecasting, her coherent and persuasive reports contributed to some stunning triumphs. One such success was the Allied landings on Luzon in the Philippines in January 1945. The surf was low on the western part of Lingayen Gulf in western Luzon, making it the most attractive location for an invasion. The Japanese were well aware of that and fortified the area heavily. With good weather data and wave refraction charts, Sears and her team produced a report indicating that the surf on the less heavily defended eastern part of the gulf would be less than six feet high, making it safe to go ashore there. Thanks in part to this report, Allied troops landed on the flank of the Japanese positions, rolling back the forces that had invaded the Philippines three years earlier. This helped set the stage for the final defeat of Imperial Japan.

Since the end of World War II, the Normandy landings in June 1944 have received a great deal of popular attention. Many know the

story of the meteorologist on whose weather forecast General Eisenhower depended for the final decision to go ahead with D-Day. Yet almost no one knows how, six months later, a critical amphibious operation in the Philippines was facilitated by a small group of marine biologists. Nor are they aware that a woman working at her desk in Washington was responsible for compiling a report indicating where the Okinawa invasion forces could land on 1 April 1945 with least danger from currents and surf.

A pioneer in the application of oceanographic intelligence to operational problems, Sears had been steadily promoted during the war, finally attaining the rank of lieutenant commander. Though only brought into the U.S. Navy because of her scientific expertise, she served it well. She and her team proved the worth of oceanographic information, and in 1946 their small unit became a full-fledged Hydrographic

Office division headed by Sears until her separation from active duty that June.

Although her full-time service in the U.S. Navy was brief, Sears did not hang up her uniform at the end of the war. Returning to work at Woods Hole, she remained in the naval reserve for the next seventeen years, commanding the local Naval Reserve Research Company. She continued to exercise her formidable skills of analysis and synthesis in the service of the U.S. Navy.

Suggested Reading

Bates, Charles C., and John F. Fuller. *America's Weather Warriors*. College Station: Texas A&M University Press, 1986.

Broome Williams, Kathleen. "Mary Sears: Oceanographer." In *Improbable Warriors: Women Scientists and the U.S. Navy in World War II*. Annapolis, Md.: Naval Institute Press, 2001.

About the Author

Dr. Kathleen Broome Williams teaches history at Bronx Community College, City University of New York, and is a member of the history doctoral faculty at the CUNY Graduate School and University Center. She received a doctorate in military history from CUNY in 1992. In addition to articles and reviews, she is the author of *Secret Weapon: U.S. High-Frequency Direction Finding in the Battle of the Atlantic* (Naval Institute Press, 1996), *Improbable Warriors: Women Scientists and the U.S. Navy in World War II* (Naval Institute Press, 2001), and *Grace Hopper: Admiral of the Cyber Sea* (Naval Institute Press, 2004).

26

Lewis W. Walt
Presence

Colonel Jon T. Hoffman

Defense Department Photo (Marine Corps)

The leading elements of the 1st Marine Division stormed ashore at Cape Gloucester on the western end of New Britain Island on 26 December 1943. As they crossed the narrow sand beach and entered the dense, fringing jungle, they met no enemy resistance but soon discovered why. Barely a few feet beyond, in the area marked on the maps as "damp flats," they encountered a swamp that often put them neck deep in fetid water. The Japanese had been expecting an amphibious assault against their nearby airfields, but never at this poor location for a landing. Both sides were surprised, but the Marines got the better end of the deal, making the initial landing with no casualties. As they pushed outward to expand their beachhead, they finally reached dry ground, though this was only a marginal improvement. The jungle was so thick in places that it was difficult for even infantrymen to move, let alone tanks, artillery pieces, and supply vehicles. Rain was frequent and often torrential during this monsoon season. Lightning and falling trees soon became a deadly threat adding to that from enemy bullets and shells. During the brief interludes without rain, the equatorial heat and humidity was oppressive.

Dubbed the "Green Inferno" by some who fought there, Cape Gloucester proved to be one of the worst environments experienced by the Marines in World War II. It took determined leadership at all levels to fight the forbidding weather and terrain as well as a tenacious foe. An effective tool for commanders in this challenging situation was presence, defined by one writer as the use of "personal example and force of character to bring order out of potential chaos during a critical turn of events" or the direct inspiration of subordinates to accomplish the mission. Such acts by commanders can swing the pendulum very quickly from looming defeat to certain victory. General Lemuel C. Shepherd Jr., the twentieth Commandant of the Marine Corps and a decorated hero in two world wars, would look back at Cape Gloucester at the end of a long career and identify what he considered to be one of the greatest examples in his experience of one man's presence affecting the outcome of a battle.

On the thirteenth day of the long campaign, the Marines were pushing their perimeter southeast along the coast to protect their newly acquired airfields from enemy artillery fire. Brigadier General Shepherd, the assistant division commander, was in charge of this portion of the offensive. A captured Japanese order stated that the remaining Imperial forces were to hold on to Aogiri Ridge at all costs, but the crude drawing accompanying the document provided no clue to the location of this apparently important feature. Even from the vantage point of high ground in the rear, the Marines could not identify any prominent hill in the jungle-covered washboard contours ahead of them. A predawn thunderstorm that morning had brought flash floods cascading down from the interior mountains to wash out units struggling to prepare for another attack into the nightmare terrain. Through the course of the day, the center of the Marine line made little headway against sometimes heavy Japanese fire that seemed to erupt from nowhere in the dense foliage. The 3rd Battalion, 5th Marines (3/5), operating in support of the 7th Marines, took the brunt of this determined resistance. As the command group began to set up in a rare clearing, it came under sniper fire; the battalion commander, the executive officer, and several other key personnel were hit. The combination of harsh natural conditions and hard fighting against a largely unseen enemy was taking its toll on the battalion, and the loss of leaders only made it worse. Shepherd recalled, "Their morale was pretty well shaken. They were wavering and lacked the will to move forward in the attack. I desperately needed a forceful leader to take command of this battalion."

Shepherd briefly put the battalion under control of the incomparable Lieutenant Colonel Lewis B. "Chesty" Puller, who already was commanding the adjacent unit, 3rd Battalion, 7th Marines (3/7).[1] But Shepherd needed someone who could devote his full attention to leading 3/5 into the fight again. He had no hesitation in ordering the 5th Marines to send up Lieutenant Colonel Lewis W. Walt, one of the youngest officers of his grade in the history of the Corps.

Walt was born in Kansas in 1913. He began his military career by enlisting in the Colorado National Guard in 1929 while he was still in high school. He remained an infantryman in his guard unit for the next six years, reaching the rank of sergeant even as he worked his way through Colorado State College as a miner and salesman, won acclaim as a football player, and earned honors as the top graduate of the school's Army Reserve Officer Training Corps program. At graduation in 1936, he received a commission as an artilleryman in the Army Reserve but within a month accepted the Corps' offer to go active duty as a Marine second lieutenant. His first mentor in the Corps was one of his Basic School instructors, Chesty Puller, already well known as one of the finest combat leaders in the Corps.

As a Marine, Lieutenant Walt saw action quickly, going to Shanghai with the 6th Marines in 1937 during one of the Sino-Japanese flare-ups. He was an instructor at Officer Candidates School in Quantico, Virginia, when the Japanese bombed Pearl Harbor, and he soon managed a transfer into the 1st Raider Battalion, a unit promising the first chance to hit back at the enemy. He learned a great deal more about leadership from his battalion commander, Merritt A. "Red Mike" Edson, who set the example of leading from the front throughout a distinguished career. In Walt's first real battle at Tulagi in the Solomons, he received the Silver Star for his actions as a company commander. When Edson took charge of the 5th Marines on Guadalcanal soon after, Walt became the regimental operations officer and then the commander of 2/5. For his outstanding service in this campaign, he quickly won promotion to major and then to lieutenant colonel, the latter at the age of twenty-nine. After Guadalcanal, he spent long periods in the hospital for malaria and multiple surgeries to repair damage to both shoulders (a legacy of his football days aggravated by combat and demanding training). He returned to full duty in time to lead his battalion into its second major campaign of the war, at Cape Gloucester. He had just been elevated to regimental executive officer the day before he received the call to take command of 3/5.

The simple act of getting forward to his new unit became an ordeal. Receiving the order late in the afternoon, Walt made his way through the jungle's lengthening shadows with one corporal to provide security. The pair had to struggle across two flood-swollen streams, nearly getting swept out to sea at one point. They reached the command post of the 7th Marines after dark, where the regimental commander told them to hold up till daylight.

Walt made it to the battalion the next morning where Puller briefed him on the situation. Every time the Marines moved forward they met intense fire from hidden machine guns, supported by sniper fire coming from high in the trees. For the balance of the day, the Marines of 3/5 and the battalions on the flanks tried to inch forward through the tangled growth, sustaining mounting casualties for little gain. Shepherd came forward to see the new battalion commander and found him crouched in the massive roots of a banyan tree right in the front lines, trying to assess the situation firsthand. A burst of machine gun fire raked the tree. One round penetrated the roots and Walt's pack, knocking him into the general but not wounding the young lieutenant colonel. The sole result of the day's action was the realization that the ground was now sloping steadily upward. Coupled with the die-hard defense, it was obvious the Marines finally had found Aogiri Ridge.

Unknown to the attackers, the enemy had dug in heavy weapons in a series of log bunkers well camouflaged along the forward crest of the jungle-covered ridge. The canopy of trees above reduced the effectiveness of artillery against this formidable position. The desperate fight required the aid of tanks and the direct fire of their heavy guns, but none could get forward in this terrain; however, during the course of the day, Walt's Marines managed to drag up a single 37 mm antitank gun. On the morning of 9 January 1944, Shepherd launched a fresh assault on the critical objective. The battalion on the left made no progress, but Walt's outfit on the right began to inch ahead with the support of their single 37 mm. The shotgun effect of its canister rounds suppressed enemy fire long enough to allow Marines to move forward a few yards with each blast.

The Japanese reacted to this new threat with intensified fire against the gun. All six men of its crew were soon dead or wounded. From his post in the thick of the fighting, Walt called for volunteers to take over the weapon, but no one responded. He moved out to the gun himself and began pushing the heavy carriage into position for the next shot. His runner joined him, only to find that the battalion commander had pulled both arms from their sockets in trying to maneuver the piece by himself. Walt instructed him how to reset them, but the young Marine had success only with one.

Walt was effectively crippled now, but it no longer mattered. His willingness to put his own life on the line at the most dangerous spot on the battlefield brought forth a surge of Marines to man the gun. Inspired by his example, they alternately fired the gun and pushed it up the slope. More men fell around the 37 mm, but Walt remained with it as it inched ahead, clearing a lane into the heart of the enemy defenses by evening. As darkness fell, the Marines owned several of the bunkers, and the battalion commander worked feverishly to arrange his men and weapons to ensure they had a secure foothold. He placed every man of the battalion headquarters into the front lines to support the depleted infantrymen, setting up his own command post with a single runner just a few yards behind.

The Japanese were well aware that the tide was turning against them and they had to deal with this penetration of their vital position. After midnight, they began a rising chant to stoke their courage and strike fear into their opponents. The Marines waited in the pouring rain for the impending counterattack, which began just after 0100. The fighting was furious and close. Five times in the ensuing few hours the Japanese charged the American lines. Walt directed repeated barrages from mortars and artillery, finally bringing the fire to within fifty yards of his own position. As the first light of dawn filtered down through the foliage, the few surviving enemy fell back, and the battle was essentially over. The Marines moved forward and captured the remainder of the ridge against little opposition.

Patrols soon discovered the importance of the ridge to the Japanese; just behind it was the main trail network that entered the area from eastern and southern New Britain. With the high ground now in American hands, the Japanese would find it increasingly difficult to feed more units into the fight to regain the airfields. Although the Cape Gloucester campaign would drag on for several more months, the battle of Aogiri Ridge essentially ended any faint hope the Japanese had of winning. Senior Marine officers toured the scene of the vicious fight on the day it ended. The commander of 5th Marines noted one of Walt's arms still hanging limply, but Walt refused to be evacuated. Shepherd walked over the ground, heard the tales of courage that carried the day, and renamed the key terrain Walt's Ridge. Months later Walt received a Navy Cross for his actions that day and night.

Soon thereafter, he was leading another battalion in combat on Peleliu and earning his second Navy Cross. He went on to command a regiment in the Korean War and lead Marines in Vietnam during the first two years of that war. But battle-hardened Shepherd never forgot Walt's performance as the commander of 3/5 at Cape Gloucester: "It was the greatest demon-

Defense Department Photo (Marine Corps)

stration of leadership I have ever witnessed. It showed how the will of the commander demonstrated by his courageous action can influence a whole battalion."

Note

1. Its leader was relieved earlier in the campaign for an inability to break through similar enemy resistance in equally terrible terrain.

Suggested Reading

Hoffman, Jon T. *Chesty: The Life of LtGen Lewis B. Puller.* New York: Random House, 2001.

———. *Once a Legend: "Red Mike" Edson of the Marine Raiders.* Novato, Calif.: Presidio, 1994.

———. *Warrior: The Life of Gen Lewis W. Walt.* New York: Random House, forthcoming 2006.

Wood, W. J. *Leaders and Battles: The Art of Military Leadership*. Novato, Calif.: Presidio, 1984.

About the Author

Colonel Jon T. Hoffman, USMCR, has spent his entire career as an infantry officer and military historian. He most recently served as the deputy director of the Marine Corps History and Museums Division. His books include two biographies of Marines: *Once a Legend: "Red Mike" Edson of the Marine Raiders* and *Chesty: The Life of LtGen Lewis B. Puller*.

27

Marc A. Mitscher
Skilled Warfighting

Lieutenant Commander
Richard R. Burgess

Naval Photographic Center

Marc A. "Pete" Mitscher attended the U.S. Naval Academy—twice. Not particularly motivated to attend, he "bilged" out in 1906. His father managed to get him readmitted, but Mitscher's second matriculation was almost as lackluster as the first. He ranked 113 out of 131 when he graduated with the class of 1910. Despite his academy performance, his career developed into a classic exception to the notion that institutional academic excellence translates into warfighting skill.

Mitscher was an aviator's admiral. Fleet Admiral Ernest J. King, Admiral William F. Halsey Jr., and Admiral John S. McCain, some of the senior aviation flag officers who led the U.S. Navy during World War II, earned their wings late in life as senior officers. In contrast, Mitscher was Naval Aviator Number 33, present almost at the creation of naval aviation. Few officers were as prepared as Mitscher to conduct carrier warfare.

Mitscher served for five years in armored cruisers, destroyers, and gunboats before entering flight training. He was designated a naval aviator in June 1916 and thereafter tested aircraft catapults. During World War I the young officer commanded two naval air stations. In 1919, he piloted the flying boat NC-1 during an attempt to cross the Atlantic. Although he was unsuccessful in his flight, he earned the Navy Cross for distinguished service.

As executive officer of USS *Langley*, the U.S. Navy's first aircraft carrier, Mitscher gained valuable operational experience, to which he later added during his service onboard carrier USS *Saratoga*. In 1934, Mitscher organized and led a four-ship formation of flying boats on the first nonstop flight from the West Coast to Hawaii. He also commanded the seaplane tender USS *Wright* and Patrol Wing 1. As assistant chief of the Bureau of Aeronautics during the late 1930s, Mitscher helped develop the naval aviation organizations, doctrine, and tactics employed so successfully in World War II.

Marc Mitscher participated in the U.S. Navy's long and bloody advance across the Pacific Ocean from the beginning of America's war against Japan. He commanded USS *Hornet* when she launched U.S. Army Air Forces General Jimmy Doolittle's bombers on their April 1942 air strike against Tokyo. His ship and its air group helped secure the decisive victory over the Imperial Japanese Navy at the June Battle of Midway. Mitscher was a leader who demanded more of himself than anyone else. He was his own harshest judge. While other Americans praised the performance of the forces at Midway, Mitscher criticized his handling of *Hornet* and her air group.

While hard on himself, Mitscher often forgave the mistakes of subordinates, especially young, green aviators. He wanted them to learn from their experiences, properly direct their energy, and develop professional skills. The men who served under Mitscher appreciated his forbearance and rarely betrayed his trust in them.

Mitscher was protective of his aircrews. Having floated in the ocean in the disabled NC-1 awaiting rescue, Mitscher knew what it was like to be in peril on the sea. On one occasion before the war, a seaplane he sent on a round trip from Long Beach, California, to San Diego failed to return. When notified the plane was overdue, Mitscher set off down the coast in a motor whaleboat and rescued the crew. He mourned the loss of those who failed to return from combat missions. For example, the deaths of Lieutenant Commander John P. Waldron and all but one man of his Torpedo Squadron 8 at the Battle of Midway devastated him.

In 1943, Mitscher was assigned command of U.S. and Allied Air Forces operating over Guadalcanal and the other Solomon Islands. His leadership was instrumental in the eventual victory over Japanese air and naval forces in the South Pacific Command. Not only was he proud of his command's destruction of enemy forces; he was also pleased with the successful rescue of 131 downed Allied crewmen.

After the stressful Solomons campaign, the U.S. Navy ordered Mitscher, malaria stricken

and visibly aged, to command Fleet Air West Coast where he feared he would spend the rest of the war. The following year, however, Mitscher was given command of Carrier Division 3, and then Task Force 58, the Fifth Fleet's fast carrier task force.

At the helm of Task Force 58, Mitscher earned lasting fame as a combat commander. His four-division carrier task force destroyed hundreds of enemy aircraft ashore and afloat, neutralized Japanese airfields, sank enemy warships and merchantmen, and covered central Pacific amphibious landings. During the June 1944 Battle of the Philippine Sea, also known as the Marianas Turkey Shoot, Mitscher skillfully led his units in the destruction of Japan's carrier air arm.

Mitscher is perhaps best known for his decision to turn on the lights in that battle, as he had done at Midway, when his air groups returned from their missions and struggled to find their carriers in the dark night. By illuminating his ships, he risked their loss to Japanese submarines, but he took that risk to save his men. It was vintage Mitscher.

Task Force 58 went on to further glory, devastating Japanese land-based air power in the Philippines and sea power at the Battle of Leyte Gulf. For the first five months of 1945, Mitscher skillfully led the task force in attacks on Iwo Jima, Okinawa, and Japan, in the process countering the fearsome kamikaze suicide plane assaults. He had to shift his flag from three carriers that were struck by Japanese aircraft.

In July 1945, following the victory at Okinawa, the U.S. Navy posted Mitscher to Washington and named him Deputy Chief of Naval Operations for air. Secretary of the Navy James V. Forrestal offered him the post of Chief of Naval Operations, but the unassuming officer turned it down. Instead, he accepted command of the U.S. Eighth Fleet and then the U.S. Atlantic Fleet. Marc A. Mitscher, the consummate carrier leader, died of a heart attack on 3 February 1947. After enduring years of wartime stress and tropical diseases, his body finally gave out.

U.S. Naval Institute Photo Archive

The words of Admiral Arleigh Burke, Mitscher's wartime chief of staff and later Chief of Naval Operations, highlighted his superior's leadership qualities: "He spoke in a low voice and used few words. Yet, so great was his concern for his people—for their training and welfare in peacetime and their rescue in combat—that he was able to obtain their final ounce of effort and loyalty, without which he could not have become the preeminent carrier force commander in the world. A bulldog of a fighter, a strategist blessed with an uncanny ability to foresee his enemy's next move, and a lifelong searcher after truth and trout streams, he was above all else—perhaps above all other—a Naval Aviator."

Suggested Reading

Coletta, Paolo. *Admiral Marc A. Mitscher and U.S. Naval Aviation: Bald Eagle.* Lewiston, N.Y.: Edwin Mellen, 1997.

Taylor, Theodore. *The Magnificent Mitscher.* New York: W. W. Norton, 1954. Reprinted with a new introduction by Jeffrey G. Barlow. Annapolis, Md.: Naval Institute Press, 1991.

About the Author

Lieutenant Commander Richard R. Burgess, USN (Ret.), has served as the managing editor of *Sea Power* magazine since 1997. He served as a Naval Flight Officer in P-3C patrol aircraft, and as an intelligence analyst, carrier department head, and editor of *Naval Aviation News*. He holds a degree in aviation management from Auburn University and a master's degree in strategic intelligence from Defense Intelligence College. He is the author of numerous articles on naval aviation and the editor of two books, *The Naval Aviation Guide* (Naval Institute Press, 1996) and *U.S. Naval Aviation* (NAMF, 2001), and coauthor of a third, *P-3 Orion in Action* (Squadron/Signal, 2004).

28

Willis A. Lee Jr.
Tactical Proficiency

Paul Stillwell

U.S. Naval Institute Photo Archive

The fortunes of war often determine which individuals in the naval service are widely known by future generations. Willis A. "Ching" Lee is an officer who is relatively obscure today despite a long and substantial naval career in the first half of the twentieth century. His peers, Chester Nimitz and William Halsey, regarded Lee so highly that he was assigned in the Pacific battle zone throughout the large part of World War II. Lee was positioned to lead battleships in a surface action against the Japanese if the occasion arose; he was also Halsey's potential replacement as Commander, Third Fleet. Because of circumstances, aircraft carriers had become the preeminent combatants by the time he got on the scene.

Lee possessed a reputation as a leader because of his tactical expertise, thorough professional knowledge, and calmness during periods of stress. Lee was unpretentious and approachable. Subordinates felt comfortable with him because of his easy manner, sense of humor, and friendliness. He also had an ability to focus on the important, leaving less important things to others. He was not fussy about military appearance; in fact, a junior officer teased him about being the first officer selected for admiral who didn't have his necktie two-blocked to his collar. Though he had a great deal of intellectual curiosity and read voraciously, Lee considered paperwork drudgery and avoided it whenever he could. His passions were gunnery, radar, ship handling, tactics, and mathematics.

Even as a boy, Lee had a great interest in guns. He grew up in the town of Owenton amid the farm country of north central Kentucky. From an early age, he began to develop his shot on whatever he could find: animals, weather vanes, and other targets of opportunity. He entered the Naval Academy in 1904 at the age of sixteen and starred on the academy's rifle team. In 1907, he won the national rife and pistol championships. Later, in the 1920 Olympics, when he was a lieutenant commander, Lee earned five gold medals, one silver, and one bronze for his shooting.

As a junior officer, Lee had an unusually early exposure to combat. In 1914, during a period of revolution in Mexico, President Woodrow Wilson ordered landing parties of Marines and Sailors ashore at Vera Cruz. Included was Ensign Willis Lee of the battleship *New Hampshire*. Snipers rarely showed themselves, so Lee calmly sat down with his rifle on his knees, offering himself as a target. It ended as "a competition in which there were no return matches," author Jack Sweetman later wrote.

Lee also developed his seamanship. During the 1920s, Lee commanded three different destroyers. A friend remembered that Lee was fond of ship handling. For his own enjoyment, he would try to bring the bow of his destroyer up close enough so that it would just kiss the stern of a ship ahead. In the years that followed, he had a variety of duties at sea and ashore. In the 1930s, he served several tours of duty in Washington in the Navy Department's Division of Fleet Training. The division was not concerned with personnel training, rather with supervising the fleet in its preparation for battle. When he went back to sea in 1936 as a captain, Lee became commanding officer of the antiquated light cruiser *Concord*. Crew members from the *Concord* considered her a happy ship because of Lee's friendly style of leadership and interest in the men. The crew also won the Battenberg Cup for winning races with pulling whaleboats, a remarkable feat for a cruiser in competition with the battleships and carriers that had much larger crews.

In the late 1930s, Lee served on the staff of Rear Admiral Harold Stark, Commander, Cruisers Battle Force. The white-haired Stark had seven staff officers, so the group acquired a nickname, "Snow White and the Seven Dwarfs." Lee, who had notoriously bad eyesight and wore heavy glasses, was nicknamed "Doc" after one of the dwarfs. When Stark became Chief of Naval Operations in 1939, Lee accompanied him to Washington and became assistant director of fleet training. Europe was soon at war, and Lee focused on getting ships as well equipped as possible with radar and antiaircraft guns. New classes of ships were emerging from the nation's shipyards, and Lee often went to inspect them to make sure the designs prepared by the engineers were suitable for operation by war-fighters.

In the autumn of 1941, Lee was selected for rear admiral, more than thirty-three years after he had graduated from Annapolis. When Admiral Ernest J. King came to Washington in December, in the wake of the attack at Pearl Harbor, Lee became his assistant chief of staff for readiness. But Lee preferred being a fighter much more than an administrator, so it was with a great deal of satisfaction that he reported to USS *South Dakota* in the summer of 1942 as Commander, Battleship Division Six, the first of the U.S. Navy's new fast battleships to go to the South Pacific.

In August of 1942, U.S. Marines invaded Guadalcanal and Tulagi in the Solomons in order to control an airstrip known as Henderson Field. The Japanese fought back desperately in an attempt to retake the island; their aircraft and ships made frequent attacks. The fast battleships were ordered into the aircraft carrier formations to provide antiaircraft protection, but the Americans also needed a way to counter the Japanese battleships and cruisers that pounded Guadalcanal with shore bombardment.

On the night of November 12–13, a U.S. cruiser force staved off a bombardment, but two American admirals were killed, in part because of unfamiliarity with how to use radar in a surface action. Two nights later, it was Lee's turn to lead a scratch force of two battleships and four destroyers in a night action between Savo Island and Guadalcanal. Lee's flagship *Washington* opened fired shortly after midnight. Projectiles zinged back and forth at close range, less than ten thousand yards. Years later, Admiral Crutchley described it as looking like "a red snowball fight." In the battle, Lee's force sank the battleship

Kirishima and destroyer *Ayanami*. The planned Japanese bombardment was stymied through Lee's superior tactical knowledge. The victory helped turn the tide in the Guadalcanal campaign.

Prewar doctrine for both the Americans and the Japanese anticipated that such gun battles would be an inevitable part of a Pacific war, and both sides continued to prepare for that possibility. In 1943 Lee became Commander, Battleships Pacific. As planners geared up for the Central Pacific island-hopping offensive spearheaded by carriers and amphibious forces, the fast battleships became heavily armored antiaircraft platforms. But Lee's ships were held in readiness in the event that the Japanese battle line emerged. In the spring of 1944, Lee was promoted to vice admiral and became the surface counterpart of Vice Admiral Marc Mitscher, who led the fast carrier force.

Commodore Arleigh Burke, Mitscher's chief of staff, considered the pair of them tops in their field tactically. But the opportunity to engage the Japanese ships eluded Lee. In June 1944, at the Marianas, he declined a proposed night surface action because his ships in the carrier screens had not had an opportunity to practice together in the high-speed night maneuvering that would be necessary. In October 1944, in the Battle of Leyte Gulf, Lee had his ships ready to take on the Japanese battle line, but he was denied the opportunity when Admiral Halsey took the battleships and carriers north to engage a decoy force of Japanese carriers devoid

Naval Historical Center, FADM C. W. Nimitz

of planes. The man who had prepared for this engagement his entire professional career was a passenger as *Washington* and the battleships with her steamed three hundred miles north and three hundred miles south without firing a shot.

In a sense, everything after Guadalcanal was anticlimactic. In June of 1945, Lee was ordered back to the United States because his analytic and tactical skills were needed to find new methods for defending against kamikaze suicide aircraft as the fleet prepared for the planned invasion of Japan in late 1945. He was eager to get back to the fleet for that final push, but it never came. Instead, the use of two atomic bombs led to the Japanese surrender in mid-August. Lee died of a heart attack a week and a half later at the age of fifty-seven. He had spent himself in the cause of victory.

Suggested Reading

Sweetman, Jack, ed. *Great American Naval Battles*. Annapolis, Md.: Naval Institute Press, 1998.

Reynolds, Clark G. *The Fast Carriers: The Forging of an Air Navy*. Annapolis, Md.: Naval Institute Press, 1992.

About the Author

Paul Stillwell is director of the history division of the U.S. Naval Institute. In 1969 he served in the crew of the *New Jersey*, which had been one of Lee's flagships in World War II. Stillwell has written a number of books on battleships, including individual histories of the *New Jersey*, *Missouri*, and *Arizona*. He is at work on a biography of Willis Lee.

29

Ernest J. King
Ambition

Captain Robert S. Burrell

Navy Department Photo in the National Archives

The U.S. Navy has not often looked to Fleet Admiral Ernest J. King as a premier example of naval leadership. With the major exception of King Hall at the U.S. Naval Academy, few historical landmarks bear his name today. One explanation for this likely derives from King's abrasive character. Army General George C. Marshall once declared, "I had trouble with King because he was always sore at everybody." One of King's own daughters mused that he was "the most even-tempered man in the Navy. He was always in a rage." The admiral certainly rubbed many of his officers the wrong way and did not seem to care very much if his subordinates feared his temper. Nevertheless, many of King's traits made him an effective leader. Fleet Admiral Ernest J. King not only led the United States to victory over Germany in the Atlantic and over Japan in the Pacific during World War II; he was also one of the most powerful naval officers in history, bearing such a senior rank in time of war. Perhaps the leadership traits that most facilitated King's exceptional accomplishments were his ambition and determination.

Oddly, ambition does not usually receive much attention by institutions imparting leadership qualities. Yet, as in most vocations, it certainly remains a necessary component to long-term success in the naval officer corps. In King's case, he started from humble beginnings in the small town of Lorain, Ohio, where his father performed maintenance in railroad yards. Perhaps his experiences growing up in a hard-working middle-class family served as impetus to take advantage of every available opportunity in life.

After graduating from high school, King secured an appointment to Annapolis in 1897. Remarkably, as a mere midshipman, he served aboard the USS *Mississippi* in 1898 and saw combat action during the Spanish-American War. Following the conflict, King returned to the Academy's academic curriculum in which he excelled. He later served as battalion commander during his first-class year; in 1901, he graduated fourth in his class. Despite his final order of merit, King refused to concede that anyone had outperformed him and later insisted that he could have been honor graduate but had chosen not to look conspicuous.

During the next forty years of King's extensive naval career, he consistently volunteered for the most demanding assignments—those that would best prepare him for future positions of authority. Initially a surface warfare officer, he served on a variety of ships. As a junior officer, his opinionated disputes with superiors earned him a number of black marks on evaluations. Nonetheless, this same vigorous bearing gained King the respect of Admiral William S. Sims, who in 1914 recommended King for command of a division of destroyers. During World War I, he worked on the staff of Admiral Henry Mayo. After his promotion to captain, King switched warfare specialties and attended submarine school in 1922. He subsequently commanded a submarine flotilla and base until 1926.

Recognizing the shortage of high-ranking officers in the ever-expanding aviation community, King laterally transferred again, attending flight school in Pensacola in 1927. At this point, his career soared for a decade with a variety of prominent command positions in the naval air arm—rising through the ranks to vice admiral. He eventually reached four-star rank in 1941, when he was charged with the Atlantic Fleet and the difficult task of protecting American shipping against German submarines.

On 7 December 1941, when the Japanese Imperial Navy dealt an almost crippling blow to the Pacific Fleet, the U.S. Navy direly needed strong leadership. The Navy's prewar battleship philosophy sunk with its ships at Pearl Harbor, and many aging admirals had little understanding of carrier warfare. The platforms the United States most needed, carriers and destroyers, were in short supply. Distinctively, the brilliant and aggressive Admiral Ernest J. King had commanded surface ships and submarines *and* flown

aircraft. Because of his experience, President Franklin D. Roosevelt asked King to serve as the new Commander in Chief, U.S. Fleet. He was eminently qualified to lead the U.S. Navy into war.

Once appointed, King immediately began consolidating his power. Instead of setting up headquarters aboard a flagship at sea as his predecessor had done, King procured office space in Washington, where he could directly fight the bureaucratic struggles over national strategy and limited resources. In addition, he effectively contested his position's responsibilities and those of Chief of Naval Operations (CNO) Admiral Harold Stark. President Roosevelt finally resolved the controversy in March by sending Stark to London and making King both Commander in Chief, U.S. Fleet, and CNO—the first and only time one man would hold both positions simultaneously, giving King unprecedented power.

As CNO, King demonstrated a dogged determination to launch an American offensive in the Pacific, despite the official strategy of containing Germany first. Initial setbacks in the South Pacific in 1942 failed to deter him. Rather than waiting for America's industrial superiority to overcome the Japanese, King demanded immediate results with the parity of forces available. His insistence resulted in earlier than expected victories at Midway in 1942 and Guadalcanal in 1943, which turned the tide of war in the Pacific. In a further resolution, King demanded extremely aggressive unrestricted submarine warfare. Regardless of the vast distances involved and technical difficulties with some components of American submarines, the CNO required successful missions and dealt with failures harshly.

By the end of 1944, the U.S. Navy had assembled such a vast fleet that it controlled the world's oceans, veritably uncontested. The U.S. Navy demolished the German submarine threat in the Atlantic, seized thousands of miles of Japanese territory in the Central Pacific, fought the largest naval battle in history against the Imperial Japanese Navy at Leyte Gulf, and facilitated the

U.S. Naval Institute Photo Archive

breaching of "Fortress Europe." And no single man exercised more influence over these results than Admiral Ernest J. King.

With the war in both the European and Pacific theaters nearly won, President Roosevelt promoted King to the new five-star rank of Fleet Admiral in December 1944. Germany surrendered in 1945 and Japan a few months later, ending the tragic contest for the U.S. Navy.

Reflecting on the most expansive naval war in world history, the United States was fortunate to possess a leader of King's forceful temperament and diverse experience. During this time of national emergency, King provided the centralized leadership to wield a U.S. Navy of unprecedented size to satisfy competing national objectives in the face of opposition around the globe. His drive, ambition, and knowledge helped to establish the course of the American war with Japan. More than any other student of prewar naval planning, he determinedly applied the U.S. Navy's theories and made them a reality. Despite colossal adversities, King doggedly pursued victory. At the age of sixty-eight, King retired from the U.S. Navy in 1946 and died ten years later in 1956. He is buried at the U.S. Naval Academy cemetery, ending his incredible naval journey in Annapolis where it had begun.

Suggested Reading

Buell, Thomas B. *Master of Sea Power*. 1980. Reprint, Annapolis, Md.: Naval Institute Press, 1995.

Graybar, Lloyd J. "Ernest J. King: Commander of the Two-Ocean Navy." In *Quarterdeck and Bridge: Two Centuries of American Naval Leaders*, edited by James C. Bradford. Annapolis, Md.: Naval Institute Press, 1997.

Love, Robert W. "Ernest J. King." In *The Chiefs of Naval Operations*, edited by Robert W. Love. Annapolis, Md.: Naval Institute Press, 1980.

About the Author

A widely published author, Captain Robert S. Burrell has a master's degree in history from San Diego State University and has taught Navy, Marine Corps, and Pacific War histories at the U.S. Naval Academy.

30

Charles B. McVay III

Accountability

Commander Mary Kelly

U.S. Naval Institute Photo Archive

Two torpedoes hit the USS *Indianapolis* shortly after midnight on 30 July 1945. Sixty-five feet of the ship's bow were completely demolished by the first torpedo, taking Sailors and Marines with it. The second torpedo pierced the four-inch steel below the bridge, affecting both boiler rooms. The impact of the two torpedoes boring into the starboard side actually lifted the ship out of the water. With the bow gone, seawater was flooding the ship at an incredible rate. For the ship's commanding officer, Captain Charles B. McVay III, his worst fear had come true. He was living a nightmare that would not end until 2001.

No stranger to warfighting and the pressures of war, Captain McVay commanded the USS *Indianapolis,* a cruiser and the Fifth Fleet flagship, through the Battles of Tarawa, Woleai, Iwo Jima, and during the bombing of Okinawa. At Okinawa, the USS *Indianapolis* was hit by a kamikaze. Without McVay's prescient focus on damage-control training and calm, confidence-inspiring leadership, the USS *Indianapolis* probably would have been lost long before that night.

Part of a well-known U.S. Navy family, McVay was expected to keep naval tradition and honor alive. His father, Admiral Charles McVay II, was an 1890 U.S. Naval Academy graduate and commanded the Asiatic Fleet. Captain Charles McVay III was a 1920 Naval Academy graduate with his own stellar career in the making. By 1945, he was experienced in command and warfighting tactics. He had just completed a record-setting transit to Tinian, delivering vital parts for the atomic bomb that was dropped on Hiroshima. USS *Indianapolis* was now en route to Leyte Gulf from Guam for weapons training and, presumably, more combat operations under Admiral Raymond Spruance, Commander, Fifth Fleet.

On 30 July 1945, that all changed. After taking two lethal torpedo hits from the Japanese submarine *I-58,* the USS *Indianapolis* began to sink. The captain gave orders to radio for help, and then to abandon ship. Precious minutes and seconds flew by as the men of *Indy* struggled away from the confines of the ship that would become their coffin if they could not escape. They scrambled to get over the side and away from the cruiser before the vacuum of the sinking ship pulled them below with it.

Of the 1,198 Sailors and Marines onboard that fateful night, about 300 either died in the torpedo attacks and the ensuing fires and explosions or were trapped in the ship and died as she went under.

For the almost 900 men floundering in the Philippine Sea, panic set in as they struggled in the darkness to find other survivors and whatever precious survival gear they could find in the carnage of their lost home. Men, body parts, and pieces of the ship were scattered for miles in the cold and murky water.

Many men were severely injured by the ensuing explosions that tore apart the ship. The thick layer of oil floating on the seawater compounded the initial burns and injuries men received from the blasts and from escaping the ship. Men found themselves covered in oil; those who swallowed it were retching violently. Sailors clung to each other and whatever floating wreckage they could find while continuing their search for better-suited life jackets and lifeboats. As time passed, what was left of the crew was now spread out over several miles, in the dark, and utterly alone in the middle of the Pacific Ocean.[1]

As the night progressed, men treaded water while tending to the wounded, comforting each other, and waiting for the warmth of the morning sun. Surely the U.S. Navy received their distress message and help was on the way.

But it was not.

The radio messages were received but ignored. One command did send boats to look for them, but all of them were recalled because there was no message confirmation. Some believed it had to be a Japanese hoax.[2] No one realized that the USS *Indianapolis* and her crew of 1,198 people were lost at sea.

The men finally managed to gather themselves into five groups. Two were composed of over 300 men. One of those was lead by Ensign Harlan Twible, who had graduated from the Naval Academy just two weeks before reporting to the USS *Indianapolis*.[3] Another was lead by Captain Edward Parke, USMC; Father Thomas Conway; and Lieutenant Commander Lewis Haynes, the ship's doctor.[4] A third group split into two when the groups in the life rafts could not agree on what to do. The last group included Captain McVay. Those in the smaller groups were fortunate to have life rafts. Except for the group that split, each of the groups believed they were the only survivors. The night passed slowly.

Hope was higher when dawn broke Monday morning. Men buoyed each other, offering encouraging words of certain rescue. The U.S. Navy must know where they were, and a ship was certainly on a search and rescue mission by now. Realizing what they had survived, the morale was relatively high. But they were fatigued from treading water all night, and the sun baked their unprotected skin. For those who sustained burns and injuries from the ship, the additional exposure to sun and salt was pure agony. Monday slowly passed without sighting planes or boats arriving to assist. The men reluctantly steeled themselves for another chilling night in the cold Pacific waters.

Could it possibly get worse? For the men of the USS *Indianapolis*, it did. The smell of blood and debris attracted sharks by the hundreds. At first, the sharks seemed content to feed on the dead, but the thrashing, injured, and bleeding men made easy prey as well. Cries of the victims sent waves of terror throughout the remaining groups of survivors. All through the night, injured men continued to fall victim to the circling sharks.

The fear of shark attacks made the second night seem endless. Exhaustion slowly set in. The cries of pain broke through the dark as more men were attacked and pulled underwater. Men tried to think of anything besides water to drink and being safe and dry.

On Tuesday, intense sunburn also added to the adversities of the USS *Indianapolis*'s crew. Although trained to the contrary, some drank the seawater and became ill. Once the survivors were safely home, Lieutenant Commander Haynes, the ship's doctor, was the first to record the events. He described the effects caused by drinking seawater: "Seawater has twice the salinity the human body can process. As sodium is ingested, the cells shrink, expand, and explode, sacrificing precious remaining free water in an effort to purge the sodium. This is called hypertremia and it impairs the neurons in the brain. The body's electrical activity stops as cells are destroyed. The only cure is massive rehydration. Hallucinations, delusional talk, and certain death follow."

Even without deliberately drinking seawater, men were massively dehydrated and were losing their ability to think rationally. The situation was growing dire. Many began to die because they slowly lost the will to live. Those who survived this ordeal claimed that fighting against the temptation to give up was the most physically and mentally exhausting challenge they faced.

A precise combination of miscalculations and catastrophic circumstances led to this tragedy. First, Captain McVay tried to protect his ship to the best of his ability, but he was not advised of Japanese submarine activity in the area (although select staff members knew about it), and he was denied an escort ship he requested. Second, due to previous message-routing problems and confusion about the follow-on assignment for the USS *Indianapolis*, no one knew when they were expected to arrive at Leyte, so their absence was not missed. Rear Admiral Lynde McCormick, from Task Force 95, to whom the USS *Indianapolis* was to report, simply assumed that the *Indianapolis* either changed her course or was diverted from her original orders by Admiral Raymond Spruance, Commander, Fifth Fleet.[5] Third, the distress message that Captain McVay ordered transmitted was treated as a hoax; as a result, no one initiated a rescue. And finally, Chief of Naval Operations Admiral Ernest King

had suspended the procedures for reporting ships' arrivals—and presumably non-arrivals—by port operations.[6]

For five painfully long, agonizing days, the remaining survivors of the USS *Indianapolis* held hope against hope that they would be found.

The survivors were discovered, accidentally, on Thursday, 2 August. Lieutenant Chuck Gwinn, flying a PV-1 bomber on a routine patrol off Peleliu spotted what he thought was an oil slick and flew lower to investigate. It was a group of survivors frantically waving from the water. They had finally been found. On receiving the radioed information, Gwinn's boss, Lieutenant Commander George Atteberry, immediately requested the launch of a Catalina, a PBY plane equipped with floats to land on water. He was denied, so he and his crew launched another bomber to relieve Gwinn, who was short on fuel. Meanwhile, radio dispatches were heard by Lieutenant Adrian Marks, part of the Catalina squadron. Marks decided the situation warranted an emergency and launched the alert plane. Once on scene, Marks made a daring sea landing to provide shelter and water to as many survivors as possible. With the disaster and location known, rescue efforts were directed to the area. The Catalina was aided by the eventual arrival, first, by destroyer escort *Cecil J. Doyle*, and later by the transports *Bassett* and *Ringness*, destroyers *Ralph Talbot* and *Madison*, and destroyer escort *Dufilho*. The last survivors were pulled from the water on Friday, 3 August, after five days in the ocean. Only 321 were alive to be rescued, and 4 of those died in the hospital shortly after arrival.

That anyone survived this terrible ordeal at sea is a miracle. Those who survived, in their own words, did so by courage and determination. It took mammoth efforts of everyone to fortify the rest of the men on the USS *Indianapolis* through the terrible ordeal. Men swam through the shark-infested waters to recover the injured. Some literally carried the unconscious as they treaded water for days. Others repeatedly gave their life preservers to others and went without until they found another. The mental and physical stamina required to survive those harrowing days at sea is difficult to imagine, and every survivor deserves recognition and admiration.

After the rescue, Captain McVay was court-martialed. He was the only commanding officer of a warship in the history of the U.S. Navy court-martialed for negligence resulting in the loss of his ship in a time of war. McVay was found guilty of "failing to zigzag" the ship.[7] The court failed to acknowledge that the ship had been zigzagging prior to bad weather, and per required procedures, discontinued the maneuver with plans to resume once weather permitted.

Throughout the entire ordeal, even though subsequent investigations proved there was nothing he could have done differently to avoid those torpedoes, Captain McVay accepted the full responsibility of command. He took each and every death hard and was plagued by guilt and nightmares for the rest of his life. Captain McVay, always the consummate professional, accepted the U.S. Navy's decision with dignity and mental courage and continued to serve in the U.S. Navy for four more years.[8]

In an October 1999 *Proceedings* article, Commander William Toti commented, "There was nothing he could have done to prevent that misfortune, and he should have never been prosecuted in the first place." A seven-member board seemed to agree and therefore recommended clemency. Upon review of the board findings, Fleet Admiral King restored McVay to full duty, but the previous guilty conviction stood as blemish on Captain McVay and the entire crew's record.

Captain McVay's story is inspirational because his story transcends him. The tale, while heartrending and sad, illuminates the heroism and courage of his crew, both during those horrific five days in the sea and in the many years that have followed. The crew of the *Indianapolis* wanted their commanding officer's name cleared. They petitioned Congress, wrote letters, and provided testimony to get the court-martial decision reversed. McVay had accepted his reprimand as part the responsibility of command. But

his men felt he had been wronged. In a telephone interview, Woody James, one of the survivors, said he was taught that "you fight just as hard, if not harder, to right a wrong done to someone else as you would for yourself." He explained that the crew felt an injustice was committed and they demonstrated the same tenacity and courage that sustained them through those five harrowing days—and they finally persevered.

The impetus for further investigations came largely from the other survivors, who held their skipper blameless. In 2001, U.S. Navy leadership took action to right a fifty-six-year-old wrong. Secretary of the Navy Gordon England ordered McVay's record cleared of all wrongdoing. Charles McVay was finally absolved. It may have been personally too late for Captain McVay,[9] but it restored honor to the courageous survivors who had lived under a shadow since the court-martial. The U.S. Navy realized Captain McVay was wronged and corrected it. In the process, the crew of the *Indianapolis* was awarded a Unit Citation for its role in the delivery of the components of the Little Boy bomb.

The courage of the crew during their difficult mission and throughout those days of horror in the Philippine Sea is a testimony to each and every one of them. The common thread among the survivors was their determination to live through the horror, when death seemed much easier. When asked to provide advice to young leaders, Woody James cautions, "Never, ever, give up. Always fight to do the right thing."

Captain McVay's exceptional leadership record was never in dispute. What is so notable about him is how he faced adversity. Captain McVay had the authority of command and accepted full responsibility, even though he was blameless. The truth of what he and the crew of the *Indianapolis* survived is more incredible than any fiction and is a reminder of what true courage under fire really means.

Those assigned to the USS *Indianapolis* on 30 July 1945 all suffered. Those who died made the ultimate sacrifice, and those who survived lived to fight for justice and to clear the name of

Charles McVay, restoring honor to the USS *Indianapolis*, her crew, and the justice and dignity of the U.S. Navy.

Notes

1. The term "crew" in this narrative includes the Sailors assigned to the USS *Indianapolis* as well as the thirty-nine members of the Marine detachment.
2. The Japanese would sometimes send a call for help to lure American ships. It seems likely that this is why no one responded to the distress call.
3. Harlan Twible said he survived by applying what he learned at the Naval Academy, and if that didn't work, what he learned in Sunday school (quoted in Kurzman, *Fatal Voyage*, p. 310).
4. Of the three, only Lieutenant Commander Haynes survived. Captain Parke exhausted himself helping others. He repeatedly gave up his own life jacket and treaded water until he could find another, all the while keeping men together. He had apparently absorbed too much seawater through his skin, experienced hallucinations from hypertremia, and swam away from the group he held together. Father Conway prayed and administered last rites for three days until delirium set in and he died in Lieutenant Commander Haynes's arms.
5. The USS *Indianapolis* was the flagship of the Fifth Fleet. While on the *Indianapolis*, Admiral Spruance directed the campaigns that cap-

Courtesy of Capt. H. H. Smith-Hutton, USN (Ret.), via Capt. Paul B. Ryan, USN (Ret.)

tured the Gilberts, Marshalls, Marianas, Iwo Jima, and Okinawa and defeated the Japanese fleet in the June 1944 Battle of Philippine Sea.

6. This policy was changed that week. To reduce message traffic as well as increase security around ship movements, Admiral King had directed policy 10CL-45, which instructed, "arrival of combatant ships shall not be reported." It was interpreted that the non-arrival of combatants was also unreported.

7. Zigzagging was an antisubmarine tactic used under attack per standard operation procedures and was considered an evasive maneuver. The commanding officer of the *I-58*, Commander Mochitsura Hashimoto, testified at the courts-martial that zigzagging would not have helped the USS *Indianapolis*.

8. In 1949, Captain McVay was discharged from the U.S. Navy, but as a rear admiral. Such eleventh-hour promotions are called "tombstone" or "graveyard" promotions, which in McVay's case meant he was allowed all customs and traditions and retirement pay as a rear admiral. He reportedly preferred to be addressed as "Captain." According to Dan Kurzman's book, *Fatal Voyage*, "he was an honest-to-goodness captain and never was a rear admiral" (p. 318).

9. Charles McVay shot himself on 6 November 1968. He had been devastated when his beloved wife, Louise, died of cancer. He later remarried but still desperately missed Louise, his soul mate. In the end, the additional loss of his grandchild to a brain tumor and the guilt from his part in the loss of so many lives became too much.

Suggested Reading

James, Woody. USS *Indianapolis* crew member. Interview by Commander Mary Kelly, 5 July 2004.

Kurzman, Dan. *Fatal Voyage: The Sinking of the USS Indianapolis*. New York: Atheneum, 1990.

Stanton, Doug. *In Harm's Way*. New York: St. Martin's, 2001.

Toti, William J. "The Sinking of the Indy and the Responsibility of Command." U.S. Naval Institute *Proceedings* 125, no. 10 (October 1999): 86–94.

About the Author

Commander Mary Kelly, PhD, is an instructor at the U.S. Naval Academy and publishes a series of management and finance articles.

31

Chester W. Nimitz
Loyalty

Dr. Jeffrey G. Barlow

U.S. Naval Institute Photo Archive

The U.S. Navy's role in the Pacific during World War II is invariably linked with Fleet Admiral Chester W. Nimitz. He served as Commander in Chief, Pacific Fleet, starting on 31 December 1941 and, beginning on 30 March 1942, concurrently served as Commander in Chief, Pacific Ocean Areas (one of two theater commands in the Pacific). Nimitz was the senior U.S. naval officer directly engaged in the war against Japan from shortly after the Japanese attack on Pearl Harbor through the signing of the surrender documents on the deck of the battleship *Missouri* in September 1945.

Imperturbable in manner, the white-haired, blue-eyed admiral most often projected an almost fatherly mien to his subordinates. Although credited with having violent outbursts of temper on occasion as a youngster, Nimitz had long since learned to curb his darker emotional impulses in the interest of furthering mission accomplishment. The leadership trait that Chester Nimitz most exhibited as a senior officer was loyalty—to his superiors and to his subordinates.

Of German-American stock, Chester Nimitz was born in Fredericksburg, Texas, in February 1885, some months after the death of his father. Raised by his mother and his gregarious, tall-tale-telling paternal grandfather, he quickly learned the simple virtues conveyed by a life filled with regular physical activity and manual labor.

Determined to seek a life beyond the confines of a small Texas town, he applied to his local congressman for an appointment to the U.S. Military Academy. When the congressman told him that all of the appointments to West Point were filled but that there was an opening at the U.S. Naval Academy, Nimitz jumped at the chance to apply for it. Following some extensive tutoring in a variety of academic subjects, the young man took the local entrance exam for the Naval Academy and emerged with the highest score of those competing. During his years at Annapolis, Nimitz proved strong in academics as well as in leadership skills. He stood seventh out of the 114 men who graduated in the class of 1905.

Nimitz spent the first years of his naval career in the Philippines, onboard ships of the Asiatic Fleet. He received command of the gunboat *Panay* as an ensign in January 1907, and a few months later Nimitz commanded the four-stack destroyer *Decatur*. During this latter assignment, the young officer ran his ship aground on a mud bank in Batangas Harbor. Dutifully informing his seniors about the accident, Nimitz was court-martialed for "culpable inefficiency" but received only a public reprimand by the admiral commanding U.S. naval forces in Philippine waters on the reduced charge of "neglect of duty." Fortunately, the incident did not harm his career.

First assigned to submarine duty in 1909, Chester Nimitz became an advocate for replacing the U.S. submarines' dangerous gasoline engines with diesels in the days before World War I. In the latter half of the 1930s, Nimitz interspersed sea duty as skipper of the cruiser *Augusta*, Commander, Cruiser Division Two, and Commander, Battleship Division One, with shore tours as assistant chief and later chief of the Bureau of Navigation (later renamed the Bureau of Naval Personnel). While heading the Bureau of Navigation in mid-December 1941, in the aftermath of the Japanese attack on Pearl Harbor, Nimitz was informed by Navy Secretary Frank Knox that he would be sent out to command the battered Pacific Fleet.

Nimitz demonstrated his concept of loyalty on the day he assumed command of the Pacific Fleet. Assembling the staff officers of Admiral Kimmel (the officer who had been in command at the time Pearl Harbor was attacked) and Admiral Pye (the officer designated as the interim commander until Nimitz's arrival in Hawaii), Chester Nimitz told the men that he did not blame them for what had happened to the fleet. He then said that he wanted them to stay on as members of his staff, because he had complete confidence in their abilities and needed

them in place to provide continuity to the command over the difficult months to come.

A second instance of the admiral's loyalty was in connection with the reassignment of Commander Joseph J. Rochefort from his job as head of the 14th Naval District's Combat Intelligence Unit (designated Station Hypo). During the initial months of the Pacific fighting, Rochefort and his people were heavily involved in breaking into JN-25—the Imperial Japanese Navy's General Purpose Code. Their success in being able to decrypt significant portions of this code and thus to read essential portions of high-level Japanese navy messages by April 1942 led in large part to the U.S. Navy's partial success in the Battle of Coral Sea in May 1942 and to its pivotal victory at Midway in early June.

The success of Station Hypo in the days leading up to the Battle of Midway in breaking the important Japanese messages and correctly analyzing from these intercepts what the Japanese Combined Fleet planned to do sharply contrasted with the woeful cryptanalytic efforts of the radio intelligence unit in Washington at that time.

Embarrassed by this circumstance, the director of naval communications was determined to get rid of Commander Rochefort, and he convinced the Vice Chief of Naval Operations, Vice Admiral Frederick J. Horne, to direct the reorganization of the U.S. Navy's intelligence setup in Hawaii and order Rochefort back to the states for other duty. When he received Horne's directive, Admiral Nimitz wrote personally to Admiral Ernest J. King, the Commander in Chief, U.S. Fleet, and Chief of Naval Operations (CNO), in an attempt to reverse the reorganization scheme and keep Rochefort in Hawaii. Although he was ultimately unsuccessful in this effort, his attempt demonstrated the strength of his loyalty to valued subordinates.

Given this leadership trait, it is little wonder that Fleet Admiral Nimitz was held in high esteem by the officers and enlisted who served with him during the war and during his final two years of active duty as CNO. Leaving active

U.S. Naval Institute Photo Archive

service in December 1947, he and his wife eventually settled in California. He died there in 1966 and was laid to rest in the Golden Gate National Cemetery, south of San Francisco.

Suggested Reading

Lundstrom, John B. "Chester W. Nimitz: Victory in the Pacific." In *Quarterdeck and Bridge: Two Centuries of American Naval Leaders*, edited by James C. Bradford. Annapolis, Md.: Naval Institute Press, 1997.

Potter, E. B. *Nimitz*. Annapolis, Md.: Naval Institute Press, 1976.

———. "Fleet Admiral Chester William Nimitz: United States Navy 1885–1966." In *Men of War: Great Naval Leaders of World War II*, edited by Stephen Howarth. New York: St. Martin's, 1993.

Ross, Steven T. "Chester William Nimitz." In *The Chiefs of Naval Operations*, edited by Robert W. Love Jr. Annapolis, Md.: Naval Institute Press, 1980.

About the Author

Dr. Jeffrey G. Barlow has been a historian with the Contemporary History Branch of the Naval Historical Center since 1987. He received a doctorate in international studies from the University of South Carolina in 1981. An expert on the U.S. Joint Chiefs of Staff and twentieth-century American military policy and strategy, he has written chapters for more than a dozen books dealing with the events of World War II and the Cold War. He is the author of *Revolt of the Admirals: The Fight for Naval Aviation, 1945–1950* (Naval Historical Center, 1994).

32

Raymond A. Spruance
Analytical Thinking

Dr. Jeffrey G. Barlow

Naval War College Historical Center

One's attention is not often directed toward senior naval officers who are quiet and deliberate in their manner of leadership. Instead, officers who display attributes of an outgoing personality and a visible confidence, even cockiness, in their attitudes and actions as leaders receive the attention. Admiral Raymond Ames Spruance was not one of the typical attention-getting officers. Throughout most of his naval career, Spruance displayed unsmiling yet serene self-control in his outward demeanor toward his contemporaries and subordinates. Nicknamed "Old Frozen Face" by some of his friends, Spruance was actually a sensitive, emotional, and shy man who had learned to suppress his emotions. During his years as a naval officer, his most prominent leadership quality was devotion to analytical thinking.

Born in July 1886 to financially comfortable parents who proved too distant or otherwise preoccupied to attend to the needs of their first-born son, Raymond Spruance was raised by his mother's parents and her sisters. He entered the Naval Academy in July 1903, a day before he turned seventeen. While there, Spruance excelled at academics. Graduating early in September 1906 with those in the top third of the class of 1907, he stood twenty-fifth out of 209 passed midshipmen. After an initial battleship tour, Spruance applied for and was accepted for postgraduate training in electricity.

As a lieutenant, Spruance first commanded the destroyer *Bainbridge*, based in the Philippines. Then he toured as the electrical officer on the battleship *Pennsylvania*. Afterward, Spruance spent the final year of World War I as an engineering duty officer assigned to the Brooklyn Navy Yard, responsible for the installation and testing of gunnery fire control systems. By now convinced that his engineering duty qualifications kept him from being selected for wartime sea duty, he never again sought an electrical engineering assignment.

When he was assigned as a student at the Naval War College in 1926, Raymond Spruance acquired the devotion to analytical thinking that held him in good stead once he became a flag officer. The course of study in which Spruance and his colleagues at the War College enrolled included an intensive instruction in naval warfare problems and war games as well as strategy and naval history. These problems provided an intellectual challenge for Spruance. Deriving sound operational and doctrinal solutions offered him a new outlet for his sharp intellect. After World War II, according to his biographer Tom Buell, Spruance remarked, "I believe that making war is a game that requires cold and careful calculation. Each operation is different and has to be analyzed and studied in order to prepare the most suitable plans for it. That is what makes the planning of operations in war such an interesting job."

When the Japanese attacked Pearl Harbor on 7 December 1941, Rear Admiral Spruance was serving as commander of the Pacific Fleet's Cruiser Division Five. As Japanese bombs were falling on the battle line docked at Ford Island, Spruance and his cruisers were some two hundred miles westward of Honolulu, escorting Admiral William F. Halsey's *Enterprise* task force, which was returning from delivering Marines to Wake Island. Almost exactly six months later, at the Battle of Midway, Spruance displayed his successful analytical thinking. At Midway, Spruance was commanding Halsey's task force, composed of the aircraft carriers *Enterprise* and *Hornet*, while Halsey was in the hospital suffering from an attack of acute dermatitis. During the afternoon of the first day of the battle, when the carrier *Yorktown*, the flagship of the officer in tactical command of the U.S. forces (Rear Admiral Frank Jack Fletcher), was badly damaged by attacking Japanese aircraft, tactical command was handed over to Spruance.

Through a combination of luck and skill that day, American naval aviators from the three carriers had managed to sink all four of the Japanese aircraft carriers. Late that afternoon the exuberant aviators on the staff pressed Admiral Spruance to head west after the remaining enemy fleet so that the American aircraft could be launched at short range against the Japanese surface forces at first light. After analyzing the situation, Spruance demurred. He was aware that his primary mission remained preventing the capture of Midway Island, and he was also aware that in the dark, his under-protected carrier force could unintentionally come within range of the unscathed Japanese battleships and cruisers that were some one hundred miles to the west. Assessing the benefits and the risks, he chose the conservative path of avoiding a possible surface melee in the dark. He ordered the task force to head eastward until midnight and then to turn north for an hour, before again heading westward in order to be in a position at daybreak to both defend Midway and attack the remaining enemy forces. In so doing, he unknowingly avoided the trap that Japanese Combined Fleet commander Isoroku Yamamoto was attempting to set for him. If he had done as the naval aviators on his staff had requested, Spruance might well have had his victory of the previous day turned into a defeat by the highly effective Japanese surface forces present in the area.

A second example of Spruance's highly successful analytical leadership style was demonstrated during the invasion of the Marshall Islands in early 1944. Spruance was a firm believer that once an operational plan had been carefully staffed out and thoroughly discussed with the commanders responsible for executing it, the plan should be followed and the commanders entrusted to do what was necessary to make it succeed. During the landings on Roi and Namur, the LVTs and landing craft of Rear Admiral Richard L. Conolly's Third Amphibious Group were milling about offshore due to the inexperience and fatigue of their crews. Even though all of the assault elements were not in position for the landing on Namur, Conolly

U.S. Naval Institute Photo Archive

ordered the assault to begin. The disorganized mass of craft headed for shore and hit the beach to find little Japanese opposition. Watching the scene from his flagship *Indianapolis*, Admiral Spruance turned to one of his staff officers after seeing the chaotic situation restored to order and said, "Seeing this proves that you can put complete faith in the men you have selected to do a job."

Spruance's quiet but determined leadership marked him as one of the outstanding U.S. naval commanders of World War II. Retiring from the U.S. Navy in July 1948, following a final tour as president of the Naval War College, Raymond Spruance and his wife settled in Pebble Beach,

California. He died in 1969 at the age of eighty-three and was buried alongside Fleet Admiral Chester Nimitz and Admiral Richmond Kelly Turner in Golden Gate National Cemetery.

Suggested Reading

Buell, Thomas B. *The Quiet Warrior: A Biography of Admiral Raymond A. Spruance.* Boston: Little, Brown, 1974.

Wukovits, John F. "Admiral Raymond A. Spruance: United States Navy 1886–1969." In *Men of War: Great Naval Leaders of World War II*, edited by Stephen Howarth. New York: St. Martin's, 1993.

About the Author

Dr. Jeffrey G. Barlow has been a historian with the Contemporary History Branch of the Naval Historical Center since 1987. He received a doctorate in international studies from the University of South Carolina in 1981. An expert on the U.S. Joint Chiefs of Staff and twentieth-century American military policy and strategy, he has written chapters for more than a dozen books dealing with the events of World War II and the Cold War. He is the author of *Revolt of the Admirals: The Fight for Naval Aviation, 1945–1950* (Naval Historical Center, 1994).

33

Victor H. Krulak
Vision

Major Shawn P. Callahan

Marine Corps History and Museum Division

Like all of the nation's most successful leaders, Lieutenant General Victor H. Krulak possessed a combination of admirable traits that contributed to his success. The prescient vision with which he focused his talents, however, made his contributions so remarkably influential. Victor Krulak looked at the world around him and saw opportunities for serving his country in new and more effective ways. By envisioning a better future for the Marine Corps and seeing that vision through, he made very significant contributions to national security on a number of occasions and helped the nation overcome several crises.

Victor Krulak was born in Denver, Colorado, on 7 January 1913. He grew up in San Diego, California. A talented boy, he earned admission to the Naval Academy when he was only sixteen years old. He began his studies at the academy in 1930 where his small frame earned him the nickname "Brute," a moniker that stuck with him for the rest of his life.

Upon graduating from the Naval Academy in 1934, Krulak served as a junior Marine officer during a period of enormous change in the Corps. Americans were becoming more aware of a new threat, Japan, whose military power was growing ominous despite negotiated limitations like the Washington Naval Arms Treaty of 1922. Marine visionaries like Lieutenant Colonel "Pete" Ellis had revised war plans, and a new role for the Marine Corps as an amphibious assault force was taking shape. In the same year that Krulak was commissioned, the Marine Corps published its *Tentative Manual for Landing Operations* (later adopted almost verbatim by the U.S. Navy and U.S. Army). In 1934, the Corps also began putting the newly formed Fleet Marine Force to the test in the first of a series of large-scale fleet landing exercises in California and on Culebra in the Caribbean. After tours with the Marine Detachment on the battleship *Arizona*, on instructor duty back at Annapolis, and with the 6th Marine Regiment, Krulak found himself in a position to contribute to this new vision of the Corps when he was transferred to the 4th Marine Regiment in China in 1937.

At a time when most Americans were skeptical about the combat capabilities of the Japanese, Krulak took them quite seriously. As a lieutenant in the intelligence section of the 4th Marines, he learned that the Japanese were also experimenting with amphibious operations. When the Japanese invaded Shanghai in 1937, he took a U.S. Navy tugboat out to observe their landing and noticed the new landing craft the Japanese were using. With specially designed bow-ramps that could be lowered to the beach, these landing craft were able to put soldiers and heavy equipment ashore much faster than the conventional landing craft of the time. Krulak compiled a series of sketches and photographs and wrote a detailed report on his observations for the Bureau of Ships, urging that the U.S. develop similar craft to improve their amphibious capability.

Unlike many who may have accepted the inertia of a bureaucratic system that did not act on new ideas, Krulak envisioned new possibilities for the Marine Corps and was aggressive in turning his vision into reality. Upon returning to the United States in 1940 to attend the Juniors Course for company grade officers, he went to find out what happened to his landing craft proposal. He eventually found the report gathering dust at the Bureau of Ships. The only indication it had ever been read was the comment, "Some nut in China" scrawled across the cover page. Krulak committed himself to seeing that the report received attention. He took it, along with a model he built of his proposed landing craft, to Brigadier General Holland M. Smith. General Smith had been charged with developing new techniques and equipment for the Marine Corps' amphibious mission and quickly recognized the value of the young captain's work. Smith had Krulak assigned to his staff and gave him the support he needed to bring his vision to fruition. Krulak soon enlisted the help of Andrew Jackson Higgins, a New Orleans boat builder who had grown famous for the shallow-draft boats that

had made successful rum runners in the swamps during Prohibition. Together, they developed a shallow-draft landing craft with a square bow and retractable ramp that became a staple of America's amphibian inventory during World War II—the landing craft, vehicle, and personnel (LCVP). Krulak supervised the operational testing of the LCVP and proved the value of his craft in fleet exercises in the Caribbean. The basic design of the vessel was adapted for carrying various types of loads and remains in use today.

As General Smith assumed command of the 1st Marine Brigade and then later the Amphibious Corps, Atlantic Fleet, Krulak served as his aide. He went on to refine another amphibious vehicle that would prove critical in the upcoming war. Donald Roebling of Dunedin, Florida, had recently developed an amphibious tractor designed for rescuing people trapped in the Everglade swamps. With its tanklike tracks, the floating vehicle could propel itself though the water, and then climb out of the water and drive across a beach, swamp, or reef. Again, working against the significant institutional inertia of the U.S. Navy and Marines Corps, Krulak was instrumental in the adoption and modification of Roebling's design and supervised the test effort in Quantico and the Caribbean. Despite the embarrassment of getting stuck on a reef when he invited Admiral Ernest J. King, Commander, Atlantic Fleet, to accompany him on a test run, Krulak's dedication to his vision won many supporters. His success with the project ultimately saved the lives of countless soldiers, Sailors, and Marines in World War II by providing them with several new landing craft purpose-built to conquer the hellish environment of amphibious assault.

Once his vision was realized and war broke, Krulak was not content to remain in the rear area as a general's aide. He volunteered for parachute training, a daring new military technique with which armies around the world had begun to experiment. As a major, he was assigned to command the 2nd Parachute Battalion, which he led in combat on Vella Lavella, Choiseul, and Bougainville. Although the "Paramarines" never jumped in combat, his unit was enormously successful at creating diversions to distract the attention of Japanese combat forces away from larger, more vulnerable landing forces. On his last raid, Krulak was wounded twice but refused to give up command until his men had all been evacuated. He was subsequently awarded the Navy Cross for his leadership and heroism.

Lieutenant Colonel Krulak served with distinction in the 6th Marine Division on Okinawa and in China after the war but then found himself recalled to Quantico. There he was assigned to study amphibious warfare on the staff of the Marine Corps Schools. In his new assignment, he continued to pioneer ideas, including the concept of vertical envelopment. In 1948, he staged the first helicopter assault operation using early aircraft that could only carry three Marines each. Although technology did not yet make his vision of large-scale heliborne attacks feasible, Krulak developed a framework for tactics that were fifteen years ahead of its time, earning wide acceptance in Vietnam in 1963.

Krulak's greatest contribution in the immediate postwar period, however, was in the fight to preserve the Marine Corps and see its mission defined in law during the armed services unification crisis of 1947–48. As part of a loose collection of Marine Corps intellectuals known as the "Chowder Society," Krulak showed his ability to mix new ideas and pragmatism to win battles in the halls of Congress as ably as he had won fights on the beaches and jungles of the Pacific. Krulak advised the Commandant of the Marine Corps and several other key agents to preserve the Marine Corps by discarding parochial arguments in favor of a new approach. The new argument was based on the idea that the United States in truth did not need a Marine Corps but in fact wanted one because the Marine Corps had earned an important place in the hearts of the American people, both as a premier fighting force and as an institution accountable for war-winning innovations. Combining a shrewd political approach that paired the anti-unification Marine position with maintaining civilian control

of the military, the argument was successful, contributing enormously to the passage of National Security Act of 1947 with a new statutory role for the Marine Corps in the Department of Defense.

Krulak's efforts soon turned from the political realm to combat. He was highly instrumental in the rapid deployment of the 1st Marine Brigade, and later the 1st Marine Division, to turn the tide of the Korean War in its early, chaotic months. After a tour as secretary of the General Staff at Headquarters Marine Corps, General Krulak was appointed to serve as a "special assistant for counterinsurgency and special activities" to the Joint Chiefs of Staff. In this capacity, he was dispatched on several fact-finding missions and had a key influence in the growing war in Vietnam from 1962 to 1964. His careful reasoning and innovative vision for the war endeared him to President John F. Kennedy, who was seeking a counterinsurgency solution for an unconventional war when so many other military men were advocating inappropriate conventional solutions. From that post, he went on to serve as the commanding general of Fleet Marine Forces, Pacific, which gave him oversight of Marine Forces in Vietnam. In this role, he spearheaded the construction of an expeditionary airfield at Chu Lai, bringing the "short airfield for tactical support" concept to fruition in its first combat application, providing operational validation of the Corps' expeditionary potential. Krulak also served as a counterweight to General William Westmoreland's frustratingly conventional strategy. Krulak guided the Marines in developing and executing the Combined Action Program by which Marines in small teams worked within the local population to provide security and win their hearts and minds, rather than focusing on the pursuit of fruitless conventional battle engagements.

Recognizing the need to preserve the martial spirit and bias for innovation that had taken the Corps so far, Krulak wrote *First to Fight: An Inside View of the U.S. Marine Corps* after his retirement. This work has become one of the fundamental resources for today's Marines to examine their

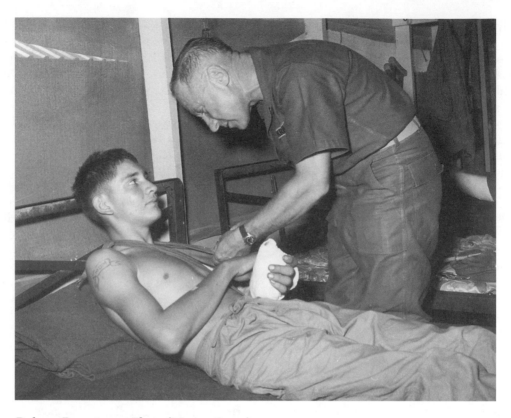

Defense Department Photo (Marine Corps)

Corps' legacy and embrace qualities such as the commitment to vision that earned the Marine Corps such a distinguished place in American history. Looking back on his life, General Krulak has a proud record as a military leader and successful father. All three of his sons served as military officers: one joined the Marines and later became a civilian chaplain, another was a twenty-five-year U.S. Navy chaplain who served with the Marines, and the last was General Charles C. Krulak, the thirty-first Commandant of the Marine Corps. Even considering this mountain of achievements, Krulak still feels that his greatest accomplishment was his work to turn his amphibious vision of the Marine Corps into a victorious reality in World War II.

Suggested Reading

Krulak, Victor H. *First to Fight: An Inside View of the U.S. Marine Corps.* Annapolis, Md.: Naval Institute Press, 1999.

Sheehan, Neil. *A Bright Shining Lie, John Paul Vann and America in Vietnam.* New York: Vintage Books, 1988.

About the Author

Major Shawn P. Callahan is a 1992 graduate of the U.S. Naval Academy. He is an F-18D weapons and sensors officer and a Marine historian who teaches American and naval history to midshipmen.

34

Joy Bright Hancock
Pioneering Spirit

Dr. Regina T. Akers

National Archives

Joy Bright Hancock spent most of her adult life proving that American women deserved to, and certainly could, serve alongside men in the U.S. Navy. As an enlisted Sailor, Navy Department civilian, and naval officer, she opened many doors for women in the naval service. She did so with a strong sense of professionalism, innovative thinking, diplomatic skill, and open-mindedness. Despite personal tragedies and setbacks that would have crushed less determined individuals, Hancock never stopped going forward to enrich her own life and to help others along the way.

Joy Bright was born on 4 May 1898 in Wildwood, New Jersey, as the third of six children born to William and Priscilla Bright. Her father sold insurance and real estate and held several state and local political positions. Joy's mother, a participant in the women's suffrage movement, often hosted discussions in their home involving leading suffragists of the time.

Joy's parents encouraged her to accomplish whatever she chose, and Joy embraced the encouragement. She repaired bikes and cars and did carpentry work, unconcerned that these were "boy's activities." When she was fourteen, her father let her supervise his office when he was out of town. After graduating from high school and later the Pierce School of Business Administration in Philadelphia, Pennsylvania, she worked as a statistician.

In 1918, Joy enlisted in the Naval Reserve as a female yeoman, or Yeoman (F). Like many other patriotic women, she wanted to serve her country in World War I. By the end of the war, she had been promoted to yeoman chief and served at naval facilities in New Jersey, including Naval Air Station, Cape May. After the war, the U.S. Navy discharged Joy and all the other women then serving except nurses.

Undeterred, Joy remained at Cape May as a Navy civilian employee and there met Lieutenant Charles G. Little, an aspiring naval aviator. They were married in 1920, but one year later, he was killed in the crash of a dirigible being tested in England. Despite her husband's death, Joy became fascinated with the U.S. Navy's lighter-than-air technology. She got a job with the Navy's new Bureau of Aeronautics (BuAer). After transferring to Naval Air Station, Lakehurst, New Jersey, she met, fell in love with, and married Lieutenant Commander Lewis Hancock, executive officer of the dirigible USS *Shenandoah*. On 3 September 1925, tragedy once again struck Joy. Her husband's air ship crashed in Ohio, killing him and many of his crewmen.

Dispirited, Hancock quit her job, traveled, and for a few years considered a career in the U.S. Foreign Service. But her heart was still in the U.S. Navy. As if to look death in the face, considering the loss of two husbands to air crashes, she earned her private flying license. She also returned to work with BuAer. Hancock edited their newsletter, later named *Naval Aviation News*, and after several years published a book, *Airplanes in Action*. By the end of the 1930s, Joy Bright Hancock earned recognition as an aviation specialist and routinely worked with John Towers, Albert C. Reed, Arthur Radford, and other naval aviation pioneers. She was even dispatched to Canada to see how the armed forces there were employing women. Impressed with her report, BuAer had her develop a plan for the employment of American women in many aeronautical fields.

As she had in World War I, Joy Bright Hancock rallied to the colors in World War II. On 23 October 1942, Admiral John S. McCain, chief of the Bureau of Aeronautics, swore Hancock into the Naval Reserve. She was then commissioned as a lieutenant. The experienced officer became the women's representative to the chief of the Bureau of Aeronautics and to the deputy chief of naval aviation. She also served as the liaison between BuAer and Commander Mildred McAfee, director of the Naval Reserve's WAVES (Women Accepted for Volunteer Emergency Service), established earlier in 1942. Hancock convinced McAfee that women should receive specialist training at all-male

schools and persuaded the personnel bureau to open the aviation machinist mate rating to women. She made many official visits to naval shore establishments to discuss aviation issues and to learn how women were faring in the Naval Reserve. She often stressed to the women with whom she came in contact that they were making an important contribution to America's fight in the war. Recognizing her outstanding performance, during World War II the U.S. Navy promoted Hancock to lieutenant commander and then commander.

After the war, Hancock became one of the leading advocates for the full integration of women in the U.S. Navy. In February 1946, she became the Assistant Director (Plans) of the Women's Reserve in the Bureau of Naval Personnel. She helped develop legislation to establish the Women's Reserve on a permanent basis. On 26 July 1946, the U.S. Navy promoted her to captain and assigned her as director of WAVES. She and her counterparts in the other services worked together to assure passage of a congressional bill enabling women to serve both as regulars and reservists. On 30 July 1948, President Harry S. Truman signed the Women's Armed Forces Integration Act (Public Law 625) into law. On 15 October that year, Hancock became one of the first female officers sworn into the regular U.S. Navy.

Joy Bright Hancock retired from naval service with the Legion of Merit on 1 July 1953, but her connection to the U.S. Navy was far from over. She married Vice Admiral Ralph A. Ostie in August 1954; unfortunately, he became ill and died shortly afterward. In the next decade, Captain Hancock studied at American University in Washington, D.C., and managed her father's company in Wildwood, New Jersey. In 1972, the U.S. Naval Institute published her second book *Lady in the Navy*, which recounted her remarkable career. She founded the Hancock Fund to help develop library collections at the University of Georgia in naval and military science, women's studies, and American history. She was also the first woman to serve on the Secretary of the Navy's advisory committee on naval history. Eventually, she moved to Vincent Hall, a U.S. Navy retirement home in McLean, Virginia.

Captain Joy Bright Hancock died on 30 August 1986 and was laid to rest in Arlington National Cemetery. During her life, she blazed a trail for women in the U.S. Navy. Through personal example—service in World War I, World War II, the Bureau of Aeronautics, and the Bureau of Naval Personnel—she demonstrated that the female American populace was capable of contributing significantly to the defense of the nation. Plagued by heart-wrenching personal tragedies, she never quit. Through balanced reasoning, in-depth knowledge, and forceful but diplomatic advocacy, she helped open naval aviation, the Naval Reserve, and the active U.S. Navy to American women.

Suggested Reading

Ebbert, Jean, and Marie-Beth Hall. *Crossed Currents: Navy Women from World War II to Tailhook.* Washington, D.C.: Brassey's, 1993.

Godson, Susan H. *Serving Proudly: A History of Women in the U.S. Navy.* Annapolis, Md.: Naval Institute Press, 2001.

Hancock, Joy B. *Lady in the Navy: A Personal Reminiscence.* Annapolis, Md.: Naval Institute Press, 1972.

Hancock, Joy Bright. Interview. U.S. Naval Institute, WAVES Volume I, 1969 and 1970.

About the Author

Dr. Regina T. Akers is the assistant branch head, oral historian, and specialist on minorities in the military in the Operational Archives Branch of the Naval Historical Center, on which staff she has served since 1987. She received a doctorate in U.S. and public history from Howard University in 2000 where she teaches women's and public history courses. She has coordinated conferences and lectures. Her publications include book reviews, chapters in books, and journal articles. Dr. Akers has appeared on BET-Television, ABC News' *Nightline*, and Maryland Cable Television and has presented papers and workshops at various historical symposia.

National Archives

35

Hyman G. Rickover
Personal Growth

Gary E. Weir

National Historical Center

They waited for him to say it, because he almost never did. They wanted him to say that they had "grown" as a professional. The desire to hear that assessment from Hyman Rickover drove scores of officers, ratings, and civilians to work harder and with greater effect than they ever imagined possible. Beginning his regular working life in Chicago before the Great War as a message runner for Western Union, this Polish-American immigrant grew into a four-star admiral as well as the premier authority on the naval application of nuclear power. Before his passing on 8 July 1986 he spent sixty-three years on active duty and served eight American presidents.

Admiral Rickover agreed with the humanists of the fifteenth-century Italian Renaissance that growth had to occur in every aspect of life for a human being to release the full potential locked inside. Commitment to scholarship, leadership, country, and community had to blend with effective communication, personal responsibility, high professional standards, and tolerance of others to form the complete person. While many people and some alleged leaders set standards against which they never measured themselves, Admiral Rickover abhorred this kind of hypocrisy and any effort to avoid personal responsibility. Leading by example, he drove himself relentlessly and effectively employed his legendary abrasive manner both to motivate others and to instill an appreciation for the regular pursuit of excellence in any worthy endeavor.

Graduating from the U.S. Naval Academy with the class of 1922, he felt very fortunate and appreciative. The U.S. Navy had provided the education that he had desperately wanted but his struggling parents had not been able to afford. It also permitted him to pursue a career in engineering while training him to understand the nature of the U.S. Navy, its complex professional and personal relationships, and the way large organizations worked. He later put all of his new knowledge and expertise to very good use. He joined his classmates in Dahlgren Hall on 2 June 1922 to receive his commission, standing 107 out of a class of 540.

After initial tours in Pacific Fleet destroyers, Lieutenant Rickover joined the engineering section of the battleship USS *New Mexico*. On his way to a career in engineering duty, Rickover's absolute attention to detail and his willingness to drive himself and his section won his ship the red "E" for excellence in engineering two years running. It also prompted one of his ensigns, who later reached flag rank and commanded the Bureau of Ships, to write an "Ode to a Senior Assistant Engineer," which concluded triumphantly,

> At last we've won the pennant
> And Rick is filled with glee
> With a forlorn screech
> And a bath on the beach
> We're off for the next year's "E."

Rickover knew all of his people and their capabilities. He knew every bolt, weld, valve, bearing, and gauge in the vessel. He knew the technical personality of his ship, her weaknesses and her strengths, so he could anticipate likely engineering problems. He did these things because he had already acquired a bit of universal wisdom that he frequently passed to others in later years: "The Devil is in the details, but so is salvation." Rickover knew that hard work helped you find those details and that salvation. Hard work was a virtue unto itself. It helped you grow.

An extended experience in the Far East in the 1930s as well as his first and only seagoing command before acceptance as an engineering duty officer provided an opportunity to lead and provided insight into world affairs and other cultures. Unfortunately, World War II quickly distracted the newly minted lieutenant commander. Rickover faced a threatening world as he left the Orient to begin his first tour in Washington, D.C., at the old Main Navy Build-

ing. He took over as assistant head of the electrical section of the Bureau of Engineering on 15 August 1939.

Once again, his hard work, attention to detail, and refusal to tolerate obstacles served him well. After obtaining a section of magnetic cable used by the British in a system designed to quickly sweep magnetic mines by detonation, he worked with General Electric on his own initiative to reverse-engineer the system. Before American entry into the war, the British would not share the generator technology that lay at the core of this approach to the mine threat. His effort succeeded, helping the bureau solve a major problem confronting the U.S. Navy in 1940. He had also directed his first successful collaboration with a commercial contractor. That same year, with a promotion to commander, he assumed direction of the bureau's electrical section.

The tasks presented by the attack on Pearl Harbor and America's entry into the war permitted him to grow further and demonstrate the absolute necessity of care, dedication, and professional excellence. The U.S. Navy needed the damaged battleships, like USS *California*, that barely survived 7 December. They also needed electrical systems that could absorb the worst possible assault and survive, even if the ship itself began to sink. Commander Rickover traveled to Pearl Harbor, visited the battleships, crawled through their spaces, and took charge of reconditioning the electric drive machinery on board *California*. He successfully created a naval-industrial team as well as a collaboration and reporting system responsible for reconditioning the vessel's electric propulsion machinery. His effort played a determining role in promptly returning the warship to the fight against Japan.

Developing battle-hardened electrical systems emerged as one of his most difficult wartime challenges at the bureau. Peacetime electrical industry standards for warships simply could not survive the test of modern battle against a worthy adversary. With the U.S. Navy expanding very quickly, even before Pearl

Harbor, to meet the requirements of a possible conflict, demand for shipboard electrical systems drew many contractors into the market. Rickover's electrical section had to devise firm standards that would come as close as possible to guaranteeing the integrity of warship electrical systems in battle. He would then have to enforce those standards with occasionally reluctant or recalcitrant contractors.

During the war, Captain Rickover conquered this formidable challenge. He designed a quality-control system that sent to sea the best electrical systems the fleet had ever seen and developed a working relationship with the American electrical industry that would serve him very well with the postwar advent of nuclear power.[1] Beginning the war with a small coterie of officers and engineers, Rickover's section grew to 341 people by

V-J Day. He commanded the largest section in what had become the Bureau of Ships.

His outstanding record in the bureau's electrical section made him a natural candidate for nuclear training once that program began in 1946 at the Massachusetts Institute of Technology (MIT). Vice Admiral Earle Mills, Commander, Bureau of Ships, eventually chose Rickover as the senior officer in the group sent to Clinton National Laboratories in Oak Ridge, Tennessee, after MIT for training in nuclear fission. That initiated the final phase of an amazing career that led to Rickover becoming the father of the nuclear Navy and the leader of the project that created USS *Nautilus* in 1955.

Once Rickover began working with nuclear energy, its possibilities for the U.S. Navy and civilian applications excited him, but the cost of

Naval Historical Center

inattention to detail and an absence of hard work spelled potential catastrophe. As his authority in the nuclear program grew, he insisted upon interviewing every officer applying for nuclear power training. Their attitude toward nuclear power, education, and hard work, as well as their personal confidence and technical qualification, assured him that the discipline imposed by this new technology, the necessity to respect the possibilities and dangers of the new power source, did not pass unappreciated. If a person worked hard enough and sought to grow in every way possible, the admiral realized that he not only brought education and experience to the engineering challenge, but he also began to appreciate the ways in which the challenge educated him. Admiral Rickover always wanted naval officers to recognize that truth, to act on it, and to grow.

Note

1. Industrial managers knew that Rickover would work hard and expect the same from his people. They also knew that he would call any chairman, any engineer, and any manager at any time of the day or night and demand the same from them.

Suggested Reading

Duncan, Francis. *Rickover: The Struggle for Excellence*. Annapolis, Md.: Naval Institute Press, 2001.

———. *Rickover and the Nuclear Navy: The Discipline of Technology*. Annapolis, Md.: Naval Institute Press, 1990.

About the Author

Dr. Gary E. Weir, a former member of the U.S. Naval Academy history faculty, is head of the Contemporary History Branch of the Naval Historical Center in Washington, D.C., and a guest investigator at the Woods Hole Oceanographic Institution. He specializes in the history of submarines, undersea warfare, and the ocean sciences. His most recent book, *An Ocean in Common: Naval Officers, Scientists, and the Ocean Environment*, a study of the U.S. Navy's role as participant and patron in oceanographic research, was selected by the Organization of American Historians as a recipient of the Richard W. Leopold Prize for 2002. Dr. Weir also teaches at the University of Maryland University College and is currently working on an official history of the U.S. Navy's Cold War deep ocean surveillance system, SOSUS.

36

Merritt A. Edson
Moral Courage

Colonel Jon T. Hoffman

U.S. Naval Institute Photo Archive

The Marine Corps reached a zenith at the end of World War II with half a million men and women in uniform and an unparalleled reputation for combat effectiveness and doctrinal innovation. Although the army had instigated efforts during the conflict to merge the War and Navy Departments, the vast majority of Marine leaders, including the Commandant, were certain, "We have no reason to worry about our place in any postwar setup." The Leathernecks were wrong. The army and the army air forces not only renewed their attempts; they found strong support from the new president—former National Guardsman Harry S. Truman—as well as from a Congress and public eager to reap the benefits of promised fiscal savings. The institutional struggle would last for two years and, in the end, the outcome would rest largely on the moral courage of one Marine officer who spoke his mind despite the consequences.

Brigadier General Merritt A. Edson saw the end of World War II from Hawaii where he served as the head of Fleet Marine Force Pacific's Service Command, but he was no armchair warrior. Prior to Pearl Harbor, he already had spearheaded the formation of what would become the 1st Marine Raider Battalion. He led that elite unit in the seizure of Tulagi on 7 August 1942, earning his second Navy Cross for the conquest of the small island near Guadalcanal.[1] A month later, Edson and his Raiders stopped a Japanese force four times their size during the two-day Battle of Bloody Ridge, for which Edson subsequently received the Medal of Honor. As chief of staff of the 2nd Marine Division in 1943, he led the planning effort for the Tarawa landing and then commanded all forces ashore for a portion of the bloody assault. Elevated to assistant division commander, he still made his way to the front lines of the tough fighting on Saipan and Tinian. His courage was matched by his organizational ability and incisive mind, for which he was transferred to

Hawaii in the latter stages of the war to sort out the logistics challenges facing a Corps twenty times its prewar size.

The army, upset by the vast expansion of the Corps, argued that a unified military department would increase efficiency by eliminating the duplication of effort. Under this plan, Marine aircraft would go to the air service while ground forces went to the land service. When Commandant General A. A. Vandegrift needed someone to lead the charge against the unification plan, he called Edson. In addition to Red Mike's stature as a hero, his intelligence, experience with Congress and the press, and reputation for fighting for his convictions made him the perfect man for the job.

Edson brought to his new task the same concerns about the future of his service that motivated the Commandant, but he soon developed much larger objections to unification. His first point of protest was the belief that a strict delineation of services based on air, land, and sea would lead to poor performance on future battlefields, because each service would focus on its own priorities to the detriment of others needing its assistance. As an example, he cited the army's experience in trying to obtain close air support from the army air forces during World War II. In Edson's view, national defense would be better served if the services had everything each judged necessary to carry out their respective missions.

The second concern also involved combat efficiency. Edson drew an analogy with economics and argued that the "effect of monopoly is to retard progress." To support this point, he cited numerous examples of equipment and doctrine developed by one service and ignored by another—equipment and doctrine that later proved useful during war. Red Mike believed the existence of independent War and Navy Departments encouraged this competitive spirit.

Edson was most worried, however, that the merger of all the services in a single executive department would deprive Congress of the open debate between the War and Navy Departments that helped inform decisions on strategy and the allocation of resources. Red Mike equated the details of the merger plan with the system from which the ideas had been copied—the German military. Once started down this road, he believed it eventually would lead to militarism and dictatorship. He also harked back to the nation's founders and seconded James Madison's argument for the separation of powers in government: "Ambition must be made to counteract ambition."

From the beginning, Edson ran a strong campaign against unification. He developed a close working relationship with a number of congressmen, providing them with advice and point papers, feeding them questions to ask during hearings and suggesting amendments to pending bills. The well-known hero also carried his views to the public. He toured the country, making speeches to any group that would listen, and met frequently with influential writers and editors. Initially, he met with little success, as one newspaper observed that there was "a near unanimity of sentiment" behind the merger legislation.

The Marine general's efforts mostly were remarkable because he undertook them in the face of Truman's express wishes that there be no military opposition to his unification plan. In speaking before Congress when presenting the first unification bill in 1945, the president declared that "further studies of the general problem would serve no useful purpose." That same day the Secretary of the Navy issued a directive forbidding naval officers from any public opposition to the plan. A few months later, Truman denounced those who did not "get into line" behind his desired policy. As the screws on dissent tightened from above, the Commandant muted his previous strong opposition and even disbanded the small staff that was assisting Edson.

Red Mike, fully aware that his actions were putting his career in jeopardy, confided to a friend: "The top brass have every reason to dislike the things I have said, and I have every reason to believe that they will pull no punches (and most of them below the belt) to get even with me." He characterized the situation as "having a bull by the tail," but "feeling as I do that the adoption of the proposed unification will be such a national calamity, I can not do otherwise." He eventually recognized that the situation could end only one way, with him resigning in protest if the legislation passed or having his career ruined if he successfully derailed it. That he was the sole senior officer still waging the fight in public made him even more defiant: "If this present bill is modified as it should be, and as I believe both CMC [Commandant of the Marine Corps] and the Navy would like to have it, it will be because I stuck my neck out when no one else would do so."

In May 1947, as the president's unification plan moved toward passage in Congress, one senator opposed to it made one last effort to stop it by calling Edson to testify before the Armed Services Committee. Red Mike forewarned the Commandant and offered his resignation, "In order to feel free to express my personal views on this proposed legislation without embarrassment to or as a representative of the Marine Corps." Vandegrift told him that was unnecessary, but also refused Edson's request for a junior officer to assist him at the hearings. The Marine general was not the only person to testify against the proposal in the Senate hearings, but he was the only active duty officer to do so, and his was the longest, strongest, and most passionate criticism. Surprisingly, his effort received no attention in the media, which continued to be in favor of the merger. The infrequent references to behind-the-scenes uniformed opposition were almost universally negative. One newspaper characterized opponents as "hidebound brass hats and stubborn, prestige-hungry military reactionaries."

Only *The Washington Evening Star* obliquely noted that not all military support was genuine. An editorial cartoon asked, "Is this shotgun marriage going to last?" It depicted the two service secretaries as squabbling bride and groom, Congress as the preacher, and Truman as the gun-toting father of the bride. When the minister noted the couple's already broken promise to live happily ever after, the president replied: "That's what I told them to say."

After the Senate committee overwhelmingly approved the merger bill, Edson focused his energy on the House. Although the relevant committee there was friendlier to the Marine viewpoint, the members found no serving officer willing to express his opposition to the legislation. Until they asked Red Mike to testify. He accepted and then tendered his resignation again, this time giving the Commandant no opportunity to reject it.

While he waited for retirement and his appearance before the House committee, Red Mike headed north to speak to fellow alumni during commencement week at the University of Vermont. He assailed the merger bill's origins within the army, as well as the steamroller tactics being used to push it through Congress: "When we have reached a point where the military are directing instead of supporting this Country's policy, we are far along the road to losing what this Country has stood for." Then he made the first public announcement of his pending retirement, citing the prospective merger as the reason. He received a vigorous ovation from the crowd.

Although he had repeated many of the same points he had made before the Senate, Edson's remarks created a much greater stir this time. *The Chicago Tribune* described the "famed leader of Marine raiders" as a man of "courage and honesty." *The Burlington Daily News* called it "an explosive speech" and editorialized: "Thank God that there are men like Edson still in Washington." A radio station declared that he had "deliberately strayed off the military reservation to deliver a well-documented attack." The only thing new in his speech was the reference to his retirement, which must have generated much of the unprecedented attention. Contrary to the stereotype of merger opponents being concerned with their own careers, here was a war hero ready to sacrifice his future to prevent an increase in the power of the military.

Three days after his Vermont speech, Edson testified before the House committee. His lengthy remarks never varied from the theme of civilian control of the military. He noted that military men had drafted the bill and that the powers of the proposed defense secretary, joint staff, and Central Intelligence Agency needed to be "carefully delineated and circumscribed." One representative declared that Edson had "tossed an atom bomb into the works." Another thought the general "should be commended for appearing before this committee and expressing his frank criticism of this measure."

The committee members soon heard more. Six days later, the Secretary of the Navy responded to growing public concern that he was preventing naval officers from speaking their minds. In a message to all hands, he stated, "I have recently become aware that a feeling of restraint may exist" regarding discussion of the merger bill. Therefore he temporarily waived previous limitations on congressional appear-ances. The result was a flood of witnesses against the administration position. Navy Vice Admiral Gerald Bogan probably spoke for his colleagues when he explained his previous silence: "We were given to understand that this legislation was favored by the high command and it was hoped that we would all support it. Being unable to support it, we had nothing else to do but keep our mouths shut." In fact, Edson had demon-strated that everyone had an option, if only they had the moral courage to pursue it. Later, he evaluated his willingness to speak out as his greatest contribution to the struggle and the pri-mary factor in generating the subsequent public opposition by other officers: "The fact remains that not a single one of them would have done so had I not led the way."

The price had been high. Edson had cut short a promising career that might have ended in his becoming Commandant. The nation had lost the

U.S. Naval Institute Photo Archive

services of one its bravest and most astute military leaders. But now fully aware of the wide range of opinion in the services, Congress drastically modified the unification legislation, preserving the Marine Corps and limiting the powers of the new Department of Defense in the 1947 National Security Act. One man's willingness to stand his ground had made all the difference.

Edson's hometown newspaper appropriately lauded his outspoken stand against the odds: "It may be true that General Edson might have been wiser had he waited until he is out of uniform on July 1 before making his speech. But Red Mike doesn't play ball that way either. He speaks his mind; he tells the truth without fear of consequences. God bless him for this forthrightness. It will keep him in good stead here in Vermont, where the truth still keeps men free."

Note

1. His first Navy Cross, along with the nickname "Red Mike," had come for a daring yearlong patrol against Sandino and his guerrillas deep in the trackless jungles of Nicaragua in 1928.

Suggested Reading

Hoffman, Jon T. *Chesty: The Life of LtGen Lewis B. Puller*. New York: Random House, 2001.

———. *Once a Legend: "Red Mike" Edson of the Marine Raiders*. Novato, Calif.: Presidio, 1994.

———. *Warrior: The Life of Gen Lewis W. Walt*. New York: Random House, forthcoming 2006.

Wood, W. J. *Leaders and Battles: The Art of Military Leadership*. Novato, Calif.: Presidio, 1984.

About the Author

Colonel Jon T. Hoffman, USMCR, has spent his entire career as an infantry officer and military historian. He most recently served as the deputy director of the Marine Corps History and Museums Division. His books include two biographies of Marines: *Once a Legend: "Red Mike" Edson of the Marine Raiders* and *Chesty: The Life of LtGen Lewis B. Puller*.

37

Charles B. Momsen

Innovative Problem Solving

Maxwell B. Uphaus

National Archives

Charles Momsen had a problematic relationship with the U.S. Navy bureaucracy. As is often the case with bold visionaries, Momsen encountered opposition from officials reluctant to develop new approaches to solving complex problems. Indeed, Momsen's innovative ideas and proposals frequently generated heated resistance from U.S. Navy organizations. As he reflected in retirement: "I guess, during my career, I steered a course a bit too much my own. . . . When an officer with initiative and imagination leaves the middle of the road, he's bound to have trouble. . . . Often when I presented a new proposal, I was made to feel like a felon committing a crime and ended up not only having to defend the idea, but myself for daring to bring it up."

Part of the problem stemmed from the fact that Momsen's branch of the U.S. Navy, the submarine service, was not considered a mainstream organization during the first decades of the twentieth century. The submarines of that era suffered from frequent mechanical failures, lack of equipment standardization, and poor safety records. Hundreds of American Sailors and twenty undersea naval vessels, then often referred to as "pig boats," were lost at sea in the years before World War II.

Charles "Swede" (as he came to be called, despite his German-Danish background) Momsen entered the U.S. Naval Academy in 1914. He failed a Spanish course and had to drop out but, undaunted, secured a new appointment from his local congressman. Two years after graduation from the academy in 1919, Momsen joined the submarine service.

Momsen soon found his life's work when he discovered that the U.S. Navy's procedures and equipment for rescuing submariners from sunken boats were totally inadequate. When the first submarine Momsen commanded, USS *O-15*, was almost lost with all hands because he could not bring her to the surface, he realized that something had to be done to rescue submariners in distress. That point was driven home in 1925 when a passenger ship struck and sank USS *S-51*. Momsen, on board nearby USS *S-1*, could only watch helplessly as the minutes and the lives of the trapped Sailors ticked away under his vessel. When salvage units raised *S-1*, Momsen discovered to his horror that some of the men had desperately tried to claw their way out of the doomed submarine. From then on, Swede Momsen was determined to develop submarine escape equipment and operational procedures.

One of his first actions was to develop a diving bell that could be lowered from the surface on cables attached to the escape hatch on a sunken sub's hull. When Momsen's base commander, future Fleet Admiral Ernest King, endorsed the design, the submariner sent it forward to the Bureau of Construction and Repair for approval. He heard nothing from the bureau. Many months later, when Momsen was assigned to the bureau, he found his plans buried under a stack of neglected paperwork. He was still unable to generate attention for his proposal.

Soon afterward, there was another submarine disaster. USS *S-4* sank in 110 feet of water. Although some of her crewmen survived for days, hammering desperate pleas for rescue on the hull of the vessel, nothing could be done for them. The U.S. Navy received a flood of outraged letters from the public. This time, the Navy listened to Momsen. He developed a device that enabled Sailors to exit a sunken submarine and float to the surface by means of a buoyant breathing apparatus that recycled exhaled air. Momsen developed the equipment on his own initiative and personally tested it, at considerable risk to his own life. The so-called Momsen Lung worked so well that the U.S. Navy ordered seven thousand of them and in 1929 awarded its inventor the Distinguished Service Medal. Now with institutional support, Momsen resurrected his diving bell idea and again personally tested the equipment. Even though the Navy named the device the McCann Rescue Chamber after an admiral

involved in the project, Momsen was gratified that they adopted it in 1930 as standard submarine rescue equipment.

From 1937 to 1939, Momsen headed an experimental deep-sea diving unit at the Washington Navy Yard, where his team pioneered the use by divers of a new mixture of oxygen and helium. This new mixture better enabled divers to avoid "the bends" caused by nitrogen narcosis and to carry out dives below the three-hundred-foot level.

The fruit of Momsen's laborious and persistent fight with the U.S. Navy bureaucracy came in May 1939 when USS *Squalus* failed to surface from a dive off Portsmouth, New Hampshire. Trapped in the vessel's forward compartments were thirty-three survivors. Momsen's team quickly deployed to Portsmouth from their base in Washington. The news that Momsen was in charge of the rescue effort cheered the survivors. "He's the man," one of them said. Through the efforts of Momsen and his team, several of whom were awarded the Medal of Honor for their heroism, and the rescue chamber, every one of the survivors made it to the surface. It was one of Momsen's proudest achievements and a validation of all he had done and endured.

Momsen also showed his mettle in wartime. During World War II, the innovative officer was determined to discover why American torpedoes failed to detonate on impact with Japanese ships. He fired torpedoes at a cliff face in Hawaii until one failed to explode and then risked instant death by retrieving and examining the dud. He found a faulty firing pin to be the culprit. During 1943 and 1944, then–Rear Admiral Momsen developed three-submarine "wolf pack" tactics and led a submarine squadron against the Japanese to test the concept. This pioneering work, which led to the sinking of five enemy ships, earned him the service's second highest award, the Navy Cross. Momsen finished his sterling career as Assistant Chief of Naval Operations and retired from the U.S. Navy in September 1955 at the rank of vice admiral. He died in 1967.

Naval Historical Center

Swede Momsen combined his humanity and inspirational abilities with creative thinking and was forever pushing the bounds of what others considered possible. His biographer, who knew him, aptly observed that "everything that could possibly save a trapped submariner . . . was either a direct result of his inventive, pioneering derring-do, or of value only because of it. . . . His deceptively composed demeanor disguised an extraordinary combination of visionary, scientist, and man of action."

Suggested Reading

Maas, Peter. *The Rescuer.* New York: Harper and Row, 1967.

————. *The Terrible Hours: The Man Behind the Greatest Submarine Rescue in History*. New York: HarperCollins, 1999.

Office of Naval Research. "Blow the Ballast: Swede Momsen." http://www.onr.navy.mil/focus/blowballast/momsen/default.htm/.

About the Author

Maxwell B. Uphaus is currently a junior at the College of William and Mary, majoring in English. During the summer of 2004, he completed a comprehensive three-month internship in public affairs at the Naval Historical Center in Washington, D.C. He earlier authored a short piece entitled "Reflections" for the April 2004 edition of *Foreign Service Journal*. In 2002, he graduated from the American International School in Dhaka, Bangladesh, where his senior honors project was on "The Evolution of Bangladeshi National Identity." He is a member of the National Society of Collegiate Scholars and Phi Eta Sigma honor society.

38

Arleigh A. Burke
Instinct

Dr. David Alan Rosenberg

U.S. Naval Institute Photo Archive

No flag officer in the U.S. Navy in the twentieth century spent more time contemplating and practicing strong, effective leadership than Arleigh Albert Burke. An outstanding World War II destroyer combat commander whose delegation of command and initiative to subordinates led to South Pacific victories, Burke was also an imaginative organizer and leader of combat staffs in Fast Carrier Task Force 58/38 in 1944–45, and in U.S. naval forces in the Korean War. From 1955 to 1961, Burke's actions in Cold War crises, and his innovations in policy and programs as the last Chief of Naval Operations (CNO) to actually command the fleets, shaped the service's course for much of the rest of the century.

A Colorado boy imbued with integrity, self-discipline, and strong principles by his farmer father and teacher mother, Burke graduated Annapolis in 1923, the very year the U.S. Naval Academy faculty compiled the first textbook on naval leadership. That book listed the essential qualities of a naval officer as personal dignity, honor, courage, truthfulness, faith, justice, earnestness, assiduity, judgment, perseverance, tact, self-control, and simplicity. At the top of the list, however, was loyalty: to country and service, but especially "up and down" to one's seniors and one's juniors. Loyalty up and down was critical because of the natural independence and self-reliance of the American Sailor, who came from a society with no established system of rank and caste. Naval officers had to earn the respect of their men through strong leadership. This philosophy became ingrained in Burke during five years in battleship *Arizona*, working jobs from inspecting and cleaning the battleship's double bottoms to leading a division that manned a fourteen-inch gun turret.

Even as a young officer, Arleigh Burke understood that technology was constantly transforming the U.S. Navy and that he needed in-depth knowledge, both technical and professional, to succeed. During three years as an ensign and lieutenant (junior grade), he completed the Naval War College correspondence course in strategy and tactics whose textbook, *The Estimate of the Situation and the Order Form*, provided a mental template for tactical and operational decision making. He also pursued postgraduate specialization in ordnance. He spent three years at the "P.G." School at Annapolis, visiting ordnance field activities, and at the University of Michigan where in 1931 he received a master's in chemical engineering, becoming a design and production specialist in ordnance explosives. This background exposed Burke to the most advanced U.S. Navy technologies of his time and would prepare him as CNO to promote the development of nuclear weapons, nuclear power, and guided and ballistic missiles. It would also lead him to support broader educational opportunities for naval officers, including the postgraduate scholarships that came to bear his name.

While technical assignments with the Bureau of Ordnance dominated Burke's early career, his abilities as a seagoing leader came to the fore in destroyers in 1937–40. He led his first command, USS *Mugford*, to the destroyer gunnery trophy in 1939 by taking the initiative to make *Mugford* a gunnery "school ship" for training other destroyer crews. Rather than resent the extra work, his crew loved the challenge, especially when Captain Burke let them take the ship to sea out of San Diego with no officers directing them. As a commanding officer Burke learned, "If you've got power, use it and use it fast, and the time to make a decision is as soon as the problem presents itself." He took that lesson into combat.

Kept in an ordnance assignment in Washington for a year after Pearl Harbor, Burke arrived in the Solomon Islands in March 1943, in command of a destroyer division. Within two months, he had completed a total reassessment of the surface warfare tactics employed in the night actions off Guadalcanal the previous year. The "doctrine of faith" he proposed to his cruiser task force commander, Rear Admiral A.

S. "Tip" Merrill, called for the destroyer screen to engage the enemy force as soon as it was sighted without waiting for orders. Tested by others in combat that summer, these tactics were employed by Burke commanding Destroyer Squadron 23 in victories at Empress Augusta Bay and off Cape St. George in November. Burke's physical courage, and a tactical genius that allowed him to carry the battle "plot" in his head and warn him of untoward enemy actions, won him the Navy Cross and Distinguished Service Medal and gave DesRon 23 the only Presidential Unit Citation awarded a destroyer squadron.

Burke completed the war as Vice Admiral Marc Mitscher's chief of staff in Task Force 58 in the campaigns for New Guinea, the Marianas, Palaus, Leyte, Iwo Jima, and Okinawa. In this job, he was one of the first surface officers to learn "the bird man's lingo" and become trusted by the naval aviators who were now leading the war in the Central Pacific. He worked immensely hard to master the ability to understand and direct forces rather than platforms. This experience would stay with him for the rest of his career and lead him to believe that pride in one's naval warfare specialty was "fine as long as the aim to make the specialty better is based on the larger desire to make the whole Navy stronger." But when an officer became an admiral, he should be "a Flag Officer in the broadest sense of the term—one who can command forces." While chafing at being away from his own combat command, he exhibited a knack for reducing staff paperwork and for making plans and action reports clear and brief. He also developed an understanding of intelligence as key to achieving victory, a quality that served him well for the remainder of his career. When the war ended, Burke was assigned as director of research and development at the Bureau of Ordnance, but Admiral Mitscher brought him back as his chief of staff in 1946 to organize America's first Cold War striking fleet, and then to run the demobilizing Atlantic Fleet.

The next nine years saw Burke exercise his staff leadership much more than his proven talent for command at sea. Although he had a cruiser command in 1948 and cruiser division commands in 1951 and 1954, it was in the Navy Department in Washington and the headquarters of Naval Forces, Far East, in Tokyo that Burke's abilities in organization and communication stood out. One other key leadership quality also emerged: his commitment to long-range planning, manifested in his ability to envision the future U.S. Navy and its requirements. While serving on the Secretary of the Navy's senior advisory body, the General Board, in 1947–48, he led the first effort to articulate the role of the Navy in national security over the next decade. In 1949, he ran Op-23, the Organizational Research and Policy Division of the Office of the CNO, where he marshaled Navy arguments to fend off legislative proposals for reducing the Navy's role in national defense and during congressional hearings over increased unification of the armed services. This assignment was followed by tours as deputy chief of staff for operations to the Commander of Naval Forces, Far East, during the first year of the Korean War, six months on the first United Nations Truce Negotiating Team, and two years as director of the Navy's strategic plans in the Pentagon championing the importance of preparing for limited wars.

Burke's comprehensive approach to leadership was articulated in a study of discipline and command he conducted for the chief of the Bureau of Naval Personnel in early 1950. In his report he championed the continuing need for loyalty to and interest in subordinates, tightness in command, and stability in personnel assignments and operations. He also championed the widest dissemination of information about Sailor's jobs, their command, and the service, to ensure that all hands understood what the service stood for and was doing. Burke believed that only in this way would "a dignified pride and self-respect" in the Navy and oneself and willingness to make personal sacrifices for the group good be achieved. When President Eisenhower promoted Rear Admiral Burke (over ninety-two

flag officers) from commander of the Atlantic Fleet's Destroyer Force to become CNO in August 1955, these views shaped the way that he ran the service. He started a monthly "flag officers' dope" newsletter to spread the word, traveled widely throughout the fleet at home and overseas, and promoted the Navy's story, including through the new medium of television. He argued, "We have to maintain in ourselves, and imbue our juniors with an ardor to keep our Navy in front. We must pass along a willingness to think hard—to seek new answers—to chance mistakes—and to 'mix it up' freely in the forums and activities around us to promote knowledge. From that knowledge we can inspire our country to have faith in us—not because the organization of the military forces is the only place to put our national faith, but because we have discharged our responsibilities in such a manner that we have justified confidence in the effective manner in which we operate."

Burke's combat and Washington experience allowed him to meet multiple challenges as CNO—including crises over Suez in 1956, Lebanon, Indonesia, and Taiwan in 1958, and Berlin in 1959—as well as to undertake the transformation of the fleet. He championed nuclear power in all future U.S. submarines as well as in aircraft carriers and surface combatants, created the Fleet Ballistic Missile Program that brought Polaris submarines from drawing board to deployment in five years, backed missiles for air defense, and started communications and intelligence programs, particularly satellites, that transformed the way the Navy communicated and tracked potential adversaries. He also strongly emphasized the professional bonds among navies by establishing the Naval Command Course at the Naval War College, which continues to bring senior foreign naval officers to Newport and expand allied and friendly links among naval officers.

As CNO, Burke understood that the U.S. Navy was an immense bureaucracy, and that it was very hard, if not impossible, to communicate his desires, much less make his commands felt.

In order to get things accomplished in the Pentagon, he decided it was "not wise to give a direct order" because if he did he would have to check whether it was carried out. Instead, he called the action officers to his office and convinced them of the importance of what he wanted. If the officer was "alert and enthusiastic" he could be counted on to follow through and do the necessary checking. This was "the main reason why" Burke believed that as CNO he could "influence things but I must get things done by persuasion and sometimes things do not get done which I think should be done." One tool Burke invariably employed in convincing his subordinates was good humor. His communications downward to Sailors, his deputy CNOs, and his fleet commanders and upward to the Secretary of Defense and even the president are filled with good natured, self-effacing humorous comments that did much to get the CNO's points across.

An almost superhuman stamina, and a determination to persevere in doing all he could to advance the mission and fortunes of the U.S. Navy at home and abroad, marked Burke's six years as CNO and indeed his entire career. He was known to regularly work seven days a week and to inspire his seniors and encourage his subordinates to do all they could to match him. Yet his service was marked with a personal humility that kept his ego in check. In fact, Burke's letters and papers from 1945 on reveal that he was prepared for and even looked forward to retirement; in fact, he had decided by 1954 that he would prefer not to be named CNO. Nevertheless, each of the three times that President Eisenhower called upon Burke to serve as CNO, his sense of duty trumped his personal desires.

Burke's ultimate conception of leadership in the U.S. Navy may best be summarized by a 1958 statement of philosophy that he put forward in arguing against increased unification of the armed forces. It highlights the special nature of leadership in a seagoing organization, where the environment demands large measures of self-reliance, flexibility, and independence of thought

Fred Freeman Collection

and action: "We believe in *command*, not *staff*. We believe we have 'real' things to do. The Navy believes in putting a man in a position with a job to do, and let him do it—give him hell if he does not perform—but be a man in his own name. We decentralize and capitalize on the capabilities of our individual people rather than centralize and make automatons of them. This builds that essential pride of service and sense of accomplishment. If it results in a certain amount of cockiness, I am for it. But this is the direction in which we should move."

Suggested Reading

Potter, E. B. *Admiral Arleigh Burke: A Biography.* New York: Random House, 1989. Most recent full popular biography, but heavy on World War II and light on Burke's postwar career.

Rosenberg, David Alan. "Admiral Arleigh Burke." In *The Chiefs of Naval Operations,* edited by Robert W. Love. Annapolis, Md.: Naval Institute Press, 1980. More complete treatment of Burke's tour as CNO.

———. "Admiral Arleigh A. Burke." In *Men of War: Great Naval Leaders of World War II*, edited by Stephen Howarth. New York: St. Martin's, 1993, 506–27. A more recent assessment of Burke's World War II service.

———. "Arleigh Burke: The Last CNO." In *Quarterdeck and Bridge: Two Centuries of American Naval Leaders*, edited by James C. Bradford. Annapolis, Md.: Naval Institute Press, 1997.

U.S. Naval Institute. *Naval Leadership with Some Hints to Junior Officers and Others.* Annapolis, Md.: U.S. Naval Institute, 1924.

About the Author

David Alan Rosenberg is a senior professor at the U.S. Naval War College and ran Task Force History for the Vice Chief of Naval Operations, compiling the Navy's operational history in Operation Iraqi Freedom and the Global War on Terror. He holds a PhD in history from the University of Chicago and is a captain in the U.S. Naval Reserve, commanding the naval reserve's largest intelligence unit.

39

Raymond G. Davis
Endurance

Lieutenant Colonel Frank G. Hoffman

U.S. Naval Institute Photo Archive

The last century was scarred by many bloody conflicts, including two world wars and wars in Korea and Vietnam. Many great Marines served the nation and their Corps with distinction. Uncommon courage was a common virtue among the Leathernecks in the twentieth century, but one particular Marine officer stands out among the many that served. He was first tested in the crucible of combat in the Pacific campaigns of World War II, where he compiled a credible combat leadership record. A company commander on Guadalcanal and a young battalion commander on Peleliu, Raymond G. Davis had seen his share of fighting. Davis had led the 1st Battalion, 1st Marines on Peleliu in some of the war's most vicious fighting. His battalion sustained 70 percent casualties in the fight for that black rock, and Davis earned the Navy Cross for conspicuous valor and intrepid leadership. Unlike most of his contemporaries, he did not return to his hometown to settle down or go to college. Instead, Ray Davis, a native of Atlanta, Georgia, stayed with the Marine Corps when he returned from the Pacific. Both his career and his combat leadership characterize the leadership traits of endurance and perseverance.

When the North Koreans crashed south across the South Korean border in the summer of 1950, Lieutenant Colonel Raymond Davis once again found himself in the thick of the upcoming fight. He was assigned as an inspector-instructor with a reserve battalion in Illinois when the North Koreans rolled over the border. But he was soon selected as commander of the 1st Battalion, 7th Marines (1/7), which absorbed a small cadre of experienced regulars, a number of veteran officers and noncommissioned officers with prior combat experience from the reserves, and hundreds of green Marines who had not yet been whipped into fighting shape. Lieutenant Colonel Ray Davis was given a week to whip a battalion of strangers into a team fit for fighting before they were shipped out.

They did not have to wait long to test themselves. The battalion landed a few days after Inchon and took its place alongside the rest of the 1st Marine Division as it swept to Seoul. After their classic amphibious victory, the Marines were swung around to the east coast of Korea in late October and landed at Wonsan. They were expected to relieve Republic of Korea units and sweep north toward the Yalu. Within a week, they bumped into a Chinese division, which they beat off in several days of tough fighting. With the People's Liberation Army (PLA) now apparently in the fight, the 7th Marines cautiously moved toward the towns of Hungnam and Hamhung. This was the starting point for a seventy-eight-mile stretch of crude highway linking those towns to the Chosin Reservoir. The Marines slowly pushed up the winding and treacherous road fighting the bitter weather until they reached Yudam-ri, the river just east of the Reservoir.

By 26 November, the 1st Marine Division had two regiments dispersed around Yudam, supported by nearly three battalions of artillery. The other regiment, Chesty Puller's 1st Marines, was fourteen miles south at Hagaru and beyond. Halfway between them was Fox Company, 7th Marines, commanded by Captain Bill Barber. Barber's 240 Marines were posted on a sharp hill guarding the critical Toktong Pass, set at the crest of a foreboding rise. They owned, somewhat precariously, the vital link between the major elements of the division. Control of that pass was critical to the communication lifeline that connected the Marines at Yudam-ri with the rest of the 1st Marines Division. It would be the site of a modern Thermopylae for Fox Company's modern-day Spartans.

The biting cold continued to hamper operations along the high ground surrounding Yudam-ri and the main supply route. Then the Ninth Army Group of the PLA struck all along the Marine column and the small enclaves connecting them to the sea. The PLA sent forward roughly one hundred thousand white-clad but poorly dressed troops, aided by very limited fire support. Nonetheless, the PLA forces threw themselves at the widely deployed Marine outposts in a series of ferocious night attacks.

After three days of such assaults, the Marine leaders were convinced that they had no choice but to concentrate their forces and reverse their march back toward the sea. What followed was one of the most famous retrograde operations in military annals and some of the most glorious pages in the history of the Marine Corps. Against long odds and temperatures that were rarely measured above zero, the Marines clawed their way back toward Hungnam, taking all their equipment and wounded with them, and as many of the dead as possible. Ray Davis played a huge role in this famous "march to the sea," all the while displaying the resolve, persistence, and indomitable will that had characterized his combat performance in World War II.

If the 1st Marine Division were to survive, it would have to overcome the persistent roadblocks and frequent ambushes of the PLA. They would also have to hold Toktong Pass. Barber's Fox Company still held that vital pass, but only barely. Like all the other Marine positions, the reinforced company was attacked in strength at night for several days and was hanging by a thread. Barber was almost out of range of artillery, he was down to his last ten mortar rounds, half his command was dead or wounded, and he was six miles from the nearest friendly unit. There was at least one PLA division between him and Yudam, and perhaps more to the south. Three times his regimental commander, Colonel Homer Litzenberg, had pushed a relief unit down the road toward Barber, and three times the force was rebuffed and returned to Yudam. Some helicopters braved withering small arms fire to deliver batteries for the radios and morphine. Air force transport planes parachuted ammunition and grenades into and around Fox Company, offering additional sustenance to Marine and Chinese combatants alike. Close air support from Marine

Corsairs and some Australian aviators was the only thing keeping Barber's outpost from being overrun.

Davis's battalion remained along a series of hills along the southern edge of Yudam. Litzenberg was out of ideas on how to save Fox Company and ensure the Marine regiments could safely climb out of Yudam. He passed the problem to Ray Davis. Davis pulled together his tired company commanders and laid out an ambitious plan. After a short hike down the main supply route to Hill 1419, now known as Turkey Hill, the battalion would hike up to the top of the mountain ridges overlooking the road network and work south to the rear of the Chinese, pinning down Fox Hill. Davis boldly ordered a night attack along several thousand yards of snow-swept wilderness to seize Hill 1520. The Chinese would not expect this route, nor a night attack from the road-bound and isolated Marines.

Davis stripped the crack battalion down to the essentials, taking only two 81 mm mortars and half a dozen heavy machine guns. His Marines carried double their normal load of ammunition and grenades. Davis planned to guide his battalion off the stars and by having illumination rounds fired. A blizzard slowed the battalion's movements, but the shrieking wind also masked the noise of five hundred troops as they cursed their way through the dark. The frequent "clank" of a mortar tube or canteen banging against a rifle was the only sound for hours as the Marines plodded along in knee-deep snow in their recently issued snow boots and parkas.

The cold numbed the reactions of the tired battalion, whose exertions were stretched past the breaking point. Exhausted, disoriented, and frozen, Davis pushed himself and his unit across the trackless terrain toward the large mass in front of them. Davis struggled to guide the battalion's arduous slog, racing up and down the line, urging his Marines forward with his quiet Georgian accent. The battalion climbed as far up

as they could go, and at 0300, 1/7 simply fell to the ground exhausted and rested. They were just outside Fox Company's reach.

Davis once again drew upon his powers of endurance to accomplish the mission. In the morning, Davis shook his tired and ragged battalion awake, and they attacked toward the surrounded Fox Company. Chinese forces were surprised as the Marines attacked them from the rear and broke the encirclement around Barber's shrunken enclave. They walked on a carpet of Chinese bodies to get into Fox Company's lines. Captain Barber and his seven officers were badly wounded. His reinforced unit had shrunken to only eighty-five effectives. Davis's arrival saved that beleaguered unit from destruction, and the heroic ordeal of both units saved the vital Toktong Pass for the epic march of the rest of the Marines. Both Barber and Davis were awarded the Congressional Medal of Honor for their inspirational leadership. However, without Davis's bold plan and persistent execution, there may not have been a Fox company to save. More importantly, without the door at Toktong Pass being held open by 1/7's overnight attack, the two Marine regiments further up the road would have been cut off.

Davis's story does not stop after Korea. He went on to take command of the 3rd Marine Division in Vietnam in 1968. Davis maintained his high standards and aggressive leadership in this conflict, his third war. Numerous major actions against North Vietnamese forces, most notably Operation Dewey Canyon, were conducted under his leadership. This tactically sophisticated campaign bore some resemblance to the ridge-running and leapfrogging operations of 1/7's fight out of the Yudami valley almost two decades earlier. In two months, the 9th Marines killed more than sixteen hundred North Vietnamese Army troops and destroyed their infrastructure in the mountains. Monsoon rains instead of freezing temperatures dogged his forces, but once again tenacious Marine aviation and innovative fire support planning proved

U.S. Naval Institute Photo Archive

crucial as did the perseverance of the Marine commander. When he finished his tour, even army generals, no lovers of the Marine Corps or its tactics in Southeast Asia, grudgingly admitted that Ray Davis was the finest division commander in Vietnam.

Davis subsequently became the Assistant Commandant of the Marine Corps with the rank of general. He retired in 1970 but stayed active in national security affairs. His sage counsel was sought whenever the tocsin sounded until his passing on 3 September 2003. A distinguished combat leader in three wars, General Davis personified all the leadership qualities, but his example of endurance and perseverance to accomplish his assigned mission was his greatest contribution and legacy to the Corps.

Suggested Reading

Alexander, Joseph H. *The Battle History of the U.S. Marines: A Fellowship of Valor.* New York: HarperCollins, 1999.

Davis, Raymond G. *Marine at War.* Raleigh, NC: Research Triangle, 1995.

Millett, Allan R. *Semper Fidelis: The History of the United States Marine Corps.* New York: Free Press, 1991.

Russ, Martin. *Breakout: The Chosin Reservoir Campaign.* New York: Penguin, 1999.

About the Author

Frank Hoffman is a Research Fellow at the Center for Emerging Threats and Opportunities, Quantico Virginia. A former Marine infantry officer, he serves as a strategic analyst and advanced concept developer for the U.S. Marine Corps. Before coming to this position, Mr. Hoffman served with the U.S. National Security Commission from 1999 to 2001, where he served as senior staffer on military and homeland security. He is a distinguished military graduate of the University of Pennsylvania (Wharton School) as well as the Naval War College. He has authored *Decisive Force: The New American Way of War* (Praeger, 1996), several government reports, and over one hundred articles on national security affairs in *Orbis, Foreign Affairs,* Naval Institute *Proceedings* and the Marine Corps *Gazette.* He routinely lectures at American and foreign military schools and consults internationally on military and national security matters.

40

James H. Doyle
Responsiveness

Dr. Donald W. Chisholm

U.S. Naval Institute Photo Archive

"I have not been asked, nor have I volunteered my opinion, if I were asked, however, the best I can say is that Inchon is not impossible." In that simple declaration, Rear Admiral James H. Doyle, Commander, Task Force 90, communicated to General MacArthur simultaneously his professional reservations about the proposed September 1950 amphibious assault at Inchon and his judgment that the operation could be successfully executed.

The true test of naval leadership comes not in the face of routine operations with adequate time and forces but in the crucible of anomaly, short time fuses, and inadequate or inappropriate forces—all of which described the major amphibious operations of 1950 in Korea. During the short months between July and December 1950 in a dynamic, continually changing battle space, Doyle successfully planned and executed four major amphibious operations: Po-Hang Dong, Inchon, Wonsan-Iwon, and Hungnam.

Absent the amphibious capability brought to bear by the U.S. Navy and Marine Corps in Korea, the war would have gone quite badly for the United Nations (UN). The first operation ensured that North Korean forces would not overrun the entire peninsula. The second was a tactically brilliant effort that perfectly fulfilled MacArthur's ingenious operational scheme: the enemy's lines of supply were severed; his troops were caught between the assault force and the advancing Eighth Army; and the South Korean capital, Seoul, was rapidly retaken. The third, conceived as an operational twin to the second, was delayed by extensive Russian and North Korean mining and overtaken by events on the ground. The last was a historically unprecedented—and still unmatched—planned redeployment of more than an entire corps and all its equipment.

Doyle proved to be well suited to face such complex challenges under the trying conditions in Korea. He melded extensive experience in planning and executing amphibious operations with consummate professionalism, intellectual rigor, hard-nosed practicality, and forthright candor with both superiors and subordinates. These traits did not necessarily endear Doyle to his contemporaries or to his seniors, but he got the job done brilliantly.

If the boy is the father to the man, the junior and midgrade officer is the father to the admiral. Doyle graduated from the Naval Academy in 1919 with the rest of his 1920 class (having served while a midshipman during World War I). Over the next seven years, he saw typical service for a black shoe of the time; he alternated between battleships, destroyers, and auxiliary types and progressed from division to department head billets. He entered George Washington University law school in 1926 and graduated with distinction in 1929. He returned to sea as executive officer of two flush-deck destroyers over the ensuing three years, followed by time in Washington with the Judge Advocate General. He then served as aide and flag secretary to Commander, Destroyers, Battle Force, followed by a tour as commanding officer of flush-deck destroyer *Sands*. From 1938 to 1940, Doyle served as aide to the Commandant, 16th Naval District, Cavite, Philippine Islands, where he came to know General Douglas MacArthur well.

For a time in 1940, Doyle, by now a captain, commanded Destroyer Squadron 67 as part of the swap with Great Britain of fifty old destroyers for long-term lease for U.S. bases. He subsequently commanded attack cargo ship *Regulus* until May 1942, when he joined Rear Admiral Richmond Kelly Turner's Amphibious Force, South Pacific staff as operations officer. He soon became brilliant, tireless, demanding, and irascible—one of Turner's most trusted officers. Doyle further developed when he became a principal planner for Operation Watchtower. Not only was he integral to planning and executing the initial landings and follow-up operations in the Solomons; he learned the inner workings of the higher levels of command, gained insights into the problems of inter-service relations,

acquired hard-won knowledge of naval gunfire support and the importance of air superiority, and discovered the intricacies of logistics.

Although Turner wanted to take Doyle with him when he returned to Pearl Harbor in July 1943 to command Fifth Amphibious Force, Doyle remained to provide continuity for Rear Admiral Theodore Wilkinson. When Doyle detached several months later, he was ordered to Washington, where he joined the Amphibious Warfare Section of headquarters, Fleet Admiral Ernest J. King's war planning staff. Here, Doyle remained a key planner through the great Central Pacific amphibious campaign of late 1943 through early 1945.

Doyle was finally ordered to light cruiser *Pasadena*, which he commanded with distinction through the Okinawa campaign, including antishipping sweeps and shore bombardments. In May 1946, he rejoined Admiral Turner on his military staff at the United Nations and in January 1948, assumed command of Amphibious Training Command, Pacific Fleet, succeeding to Amphibious Group One in January 1950.

Doyle thus acquired extensive seagoing experience over the course of four ship commands, two of them during war, combined with wartime planning experience on operational and higher headquarters staffs during the acme of U.S. Navy operational-level planning. He had worked firsthand in large-scale joint operations, directly observed the machinations of the United Nations and the problems of alliances and coalitions, and served under two of the most brilliant and hard-nosed senior U.S. naval officers of the twentieth century.

In 1950, planning and conducting those operations in Korea, Doyle and his staff ascertained the structure of the problems and devised solutions for them. Doyle quietly and forcefully ensured that he and his professionals had the leeway to devise and execute those solutions. At the same time, he granted his subordinates considerable discretion. Two incidents illustrated these points.

Remarkably, MacArthur conceived the Inchon landing only days into the war. Events on the ground and the absence of immediately available trained amphibious forces dictated, however, that it be delayed until September. Doyle and his staff nevertheless commenced a detailed study of Inchon. Neither MacArthur's staff nor the X Corps staff had "amphibious training, experience, or basic understanding of amphibious operations"—the army's plan simply assumed that the troops would be put ashore successfully to commence their drive on Seoul. In consequence, Doyle determined that Mac-Arthur should be briefed thoroughly on what the Inchon landing would entail. The general's chief of staff, who noted that the operation was "purely mechanical," and told him "the General is not interested in details," rebuffed him. Doyle insisted, however, and in late August, he and nine of his staff briefed the details of the landing, outlining the unique challenges the operation presented, Doyle's reservations, and alternative landing sites. With Army Chief of Staff General Lawton Collins and Chief of Naval Operations Admiral Forrest Sherman also present, MacArthur listened and then forcefully enumerated why the landing would be at Inchon.

Doyle had more than met his professional obligation. He took his orders and went about planning the operation, absent the normal time for preparing and executing such operations, which meant no rehearsal. Meanwhile, the commander of the assault force, Major General O. P. Smith, arrived, and together the two officers and their staffs worked closely to build a plan that would not fail. Their solutions to the myriad problems proved to be exceptional and effective in execution.

Hungnam loomed just as important, operationally and strategically, as Inchon. Following the Wonsan-Iwon operation, Doyle went to his old and close friend Vice Admiral C. Turner Joy, Commander, Naval Forces Far East, and told him that he could not and would not serve under Vice Admiral Arthur D. Struble, Commander, Seventh Fleet, in the future. When the plan for the evacuation of UN forces from Hungnam was issued on 13 November, Joy acceded to Doyle,

believing that he needed his amphibious expertise more than he needed Struble. Doyle thus reported directly to Joy, enjoying significant discretion and broadly defined duties, including redeployment, shipping protection, control of air support and naval gunfire in embarkation areas, and maintenance of the blockade along the east coast of Korea.

Admiral Sherman was uncomfortable about giving such authority to Doyle, being especially unwilling to pass control of the fast carriers to an amphibious commander and fearing disaster if the evacuation went awry. Sherman already told Joy that he favored his former deputy Struble for Inchon and Wonsan. Doyle learned only later that Sherman arranged for Lieutenant General Lemuel Shepherd, Commander, Fleet Marine Forces Pacific, to assume command at Hungnam if Doyle proved ineffective. Doyle found that "Sherman knew little, if anything, about amphibious operations." Notwithstanding Sherman's concern, Joy's decision stood.

In execution, the operation succeeded brilliantly. More than one hundred thousand UN soldiers and Marines, ninety thousand Korean civilians, 17,500 vehicles, and 350,000 measurement tons of cargo were taken off the beach during the two weeks preceding Christmas Eve 1950. In the heroic fighting withdrawal of the 1st Marine Division and attached army units from Chosin, not one friendly was left on the beach. Also, Communist forces were never able to pose a serious threat during the operation. As Doyle himself later described the event, "It was walk, don't run, to the nearest exit."[1]

The key to this remarkable military feat is found in Doyle's recognition that, although vastly experienced in amphibious operations, he and his staff had never encountered a problem remotely resembling Hungnam. The linchpin was the decision to form an ad hoc organization and devise a plan predicated on conducting an amphibious operation in reverse—an arrangement that enabled experts to exercise judgment, identify problems, generate solutions, and directly and quickly communicate with others.

National Archives

Doyle established and maintained a decentralized, self-organizing system that proved highly adaptive, flexible, and well suited to the principal constraint of time. The command arrangements clearly contravened prevailing doctrine but allowed Doyle the freedom to plan and execute as his professional judgment dictated.

Rear Admiral Doyle displayed throughout his time in Korea the basic qualities of leadership deemed the hallmark of the professional naval officer. He took initiative where appropriate, trusted his subordinates to do their jobs, and displayed keen analytic thinking and professional knowledge. Most importantly, in every situation where he believed it vital, he did not stand mute; rather, he insisted on speaking the truth. In so doing, he evidenced in stark relief the moral courage found in the best of officers. Having voiced his concerns in a highly professional manner, he then worked to make the decisions of his superiors prove sound. He thereby contributed materially to the success

of several very difficult operations and to the larger United Nations' effort in Korea.

Note

1. While Doyle directed the Hungnam operation, he was also overseeing similar redeployments from four other locations on both Korean coasts.

Suggested Reading

Buell, Thomas B. *Naval Leadership in Korea.* Washington, D.C.: Naval Historical Center, 2003.

Cagle, Malcolm W., and Frank A. Manson. *The Sea War in Korea.* Annapolis, Md.: Naval Institute Press, 1957.

Chisholm, Donald. "Negotiated Joint Command Relationships: Korean War Amphibious Operations, 1950." *Naval War College Review* 53 (2000): 65–124.

———. "Escape by Sea: The Hungnam Redeployment." *Joint Force Quarterly* (Spring/Summer 2001): 54–62.

Doyle, James H., and Arthur J. Mayer. "December 1950 at Hungnam." U.S. Naval Institute *Proceedings* 105 (1979).

Field, James A. *History of Naval Operations in Korea.* Washington, D.C.: Government Printing Office, 1962.

Heinl, Robert D. *Victory at High Tide: The Inchon-Seoul Campaign.* 3rd ed. Annapolis, Md.: Nautical and Aviation Publications, 1979.

About the Author

Professor Donald W. Chisholm joined the Naval War College in 2000. Before coming to the Naval War College, he taught at several universities, including the University of Illinois at Chicago and the University of California, Los Angeles, where he was a founding member of the School of Public Policy and Social Research. Professor Chisholm earned his AB, MA, and PhD in political science at the University of California, Berkeley. His chief fields of interest include military history, organization theory, administrative behavior, policy analysis, and American political institutions. His research has examined the planning and execution of joint military operations; cognitive and organizational limits on rationality; organizational adaptation and innovation; organizational failure and reliability, particularly in high-risk technologies; and privatization of public activities. He is the author of *Coordination Without Hierarchy: Informal Structures in Multi-Organizational Systems* (University of California Press, 1989) and *Waiting for Dead Men's Shoes: Origins and Development of the U.S. Navy's Officer Personnel System, 1793–1941* (Stanford University Press, 2001), for which he received the 2001 Rear Admiral Samuel Eliot Morison Award for Distinguished Contribution to Naval Literature. He has also published a number of articles in professional journals, including *Joint Force Quarterly*, *Parameters*, and the *Naval War College Review*.

41

Grace Murray Hopper
Technical Innovator

Dr. Kurt W. Beyer

Naval Historical Center

Humans are allergic to change. They love to say, "We've always done it this way." I try to fight that. That's why I have a clock on my wall that runs counter-clockwise.

Rear Admiral Grace Murray Hopper

On the eve of World War I, Field Marshall Ferdinand Foch, a world-renowned military strategist at the French Ecole Supériure de Guerre, pronounced, "Airplanes are interesting toys but of no military value." With similar sincerity, senior engineers at AT&T spent many hours during the 1960s trying to convince Pentagon officials that digital networks based on packet switching were a foolhardy approach to military communications. Luckily, forward-looking administrators at the Advanced Research Projects Agency ignored such authoritative advice and created the ARPANET, precursor to the Internet. So often "experts," be they senior military leadership, prominent academics, or business executives, have difficulty seeing beyond the borders of their specialty. Education, tradition, and community culture create a mental framework that helps to explain reality on the one hand, yet also hinders one's ability to see alternative approaches or adjust to ever-changing circumstances. The rare military leader looks beyond "what is" to grasp "what could be." It is even more unusual for that leader to consciously pursue that vision, often in the face of mounting organizational opposition. Rear Admiral Grace Murray Hopper was such a leader, and her commitment to computer innovation and implementation helped to shape the modern technical military.

Grace Hopper's military career and computer career ran parallel from the start. The events of 7 December 1941 at Pearl Harbor inspired the mathematics professor to radically alter the direction of her life. Within a year of the United States' declaration of war against the Empire of Japan and Nazi Germany, Hopper left her tenured position at Vassar College, separated from her husband Vincent Hopper, and attempted to join the U.S. Navy. Not knowing exactly what to do with a five-foot-three, 105-pound, thirty-six-year-old with a PhD in numerical analysis, the Bureau of Personnel turned down Hopper's request. Rejecting Hopper was made administratively easier by the fact that as of 1942 the U.S. Navy was not accepting women as officer candidates; however, rejection did not seem to hinder the obstinate Hopper. With the introduction of the WAVES (Women Accepted for Volunteer Emergency Service) on 30 July 1942, Hopper's prayers were answered and the newly minted officer soon found herself in charge of programming the world's first operational computer, the Harvard Mark I.

In many ways, Grace Hopper's naval career mirrors the rise of the Information Age. During the war years at Harvard, Hopper and her crew solved a range of military problems from ballistics trajectories to the infamous implosion problem for the first atomic bomb. Initially out of wartime necessity, these pioneers developed early coding techniques, debugging practices, subroutine principles, and batch processing procedures that confirmed the utility of the new computing technology and helped to change the nature of warfare from that point forward.

As the technology was transferred from the laboratory to primarily the defense industry and military installations in the late 1940s and early 1950s, programming loomed ever larger as the bottleneck that hindered the spread of electronic computers. The costs associated with defining an application along with writing and debugging the necessary programs began to outstrip the cost of hardware itself. Hopper, who by 1950 had become the senior mathematician for Remington Rand's UNIVAC computer and a lieutenant commander in the U.S. Navy Reserves, believed that the only way to solve the programming crisis was to teach computers to program themselves. Her key invention, one on which all modern computer languages rest, is called the

compiler. By means of a compiler program a computer could call upon relevant subroutines and manage address and memory allocation, thus relieving the human programmer from the most difficult housekeeping tasks.

Compilers, Hopper believed, were the key to "democratizing" computers. They would allow a much wider audience to communicate with the mechanical giants. Instead of forcing the human to learn machine language, she made the computer learn English, French, German, or any other human language. Much of her energy during the 1950s and 1960s was spent spreading the automatic programming gospel to the military and large corporations through lectures, articles, and conference presentations. Her concepts would eventually serve as the blueprint for COBOL, the most widely used computer language to date.

On 1 January 1967, Commander Grace Hopper was placed on the Naval Reserve retirement list. Two years prior she had stepped down as the director of Automatic Programming Development, UNIVAC division of Sperry-Rand. Though she remained with UNIVAC as a senior staff scientist and served as a visiting associate professor at the University of Pennsylvania, from all appearances the sixty-year-old Hopper was slowly making the transition to retirement. After having such a dynamic and productive career, Hopper was naturally showered during this period with numerous accolades. In 1962, the pioneering programmer was elected Fellow of the Institute of Electrical and Electronic Engineers, and two years later she received the 1964 achievement award by the Society of Women Engineers. The highlight of these tributes came in 1969 when the Data Processing Management Association named Hopper the first-ever Computer Sciences "Man of the Year."

But to the surprise of everyone—except probably Hopper—"retirement" merely signaled the beginning of a new productive phase in her life. The Navy was experiencing difficulties fully implementing COBOL throughout its growing network of computers, and Hopper was once again called to duty. What began as a six-month active duty appointment extended for twenty years. Hopper was named director of the Navy Programming Languages Group, where she remained until 1977. During this period Hopper officially retired from Sperry-Rand in 1971, and in 1973 she was promoted to the rank of captain.

From 1977 to 1983, Hopper was assigned to the Naval Data Automation Headquarters in Washington, D.C., where she monitored the state of the art in computing and recommended which technologies should be applied to existing naval systems. It was during this period that Hopper developed the fleetwide tactical data system for nuclear submarines and was awarded the prestigious Navy Meritorious Service Medal for her efforts. In 1983 by presidential appointment, Hopper was promoted to commodore, later changed to rear admiral. Rear Admiral Hopper used her elevated rank to aggressively advance technical innovation both in and outside of the U.S. Navy. She spent her final three years in the service touring and lecturing, and in 1986 the oldest active officer in the U.S. Navy retired. Hopper was immediately hired by the Digital Equipment Corporation as a senior consultant, where she worked until her death in 1992 at the age of eighty-six.

Besides becoming the first woman to achieve the rank of rear admiral on active duty, Hopper was showered with another round of awards before her passing, most notably the National Medal of Technology. On 6 January 1996, the guided-missile destroyer DDG 70 was christened the USS *Hopper*. But despite the hundreds of honors and accolades, Hopper maintained to her death that her most cherished award was her first received in the field of computing, the 1946 Naval Ordnance Development Award, presented by Howard Aiken for her superior work on the Harvard Mark I as a lieutenant junior grade during the war.

Undeniably, Grace Hopper played a pivotal role in the development of the computer indus-

try and the modern Navy. What makes her story even more compelling is the fact that her greatest accomplishments in the field came at a time when many American women were retreating from public life. Why certain women such as Hopper were able to rise to prominent positions in the face of growing postwar antipathy toward women in the workplace is not an easy question to answer.

Pearl Harbor and the ensuing mobilization for war marked a unique watershed for Hopper and many other American women. The reorganization of labor on a massive scale created opportunities for women once reserved for men. Hopper benefited from this labor shift and became an officer in the most gendered organization of its day, the U.S. Navy. Hopper's membership in the Navy, which lasted forty-three years, benefited her in a variety of ways. First, her military rank endowed her with the external trappings of authority: uniform, title, pay, privilege. In both the business and military environment, those trappings helped to neutralize societal prejudices against women in positions of public responsibility.

Hopper used her U.S. Navy membership through the 1940s and 1950s to keep abreast of the service's computational needs. Every year Hopper spent two weeks fulfilling her reservist requirements by advising naval leadership on how computer technology could be applied to U.S. Navy systems. This interaction helped Hopper foster strong ties with top brass and maintained her special relationship with the largest organizational user of computer technology. That special relationship served Hopper well; it enabled her to organize conferences and events that few others could and provided her access to confidential material.

The fact that computing was a new discipline afforded Hopper the flexibility to define her role within the emerging computer community. Oftentimes, gender-defined roles and responsibilities exist in more established fields. Hopper's programming knowledge and expertise held her

Naval Historical Center

in good standing with her peers regardless of gender, and as the relevance of computing grew, so too did Hopper's stature.

Ultimately, Hopper's ability to transcend organizational gender bias and elevate her career to uncharted heights may best be explained by her unique character. Like any woman during this period, Hopper had to deal with her share of mistreatment. In fact, by placing herself in male-dominated environments, Hopper courted abuse to some extent. Yet somehow she found the strength of character to overcome, turning harassment into self-motivation. Hopper's confidence in her abilities, leadership skills, sense of humor, and aggressive nature allowed her to win over even the toughest critics. Moreover, she cre-

ated a safe work environment for other young, aspiring female programmers. Grace Hopper became a role model for generations of women in the computing industry and the U.S. Navy. This may have been her greatest accomplishment.

Suggested Reading

Beyer, Kurt. *Programming the Future: Grace Murray Hopper and the Computer Revolution.* Cambridge, Mass.: MIT Press, forthcoming 2005.

Broome Williams, Kathleen. *Improbable Warriors: Women Scientists and the U.S. Navy in World War II.* Annapolis, Md.: Naval Institute Press, 2001.

About the Author

Dr. Kurt W. Beyer is currently Professor of Information Technology at the United States Naval Academy. His interests include understanding the socioeconomic impact of various information technologies, as well as tracking the growing IT-military nexus. Prior to receiving his PhD from the University of California, Berkeley, Dr. Beyer was a Naval Aviator, flying F-14 Tomcats out of Naval Air Station Oceana in Virginia Beach. Dr. Beyer is a graduate of Oxford University (MA Politics, Philosophy, and Economics) where he rowed and played basketball for the university, and the U.S. Naval Academy (BS Engineering, History Honors), where he played baseball and served as Brigade Commander his senior year. His first book, titled *Programming the Future: Grace Murray Hopper and the Computer Revolution*, will be published by The MIT Press in the winter of 2005.

Dr. Beyer lives in Washington, D.C., with his wife, Johanna, their son, Charlie, and their cat, Sassy.

42

Carl M. Brashear

Perseverance in the Face of Discrimination

Paul Stillwell

U.S. Naval Institute Photo Archive

In 2000, moviegoers throughout the nation saw the life and career of U.S. Navy diver Carl Brashear unfold in the film *Men of Honor*, which starred Cuba Gooding Jr. Though the movie fictionalized and exaggerated many of the elements of Brashear's life, as Hollywood often does in portraying real people, it bore enough semblance of the truth to inspire many viewers. Brashear personified a number of leadership traits, including physical courage, mental toughness, and sheer persistence. He passed the rigorous tests needed to become the U.S. Navy's first black master diver in 1970, overcoming a myriad of obstacles. He came to the Navy with limited education; he was a black man in a service that was not welcoming when he joined; and he achieved the physical requirements of diving despite the amputation of his left leg just below the knee. Brashear succeeded because he refused to surrender to roadblocks that would have stopped nearly anyone else.

The beginning of Brashear's life was modest at best. He was born in 1931 in Kentucky. His parents were sharecroppers who moved when he was a few weeks old to a farm a few miles outside the town of Sonora in Hardin County. The family home had neither running water nor electricity. On the farm, young Brashear milked cows, chopped wood, and fed livestock. Brashear attended the first through eighth grades in what he later described as "a segregated schoolhouse with broken-out windows and hand-me-down books." He did well in school but did not enjoy it, so he quit as soon as he could. He much preferred adventure to the classroom.

In 1948, just past his seventeenth birthday, Brashear set out to join the army. After an unpleasant experience with recruiters at Kentucky's Fort Knox soured him, he stopped at a U.S. Navy recruiting office in Elizabethtown, not far from his home. The chief petty officer there was reassuring and inviting, and Brashear was hooked. The reality was not always as pleasant as promised. As Brashear related in an oral history, in recruit training he stole a pie and had to do penance by hitting a pie pan with spoons and proclaiming repeatedly, "I stole a pie."[1] But there were other barriers as well. Though the armed forces were officially integrated in 1948, job opportunities for blacks were still limited. He had no choice at the outset except to be a steward, essentially a servant for white officers. And during his initial duty in Key West, Florida, black Sailors were allowed in the naval base swimming pool only three hours a week.

While at Key West, Brashear took his first steps toward his U.S. Navy occupational specialty, boatswain's mate, when Chief Petty Officer Guy Johnson arranged for him to swim out and bring seaplanes in to the beach. That exposure to seamanship provided a taste of the excitement Brashear was eager to experience. Johnson also imparted leadership lessons and pride: "Be a good man and a good sailor."

From Key West Brashear moved on to shipboard duty in the escort carriers *Palau* and *Tripoli*, where he developed his boatswain's mate skills still further. A previously kindled interest, Brashear applied to become a U.S. Navy diver while on board the *Palau*. His early requests were not approved, but in 1954 he finally reached salvage diving school at Bayonne, New Jersey. The training there was rigorous and stressful, though not as manifestly unfair as the movie depicts. Chief Petty Officer Billy Sunday, one of Brashear's tormentors in the film, was a creation of the screenwriter's imagination. In reality, Harry Rutherford, a first-class boatswain's mate from Arkansas, gave Brashear the encouragement he needed in order to keep going. The young black man had received death threats from others in the class, and Rutherford talked him out of quitting.

Brashear passed the course in which nearly half those who started failed. He was now qualified as a U.S. Navy diver and worked on a variety of salvage jobs as he served the next few years. Diving requires a great deal of coordination between the

diver below the surface and the people topside tending him and providing air. Brashear learned teamwork as an essential part of the work. He also realized that he needed more education and eventually earned his general equivalence diploma after taking a number of correspondence courses.

In 1960, Brashear went to school to become a first-class diver but failed. His failure disqualified him from diving. By his recollection, he hit rock bottom at that point. But he went back to school and became a second-class diver, a step below his earlier goal. He finally made first-class diver in 1964. The following year he was assigned to the U.S. Navy salvage ship *Hoist*, which Brashear saw as the ticket to prepare himself for the training needed to become a master diver, the top rung of the ladder for U.S. Navy divers.

His career progress came to an abrupt halt when Brashear was involved in a dramatic, life-changing incident. In January 1966, two air force planes collided, and a nuclear bomb from one of them dropped into the Mediterranean Sea near Palomares, Spain. A U.S. Navy task force began searching for the missing bomb. In March, the *Hoist* found the bomb and lifted it to the surface. While Brashear and his crew were bringing the weapon aboard ship, a line on the lifting capstan parted. As he ran to get his men to safety, a pipe broke loose and struck him just below the left knee. He suffered a compound fracture and began bleeding profusely. Two tourniquets stopped the blood flow, but he was near death.

Gradually, Brashear revived, but his leg developed gangrene and infection. Doctors laid out a recovery plan that would have taken years and left one leg shorter than the other. So Brashear, by now a chief boatswain's mate, asked to have his lower leg amputated so he could get back into action. He took inspiration from airplane pilots who had resumed flying after losing legs. Always keen on physical fitness, once he was fitted with an artificial leg in late 1966, he worked even harder. He drove himself to get into shape. He also snuck out of the hospital and went to diving school to prove that he could still do it. He had himself photographed performing diving, weightlifting, and other feats to demonstrate his fitness. In between times, he had to soak the bleeding stump of his leg in salt water because of the punishment he was giving it. When he was supposed to report to a physical evaluation board that was set to retire him from the U.S. Navy for disability, Brashear simply didn't show up.

Finally, he had the opportunity to demonstrate his capability officially, and he passed. His refusal to quit restored him to duty. After two more tours of service, Brashear reported to Washington, D.C., to go through an evaluation that led to his designation as master diver. That designation comprises fewer than one hundred divers at any given time. To reach the top of one's profession is an accomplishment under any circumstances. To do so in a physically demanding field after the loss of a leg is truly remarkable.

In addition to his diving qualification, Brashear achieved the grade of master chief petty officer, the highest grade available for U.S. Navy enlisted personnel. As a senior petty officer, he now had the opportunity to shape the lives and careers of his juniors, just as other leaders had done for him. Interestingly, in a reverse of the situations he had encountered as a young Sailor, he now had to catch himself to avoid showing favoritism to his subordinates who were black. The segregated U.S. Navy that Brashear joined in 1948 had changed greatly. By the late 1970s he was the senior enlisted man on board the salvage ship *Recovery*.

He retired from active duty in 1979 and went on to a number of jobs, both in civil service and in private industry. The story of his achievements received initial recognition through television programs and published articles. Brashear's fame became worldwide with the release of *Men of Honor*. He was sought after for public appearances and, as a result, traveled widely to tell his story. Thousands more have drawn inspiration from his example, even though they have never met him. The sharecropper's son from Kentucky made quite an impact.

U.S. Naval Institute Photo Archive

Note

1. In the movie version of Brashear's life, it was another Sailor who did the banging with the spoons.

Suggested Reading

Brashear, Carl. Oral History. Annapolis, Md.: U.S. Naval Institute, 1998.

Robbins, David. *Men of Honor*. New York: Onyx/Penguin Putnam, 2000.

About the Author

Paul Stillwell is director of the history division of the U.S. Naval Institute. In 1969 he served in the crew of the *New Jersey*, which had been one of Lee's flagships in World War II. Stillwell has written a number of books on battleships, including individual histories of the *New Jersey*, *Missouri*, and *Arizona*. He is at work on a biography of Willis Lee.

43

Thomas H. Moorer
Conviction

Dr. Edward J. Marolda

Naval Photographic Center

Throughout his service to the U.S. Navy and the nation, Admiral Thomas Hinman Moorer exhibited many attributes of a true leader: physical and moral courage, loyalty to subordinates and superiors, integrity, and determination to stand by his principles. At times when it was not politic or popular to do so, Moorer confidently presented his case to his superiors, supporting it with sound analysis and his considerable professional experience.

Thomas Moorer was born in the small town of Willing, Alabama, on 9 February 1912. As he grew older, Moorer excelled at local schools; in 1929, he started his plebe year at the U.S. Naval Academy. Two years after graduating with the class of 1933, Ensign Moorer began flight training at Pensacola Naval Air Station in Florida. The young officer wanted to make a mark in carrier aviation, the U.S. Navy's still infant but promising combat arm. From 1936 to the outbreak of World War II in Europe, Moorer served in fighter squadrons onboard the U.S. Navy's early carriers. As a member of Patrol Squadron 22 in Hawaii when the Japanese attacked Pearl Harbor on 7 December 1941, the naval aviator experienced war for the first time.

Moorer's squadron of PBY patrol planes was almost immediately sent to support Allied naval forces fighting desperately to prevent the Japanese from invading the Dutch East Indies. He first tasted combat the hard way—the enemy shot down his plane and then sank the ship that rescued him and his crew. But the wounded pilot acted with such courage and skill, landing his damaged plane and getting surviving crew members to Australia, that the U.S. Navy awarded him the Silver Star and Purple Heart. During the next several months, Moorer piloted his unarmed seaplane through skies filled with Japanese fighter aircraft. On one occasion, he delivered badly needed supplies to an Allied ground unit under attack and brought out eight seriously wounded men. His bravery earned him the Distinguished Flying Cross.

The U.S. Navy then rushed the battle-tested naval officer to another global hot spot—the Atlantic Ocean, where German U-boats were savaging the Allied merchant fleet. As commanding officer of Bombing Squadron 132 and in staff billets, Moorer demonstrated exceptional skill in devising tactics and techniques for hunting down enemy submarines. His Legion of Merit citation credited him with contributing "materially to the combat effectiveness of aircraft in anti-submarine warfare." By the end of the war, the U.S. Navy promoted the talented officer to commander.

Moorer continued his fast rise through the officer corps in the 1950s, when he served in successive naval aviation billets ashore and afloat. Promoted to rear admiral in July 1957, Moorer spent the next several years honing his intellectual skills as a strategic planner in the office of the Chief of Naval Operations in Washington. Not one to be tied to a desk, however, the dynamic and aggressive officer went to sea again as Commander, Carrier Division 6.

In October 1962, Moorer was appointed Commander, Seventh Fleet, and began a long association with Indochina. He oversaw the deployment to South Vietnam of an increasing number of naval advisors, naval commandos from two newly created SEAL teams, and naval support forces. Two years later, Moorer was promoted to full admiral and named Commander in Chief, U.S. Pacific Fleet. He was then responsible for commanding American naval forces operating in vast expanses of the Pacific Ocean and in waters off the Soviet Union, the People's Republic of China, and the Democratic Republic of Vietnam (North Vietnam).

Moorer ardently opposed the spread of Communist ideology and military power and clearly regarded U.S. naval forces as a vital instrument of the nation's containment strategy. He strongly supported actions taken by President Lyndon B. Johnson's administration to use military actions against Communist forces working to overthrow pro-American governments in Laos and South Vietnam.

But the admiral strongly objected to the way Washington, and Secretary of Defense Robert McNamara in particular, wanted to control naval operations from afar. For instance, through official channels he expressed his displeasure at how McNamara personally chose the type and number of aircraft, bomb loads, approach altitudes, and other operational details for small reconnaissance flights over Laos. He raised his voice against micromanagement of military operations throughout the Vietnam War.

On 2 August 1964, Communist North Vietnamese torpedo boats attacked the destroyer USS *Maddox* in the Gulf of Tonkin. In defense, the ship (and supporting carrier aircraft) put holes in the attacking units. Commander John J. Herrick, the officer in charge of *Maddox*'s intelligence-gathering operation, felt the ship was a "sitting duck" in the confined waters of the gulf, so he withdrew her from the area. Admiral Moorer, however, concerned that the Communists had openly attacked an American naval vessel in international waters, ordered Herrick and *Maddox* to resume the patrol, accompanied by destroyer USS *Turner Joy*. Moorer and his immediate superior, Admiral Ulysses S. G. Sharp, Commander in Chief, Pacific Command, were convinced that Communist naval units had carried out a second attack (later discounted), on the night of 4 August. The Pacific commanders called for retaliatory carrier air strikes on North Vietnam. President Johnson agreed, and it was executed on 5 August. Congress then passed the Tonkin Gulf Resolution that many Americans regarded as authorizing prosecution of the Vietnam War.

At the end of April 1965, as Pacific Fleet forces put U.S. Marines ashore at Danang, South Vietnam, Moorer took command of U.S. and NATO naval forces in the Atlantic. The president was so impressed with Moorer's ability and candid military manner that on 3 June 1967 he appointed him Chief of Naval Operations. For the next three years, the U.S. Navy deployed to Vietnam, providing naval gunfire, coastal patrol, river assault, and river patrol forces that bombed enemy targets ashore, stopped major seaborne infiltration, and established control of South Vietnam's inland waterways.

President Johnson's successor, Richard M. Nixon, was just as comfortable with Moorer's general conservatism and loyal support of the administration's war effort. As a result, on 2 July 1970, he appointed Moorer chairman of the Joint Chiefs of Staff.

Even though he did not always prevail in the councils of government, Moorer did not shy away from expressing his belief in strong military actions against the Communists. To give America's South Vietnamese allies more time to develop their armed strength, Moorer called for

slower withdrawal of U.S. forces from the war. In 1972, when the Communists frustrated negotiations to end the war, Moorer and other officials recommended inauguration of a major bombing campaign and the mining of North Vietnam's ports. This time the president agreed and ordered the Linebacker Campaign, which helped compel Hanoi to sign the Paris agreement of January 1973 that ended direct U.S. involvement in the conflict and freed American prisoners of war from captivity.

Despite focusing much of his effort on the war in Southeast Asia, Moorer worked especially hard to ensure that U.S. nuclear and conventional forces could deal with Soviet threats around the globe. In particular, he championed modernization of the U.S. Navy's submarine

Official U.S. Navy Photograph

fleet. He strongly opposed the suggested U.S. concessions to the USSR in the Strategic Arms Limitation Talks of 1972. The admiral was also a realist and understood that U.S. involvement in the Vietnam War heavily strained national resources and capabilities. During the Yom Kippur War of 1973 in the Middle East, Moorer did not sugarcoat the fact that U.S. military forces would have been hard pressed had conflict with the Soviet Union occurred.

In July 1974, Admiral Thomas H. Moorer retired as chairman of the Joint Chiefs of Staff, completing forty-one years of distinguished service to the United States. He died on 5 February 2004. Throughout his long, distinguished career in the U.S. Navy, Thomas H. Moorer had exhibited exceptional leadership qualities: moral and physical courage, intellectual honesty, and the determination to present a well-reasoned case, whether popular or not.

Suggested Reading

Baer, George W. *One Hundred Years of Sea Power: The U.S. Navy, 1890–1990.* Stanford, Calif.: Stanford University Press, 1994.

Marolda, Edward J. *The U.S. Navy in the Vietnam War: An Illustrated History.* Washington, D.C.: Brassey's, 2002.

Webb, Willard J., and Ronald H. Cole. *The Chairmen of the Joint Chiefs of Staff.* Washington, D.C.: Historical Division, Joint Chiefs of Staff, 1989.

About the Author

Dr. Edward J. Marolda is the senior historian of the Naval Historical Center, located in the historic Washington Navy Yard, on whose staff he has served since 1971. He received a doctorate in American history from George Washington University in 1990. In addition to organizing numerous conference and lecture programs relating to the history of the U.S. Navy, he has authored, coauthored, or edited eight naval histories, including *Shield and Sword: The U.S. Navy and the Persian Gulf War* (Naval Institute Press, 2001) and *The U.S. Navy in the Vietnam War* (Brassey's, 2002).

44

Ulysses S. Grant Sharp
Courage

Glenn E. Helm

Official U.S. Navy Photo

Ulysses S. Grant Sharp confronted both Axis opponents in combat and the Secretary of Defense in Senate hearings with equal courage.

Sharp was born in Chinook, Montana, on 2 April 1906 into a family noted for service to the U.S. Navy and U.S. Army. During his early years, he was an avid camper and loved the wilderness. After attending high school in Fort Benton, Montana, Sharp joined the class of 1927 at the U.S. Naval Academy. Nicknamed "Ole," he participated in sports as a runner and was noted for cheerfulness and optimism.

After graduating from the academy, he served for a year on the battleship USS *New Mexico*, with subsequent assignments to transport USS *Henderson*, destroyers USS *Sumner* and USS *Buchanan*, and aircraft carrier USS *Saratoga*. From 1934 to 1936, Sharp studied engineering at the Naval Postgraduate School in Annapolis. This tour was followed by duty on cruiser USS *Richmond* and destroyer USS *Winslow*. During 1941 and early 1942, Sharp served in the Bureau of Ships in Washington.

He then commanded the high-speed destroyer-minesweeper USS *Hogan*, which participated in the November 1942 invasion of North Africa. In January 1943, Sharp assumed command of destroyer USS *Boyd*, which operated for the next two years in the Pacific theater. His ship was involved in attacks on Wake Island, the Battle of the Philippine Sea in the Marianas, Truk, and Okinawa. The U.S. Navy awarded Sharp two Silver Stars for gallantry. In one instance, Sharp bravely conned his ship close to the Japanese-held island of Nauru to rescue an American flier reportedly downed offshore. Suddenly, enemy six-inch coastal guns opened up on the destroyer and put two rounds into the ship's forward engine room. Sharp calmly ordered the helmsman to steer a zigzag course and chase the shell splashes, because he figured the enemy gunners would try to correct their fire after each miss, and not hit the same location twice. His cool courage under fire got his ship and crew out of trouble.

After the war, Sharp attended the Naval War College, commanded the Fleet Sonar School in San Diego, and in June 1950 at the outbreak of the Korean War, took command of Destroyer Squadron 5. Temporarily detached from his unit, he served as a planning officer for the Inchon invasion. In 1951, Sharp served as operations officer and then chief of staff and aide to Commander, Second Fleet. During 1953 and 1954, Sharp commanded the cruiser USS *Macon*, served on the staff of the Commander in Chief, U.S Pacific Fleet, and took charge of Cruiser Division 3. The next several years involved duty in the office of the Chief of Naval Operations, where he rose to become the director of the Strategic Plans Division.

In February 1959, Sharp was designated Commander, Cruiser-Destroyer Force, U.S. Pacific Fleet, and a year later Commander, First Fleet. As the Deputy Chief of Naval Operations for plans and policy in Washington, D.C., Sharp was deeply involved in planning naval operations during the Cuban Missile Crisis of 1962. The following year, Sharp became Commander in Chief, U.S. Pacific Fleet, the world's largest naval command.

In June 1964, the Secretary of Defense appointed U. S. G. Sharp Commander in Chief, Pacific (CINCPAC), with responsibility for all U.S. military forces in the vast Pacific region—an operational area of eighty-five million square miles. From his headquarters at Camp H. M. Smith in Hawaii, Sharp commanded 940,000 soldiers, Sailors, airmen, and Marines; 560 warships; and 7,500 aircraft.

During the Gulf of Tonkin Crisis in August 1964, Sharp recommended to the Joint Chiefs of Staff that air strikes be launched against North Vietnamese naval bases from which torpedo boats had attacked destroyer USS *Maddox* and, as he mistakenly thought, destroyer USS *Turner Joy*. The recommendation by CINCPAC was instrumental in President Lyndon Johnson and Secretary of Defense Robert McNamara ordering retaliatory carrier air strikes on North Vietnam.

From 1965 to July 1968, Sharp was nominally in charge of the air war against Communist forces in North Vietnam and Laos. But President Johnson and Secretary of Defense McNamara closely managed the Rolling Thunder bombing campaign. They feared provoking Chinese or Soviet intervention and doubted the ability of the U.S. military to carry out an effective operation without their direction. As a result, the Washington leaders severely restricted bombing operations, for instance, prohibiting U.S. aircraft from hitting military targets in the Hanoi and Haiphong areas and along the Chinese border.

During the second half of 1967, differences relating to the conduct of the air war between Sharp and other military leaders and the Johnson administration boiled over. Sharp had become increasingly frustrated with the restrictions of the air campaign. He knew that final targeting decisions, and frequently the tactics to be employed by American pilots, were routinely decided at a Tuesday luncheon in the White House attended only by civilian leaders. Sharp was especially bothered by McNamara's well-known disdain for advice from professional military officers.

Sharp decided to air his grievances, within channels, when he testified in August 1967 before the Preparedness Investigating Subcommittee of the Senate Armed Services Committee, which was looking into the conduct of the air war in Southeast Asia. The admiral knew that Senator John Stennis of Mississippi, chair of the subcommittee, shared many of his views about the mismanagement of the bombing campaign. Recognizing their vulnerability to military criticism, on the first day of testimony Johnson and McNamara sought to moderate Sharp's testimony by giving him permission to bomb sixteen previously off-limits targets.

In Sharp's testimony, he called for an expansion of the bombing campaign and authority to strike targets around Hanoi, North Vietnam's capital, and Haiphong, the country's primary port, through which poured vital war materials from the Soviet Union and China. He also wanted to strike rail lines near the border with China that groaned under the weight of military supplies entering North Vietnam. Sharp argued that even though the enemy was suffering military, economic, and psychological damage from the bombing, the campaign could only become truly effective when most Washington-imposed restrictions were lifted.

The subcommittee's final report, which reflected the testimony of Sharp and other dissatisfied military leaders, severely criticized the administration's handling of the bombing of North Vietnam. While President Johnson did not significantly ease the bombing restrictions, the hearings helped convince him that he had to take a different approach to the war. Out of favor with the president, McNamara resigned, and the following March, Johnson halted bombing operations north

of the twentieth parallel in North Vietnam. As a courageous professional, Admiral Sharp had spoken out when it was clearly called for.

U. S. G. Sharp retired from the U.S. Navy on 1 August 1968. During the next thirty-three years, he retained a strong interest in defense matters and continued to speak out as a private citizen about the Vietnam War. Indeed, in 1995 at the age of eighty-nine, Admiral Sharp voiced strong criticism of McNamara's poor wartime leadership at a conference in the Army and Navy Club in Washington. The courageous naval officer died on 12 December 2001 at his home in San Diego, California.

Suggested Reading

McNamara, Robert S. *In Retrospect: The Tragedy and Lessons of Vietnam.* New York: Random House, 1995.

Sharp, U. S. G. *Strategic Direction of the Armed Forces.* Newport, R.I.: Naval War College, 1977.

———. *Strategy for Defeat: Vietnam in Retrospect.* San Rafael, Calif.: Presidio, 1978.

U.S. Congress. Senate. Committee on Armed Services. *Air War Against North Vietnam: Hearings Before the Preparedness Investigating Subcommittee, Part 1.* 90th Cong., 1st sess., 9 and 10 August 1967.

Naval Historical Center Collection of Adm. U. S. G. Sharp, USN (Ret.)

About the Author

Glenn E. Helm is the acting director of the Navy Department Library at the Naval Historical Center. He has lectured or given conference presentations at the Central Intelligence Agency, Office of Naval Intelligence, Georgetown University, Arizona State University, Society for Military History, and U.S. Government Printing Office. He is a contributor to the *Reader's Guide to Military History* (Fitzroy Dearborn, 2001) and the *Encyclopedia of the Vietnam War* (ABC-CLIO, 1998), as well as the forthcoming ABC-CLIO publications *Encyclopedia of World War I* and *Encyclopedia of World War II.*

45

Samuel L. Gravely Jr.

Setting the Precedent

Paul Stillwell

Photo by Milt Putnam

One hallmark of a successful leader is the ability to go where no one has gone before, to light the way, and to serve as a role model and mentor so that others may follow. Samuel L. Gravely Jr. was such an individual for the U.S. Navy. He became the service's first black commander, captain, rear admiral, and vice admiral. His steady progress coincided with dramatic changes in the nation as a whole—changes in the law and in the way America viewed the minority of its black citizens. He witnessed dramatic growth in opportunity, and by his own achievements, helped foster that growth.

When Sam Gravely was growing up in segregated Virginia in the 1920s and 1930s, the idea of a black admiral in the U.S. Navy was beyond imagination. It was not a goal for which he could hope to strive. Indeed, when he enlisted in the Naval Reserve in September 1942 the U.S. Navy did not yet have its first black officer. Opportunities began to open slightly in 1943 when the Navy inaugurated its V-12 program, which consisted of a two-year period of college education and officer training. Though the service had a long tradition of separation of the races, President Franklin D. Roosevelt directed that V-12 would include black midshipmen. Gravely studied at the University of California at Los Angeles and at Midshipman School, Columbia University, in New York. He was commissioned as an ensign in the Naval Reserve in December 1944.

Even as the U.S. Navy was commissioning its first handful of black officers, the service was unwilling to have white enlisted personnel serving under black officers. The Navy commissioned two warships with white officers and black enlisted men in their crews, the destroyer escort *Mason* and the antisubmarine patrol craft *PC-1264*. When Ensign Gravely joined the latter in May 1945, he became one of the first few black officers to serve in combatant-type ships.[1] Gravely reveled in the opportunity to serve with an open-minded skipper, Lieutenant Eric Purdon, but duty in *PC-1264* was not without its drawbacks. In one instance when Gravely was on liberty in Miami, military policemen arrested him for impersonating an officer. They did not believe a black man could hold such a rank. After the war ended, Sam Gravely returned to Virginia to complete his college education and worked for a time as a railway postal clerk.

Circumstance and timing then played their parts in Gravely's career. In 1949, after the U.S. armed services were integrated by presidential order, the U.S. Navy recalled Gravely for a one-year period of active duty as a recruiter. That planned year of service turned into more than thirty years. In 1950 the Korean War intervened, the U.S. Navy rebuilt its strength, and Gravely went on sea duty, first aboard the battleship *Iowa* off Korea and later on the heavy cruiser *Toledo*.

Though Gravely enjoyed sea duty, he found himself pigeonholed in the specialty of communications and operations. He did not have a well-rounded experience, nor had he served on destroyers, a type of duty he needed as a stepping-stone for promotion. As a pathfinder, he realized that he needed to make his own opportunities. He initiated a do-it-himself program of training to be an executive officer. He took courses and spent time onboard various destroyers as an extra man. Gravely's method was to familiarize himself with the ships, watch their exercises in action, and thus absorb lessons that can be learned only through experience. He succeeded.

In January 1960, he got orders to become executive officer of the destroyer *Theodore E. Chandler*. It marked a major advance in his career; Gravely remembered, "I was just flabbergasted, but happy as a lark." He got his first command of an operating ship in January 1962, when he became skipper of the radar picket destroyer escort *Falgout*, ported at Pearl Harbor, Hawaii. The news media played up the story, but Gravely accepted the publicity reluctantly, as he did throughout his career. He viewed himself as merely doing his job within the U.S. Navy estab-

lishment, but—like it or not—he was indeed a role model during the emerging civil rights struggles of the early 1960s. In early 1963, the U.S. Navy dispatched him from Hawaii to the Kennedy White House for a celebration of the one hundredth anniversary of the Emancipation Proclamation, issued during the Civil War to free slaves. Gravely's professional emergence came as the nation as a whole was changing.

After he left the *Falgout*, Commander Gravely and Lieutenant Commander George Thompson became the first two black officers to attend the august Naval War College in Newport, Rhode Island, as students. As he was nearing the end of the academic year, Gravely and his wife, Alma, were planning to move to Washington, D.C., for his next assignment. A real estate agent called to invite them to visit the office to see about housing. When the Gravelys showed up with their children in tow, the chagrined agent discovered that the potential clients were black and said there were no available rental places in Northern Virginia. After a great deal of looking, the family found a place on their own.

In the years that followed, Gravely continued to ascend the rungs of the U.S. Navy hierarchy. During the latter part of the 1960s, he commanded the destroyer *Taussig*, which was engaged in combat duty off the coast of Vietnam. It was a dramatic increase in operations over the role of the *Falgout*, which had served largely on detached radar picket duty. He was featured in an illustrated article in the magazine *Ebony* as being in command of the ship's entire crew—a long step forward from 1945, when whites could not serve under black officers.

Gravely then moved to shore duty in Washington to work with the U.S. Navy's emerging satellite communication program. His next wartime duty followed, this time in the sophisticated guided missile frigate *Jouett*, which used its radars and electronic tactical data system to monitor air traffic in Vietnam. The Chief of Naval Operations at the time was Admiral Elmo Zumwalt, who instituted a wide-ranging program to provide greater opportunities for minorities within the service.

Gravely was in the right place at the right time with an accomplished record in the most important area, command at sea. In the spring of 1971, a selection board chose Gravely as the U.S. Navy's first black admiral. He went on to command the Naval Communications Command, Cruiser-Destroyer Group Two, and the 11th Naval District. In 1976, he became the U.S. Navy's first African-American three-star admiral and its first fleet commander as Commander, Third Fleet, in Hawaii. He later served as director of the Defense Communications Agency, his last billet prior to retirement from active duty in 1980.

By that time, many more black officers were following in the admiral's footsteps. The selec-

tion of an African-American or other minority officer for flag rank became a part of the regular process, no longer a widely heralded exception. One such individual was Mack C. Gaston, who eventually became a rear admiral himself. In the 1960s, when he was a newly commissioned ensign, Gaston served on the destroyer *Buck*, which was once moored alongside Gravely's destroyer *Taussig*. Gaston had heard about this lone black skipper and introduced himself. As Gaston later remembered the moment, "He reached across to me and shook my hand. He was a tall man with incredible stature and presence. His handshake was firm but friendly, and somehow I knew in meeting him that he would have a profound impact on me as a naval officer, role model, and long-time friend."

Naval Photographic Center

Note

1. His contemporaries got shore duty or assignment to harbor craft from which white crew members had been replaced by black ones.

Suggested Reading

Astor, Gerald. *The Right to Fight: A History of African Americans in the Military*. Novato, Calif.: Presidio, 1998.

Gravely, Samuel L., Jr. Oral History. Annapolis, Md.: U.S. Naval Institute, 2003.

Nalty, Bernard C. *Strength for the Fight: A History of Black Americans in the Military*. New York: Free Press, 1986.

Purdon, Eric. *Black Company: The Story of Subchaser 1264*. Washington, D.C.: R. B. Luce, 1972.

About the Author

Paul Stillwell is director of the history division of the U.S. Naval Institute. In 1969 he served in the crew of the *New Jersey*, which had been one of Lee's flagships in World War II. Stillwell has written a number of books on battleships, including individual histories of the *New Jersey*, *Missouri*, and *Arizona*. He is at work on a biography of Willis Lee.

46

Ronald McKeown
Physical Courage

Dr. John Darrell Sherwood

During the early 1960s, all physically qualified midshipmen at the Naval Academy had to compete in intramural boxing, and the two best boxers in each weight class ultimately squared off in the finals. In the 1961 finals, Ronald "Mugs" McKeown fought future Marine officer Pete Optekar, class of 1963. "Pete had an anvil for a jaw. It was just solid muscle. I threw him the hardest punch I ever threw in my life and he just blinked and said, 'Now, you've pissed me off,' and he knocked me across the ring. I remember hanging on the rope and I could see about three of him coming at me." McKeown kept fighting, eventually wearing Optekar down with his speed and precision punches.

The courage and resolve exhibited by McKeown in the ring that day ultimately served him well in the rough and tumble world of naval aviation. McKeown remembered, "Boxing gave me more transferable skills than any other sport I ever played during my life. It gives you fluidity of movement, good hand-eye coordination, and great anticipation. It gives you a certain level of confidence to be able to handle things, to be able to think clearly under pressure. I mean, if somebody's banging on your head, you have to be able to think and move. Those are really very tangible and transferable skills into real life and I'm convinced, yes, that it had a lot to do with my ability in an airplane." Less than one percent of the military pilots of the Vietnam generation achieved a MiG kill. Mugs McKeown scored two in one mission. Like all good pilots, McKeown possessed an abundance of situational awareness and good stick and rudder skills, but what truly separated him from others was his courage to keep fighting even under the most difficult circumstances.

McKeown was born in 1939 in the small town of Pipestone, Minnesota. His family moved to El Paso, Texas, where McKeown played high school football. He made all-state running back at Ysleta High, which helped him gain entry to the U.S. Naval Academy.

Initially, McKeown hated the place. "I think every day of plebe year was a dead heat for the most miserable day of my life." His only saving grace was football. Football got him away from the academy on many weekends and spared him from some of the incessant hazing of freshmen year. Life as a player, however, was not without its disappointments. "I got there and was pretty confident until I found out how many players they'd recruited. They had a guy named Joe Bellino who was a classmate of mine and he went on to win the Heisman Trophy and I became old what's-his-name, the other running back with Joe." McKeown did not play in earnest until his junior year, when he made honorable mention all-American as a cornerback. But, during his senior year he played in nearly every game, including the Orange Bowl against Missouri.

Following graduation, McKeown became a U.S. Navy fighter pilot. In December 1964, he deployed with VF-154 onboard USS *Coral Sea* and took part in the earliest U.S. bombing raids against North Vietnam. McKeown flew 185 combat missions in F-8 Crusaders during his first tour. He soon began to question the sanity of what he was doing. During one twenty-four-hour period, the tail hook of his plane impaled the tailpipe, the engine flamed out in another one, and the nose gear of a third broke when he tried to extend it just prior to landing. "I had three airplanes down in the hangar bay and all within about 24 hours and I said, 'Skipper, I think I'm going to go climb in a gin bottle for a day or two. God's trying to tell me something, I better listen.'"

One night, McKeown asked himself, "How long can I keep doing this? How many times can I run down the muzzles before I get hit?" His eyes then focused upon his class of 1961 Naval Academy ring. "Mugs, you don't push spaghetti. You pull it. There's nothing you would ever do to reflect dishonor on that institution. Your purpose in life is to win wars and that is the essence of what they trained you to do and by God, you're going to do it." Pushing his doubts

aside, he made up his mind to accept his fate as a warrior.

This attitude paid off during his third Vietnam combat tour. On 23 May 1972, Lieutenant Commander McKeown and his naval flight officer, Lieutenant Jack Ensch, were flying a MiG combat air patrol for a large "alpha strike" against the Haiphong Petroleum Products site. As they sat in the cockpit of their F-4 Phantom II waiting to launch, Mugs and his back-seater distinctly remembered feeling that something was going to happen. "It was nothing we could put our fingers on, but we knew that this was not going to be an ordinary hop." The plane launched at 1800, hooked up with an aerial tanker to top off, and got ready to meet the enemy. Destroyer USS *Oswald*'s radar operator vectored McKeown and his wingman (flown by Lieutenant Mike Rabb and Lieutenant Ken Crandall) toward a bandit over Kep airfield in North Vietnam.

The radar man warned the pair of Phantoms, "They're low; they're low." Mugs and his wingman descended to fifteen hundred feet, where they spotted the MiGs near the runway. The Phantoms flew right through a section of two silver MiG-19s and then started a cross turn with Mugs going high. Suddenly, four MiG-17s in green and brown camouflage came screaming toward the Americans from above and attacked McKeown's wingman. Mugs recalled, "It seemed like they were on a pedestal turning through the sky. I initiated a break-turn into the closest MiG-17 and he rendezvoused on me. Within the next 270-degree of turn he achieved a real fine firing position. Pulling lead and firing, the MiG was not much more than 500 feet away. My instinct was to keep turning into him." McKeown had expected the MiG to fight in the horizontal plane, but this pilot insisted instead on fighting in the vertical.

Spotting a MiG-19 below him, Mugs started pulling toward it while at the same time running from the MiG-17. One of the uncanny abilities McKeown had was that he could function in both a defensive and an offensive mode at the same time. Hence, after avoiding a collision with the MiG-17, he focused his attention on the MiG-19.

"I pulled back into the MiG-19 as hard as I could. We were in a hard, nose-high turn, thirty degrees nose up, pulling around hard to the right in heavy buffet. The stick then started lightening on me," and the F-4 departed from controlled flight. As the F-4 started rolling, McKeown jammed his stick forward. "It flashed into my mind that we were going to spend the night in this little valley, eat pumpkin soup, and have our name on a bracelet. All these things entered my mind, but as soon as the thing popped out at 1,800 to two thousand feet, I got right back into the fight." Again, Mugs refused to let his close brush with disaster distract him from his central mission.

Looking up and seeing a MiG-17 in front of him, McKeown pulled behind the enemy plane, got a good radar tone, and fired an AIM-9G Sidewinder missile. In full afterburner, the MiG pilot did almost a ninety-degree turn, and the missile flew right by his tail.

McKeown then spotted another MiG firing at his wingman from behind. McKeown launched another AIM-9G, which also missed. He continued chasing the MiG in a spiral descent down to two hundred feet, when the enemy plane pulled its nose up and started to climb. McKeown got a good tone and fired a third Sidewinder. Even though the North Vietnamese pilot broke hard right to avoid the missile, it stayed with the MiG and hit the tail. The explosion flipped the MiG and brought it down.

"Holy s#&%. We've got another one at 4:30 and he's gunning!" Jack Ensch suddenly exclaimed.

McKeown decided to force the second MiG into an overshoot. "I broke real hard into him and he dug inside our turn and started ren-dezvousing on us. All of a sudden it hit me. He can't see me. The bastard can't see me!" Mugs knew he was in the MiG's blind area. "I pushed negative G, unloaded, came out of afterburner, and watched him turn inside of us. He flew right by the starboard side. When we didn't fly out in front of him, he broke back to the left with that real slow roll rate. He was nose high and we just rolled in behind him. I got behind him, had a good tone, fired a Sidewinder, and that one went right up his tailpipe. He came out and then the airplane blew up. And so that was it."

As in his boxing match with Optekar, during his air-to-air engagements over North Vietnam McKeown demonstrated an ability to fight under the worst possible odds, roll with the punches, and snatch victory from the jaws of defeat. Like all great warriors, McKeown sometimes had moments of doubt, but his courage, reinforced by his boxing and football experiences at the Naval Academy, was there when he needed it. His was a profile in battle courage.

Suggested Reading

Sherwood, John Darrell. *Afterburner: Naval Aviators and the Vietnam War*. New York: New York University Press, 2004.

About the Author

John Darrell Sherwood is a historian in the Contemporary History Branch of the Naval Historical Center. He received a doctorate in history from George Washington University and is the author of three books: *Officers in Flight Suits: The Story of American Air Force Fighter Pilots in Korea* (New York University Press, 1998); *Fast Movers: Jet Pilots and the Vietnam War Experience* (Free Press, 1999); and *Afterburner: Naval Aviators and the Vietnam War* (New York University Press, 2004).

47

Elmo R. Zumwalt Jr.

Innovation

Lieutenant Commander Thomas J. Cutler

Naval Photographic Center

Admiral Elmo R. Zumwalt Jr. summed up his tenure as nineteenth Chief of Naval Operations (CNO) when he told an audience, "I have a wonderful list of friends and a wonderful list of enemies, and am very proud of both lists." One of the most controversial naval leaders of all time, he was a Sailor who had gone in harm's way—both literally and figuratively—and changed the U.S. Navy in the process.

"Bud" Zumwalt's career included service in World War II and the Korean War; command of several ships; attendance at both Naval and National War Colleges; and two tours in Washington, one as an aide to the Assistant Secretary of the Navy for personnel and the other in the Bureau of Naval Personnel. He enjoyed the reputation of "front-runner" or "comer" in U.S. Navy argot. From his earliest days, many saw him as a future admiral. And they were right. Two years before his class was technically eligible for promotion to flag rank, he became a rear admiral.

Shortly after the Tet Offensive in early 1968, Zumwalt was ordered to Vietnam as a vice admiral to command the in-country naval forces there. He arrived in Saigon in September and found the U.S. Navy's role in Vietnam stagnant. Earlier coastal surveillance, river patrol, and combined riverine operations had driven the enemy off the major rivers and minimized his littoral operations, but now supplies were coming in from the Cambodian sanctuary and traveling uninhibited along a network of tributary waterways deep into the strategically vital Mekong Delta. To counter this, Zumwalt convened his senior commanders and staff members to work out the details of a new strategic concept he called SEALORDS, for "South-East Asia lake, ocean, river, and delta strategy." The new strategy consolidated the various elements of the U.S. Navy's in-country forces and redeployed them to interdict the flow of enemy supplies, placing the naval forces in harm's way and taking the fight to the enemy. This redeployment not only put new pressure on the enemy; it had the added effect of injecting new life into the brown water forces whose relegation to mere holding operations had seriously demoralized them. Ironically, casualties went up, and so did morale.

Because Secretary of Defense Melvin Laird and Secretary of the Navy John Chafee wanted a Chief of Naval Operations who could "bring the Navy into the modern age," they selected Zumwalt, promoting him over thirty-three more senior admirals on 1 July 1970. While he brought youth and a more dashing image to the office, he also brought less experience. At age forty-nine, he was the youngest CNO in history.

Zumwalt's three decades of experience with the U.S. Navy had taught him that traditional methods of change often led to the slow death of initiative; untraditional ideas were frequently swallowed up by a slow process of approval made slower by the reluctance of conservative senior commanders. Zumwalt came to believe that ideas that went against the grain of tradition could only survive if they were suddenly brought into the open where they could not be ignored. This philosophy soon brought unprecedented changes to the U.S. Navy but had the corollary effect of creating vehement factions when he created his so-called Z-grams, most of which were designed to counter personnel retention problems in the U.S. Navy. Responding to the mandate given him by Laird and Chafee to "bring the Navy into the modern age" and keeping to his philosophy that unconventional changes needed unconventional methods of implementation if they were to succeed, Zumwalt used the Z-gram method as a means of simultaneously communicating his changes directly to all personnel in the U.S. Navy.

The personnel changes wrought by the Z-grams were generally popular among the younger officers and enlisted personnel, less so among more senior personnel. Some senior officers and petty officers felt that the method and the content of the Z-grams had undermined their authority. Others lauded the changes but resented the use of such an unconventional method of bringing them about.

The results, however, were indisputable. Never in the history of the U.S. Navy had such sweeping changes taken place. Many of the so-called chicken regs that had long been a point of contention among naval personnel were eliminated. Suddenly the family and the individual assumed a new significance. In his first year in office, first-term reenlistments rose from 10 to 17 percent. Zumwalt succeeded in transforming the U.S. Navy from its image of a "humorless, tradition-bound, starchy institution." His successful efforts captured the attention of the national media, putting him on the cover of *Time* magazine, landing him an interview in *Playboy*, and making him the most famous admiral since Halsey and Nimitz during World War II.

One of his most significant Z-grams was number 66, which acknowledged race-related problems within the U.S. Navy and established a number of measures to correct the situation. This groundbreaking Z-gram concluded with the words, "There is no black Navy, no white Navy—just one Navy—the United States Navy."

It is difficult to assess the significance of Admiral Zumwalt's personnel policies. He was CNO at a time when all of American society was in turmoil, when terms such as "countercultural revolution" were commonplace, when racial tensions and dissension over the Vietnam War had skewed perceptions and erected barriers to reasoned debate. In truth, much of what he was attempting to achieve in the U.S. Navy was mirrored in the other armed services, but with much less flourish and without a personalized target such as he had become. It is also difficult to discern what the effects might have been had he not come along at a time when chicken regs and countercultural society were on a collision course. His opponents saw him as the instigator of permissiveness and the destroyer of discipline within the U.S. Navy, while his advocates claimed him as the "man of the hour" and the "savior of the U.S. Navy." Both views are certainly arguable, and the truth probably lies somewhere in between.

His personnel policies were not the only lightning rods of his tenure. His "high-low mix" of fleet units encountered significant opposition from various factions, including Admiral Hyman G. Rickover, father of the U.S. Navy's nuclear power program. In a time of tight budgetary constraints, Zumwalt called for the building of fewer "high-end" ships (attack carriers and ballistic missile submarines) and used the available funds to build moderate cost, moderate performance ships and systems that could be turned out in relatively large numbers for the sea control mission. Zumwalt envisioned that "in most cases seven or five or even three ships of moderate capability would contribute far more to the success of this mission than one super ship." To achieve this, he proposed the prerequisite move of decommissioning many of the older ships to free up funds and allowed the fleet to function for a time with less than the optimum number of units. This was a calculated risk deemed necessary for the ultimate achievement of his long-term goals but not without its opponents.

On 29 June 1974, the tumultuous tenure of the U.S. Navy's nineteenth Chief of Naval Operations came to a close in ceremonies held at the U.S. Naval Academy where his naval career had begun. In an interview some years later, former Secretary of the Navy and then–Senator John Warner described Zumwalt as having the courage to "raise his head above the ground" even at the risk of getting "it shot off." Zumwalt was clearly an innovative thinker and a risk taker. His methods were unquestionably radical and provocative, but they also achieved what had not been done before. Zumwalt's contention that the traditional methods were prone to failure when revolutionary changes were needed makes sense when viewed historically. An intriguing evaluation proffered in retrospect by the Center for Naval Analyses states, "The Zumwalt strategic

U.S. Naval Institute Photo Archive

revolution would have achieved greater success had Admiral Zumwalt not believed it necessary to carry out the personnel revolution simultaneously." Yet, Zumwalt did believe that his personnel revolution was necessary, even to the detriment of his strategic initiatives. Looking back, he later wrote:

> I was certain to turn over to my successor a Navy in which all kinds of important business was unfinished: strategic analysis, ship construction, weapons development, relations with other parts of the government, and so forth, ad infinitum. But if it was within my power, I was determined to turn over to him a Navy that had learned to treat its men and women, enlisted and commissioned, in a manner that recognized that, regardless of the peculiar demands military life made upon them, they were citizens of a free country in the last quarter of the twentieth century.

In hindsight, Zumwalt properly aimed his vision. The strategic situation he and the U.S. Navy faced in the early 1970s changed tremendously, but the importance of the Navy's people remains constant.

Suggested Reading

Cutler, Thomas J. *Brown Water, Black Berets: Coastal and Riverine Warfare in Vietnam.* Annapolis, Md.: Naval Institute Press, 1988.

Zumwalt, Elmo, Jr. *On Watch: A Memoir.* New York: Quadrangle, 1976.

Zumwalt, Elmo, Jr., and Elmo Zumwalt III. *My Father, My Son.* New York: MacMillan, 1986.

About the Author

Lieutenant Commander Thomas J. Cutler, USN (Ret.), is the senior acquisitions editor for the Naval Institute Press.

48

John F. Lehman Jr.
Passion

Captain Peter N. Swartz

U.S. Naval Institute Photo Archive

Unlike most of the naval leaders in this book, John F. Lehman Jr. was not a regular naval officer. Nor did he receive a commission from the U.S. Naval Academy, Naval Reserve Officers Training Corps, or Officer Candidates School. Lehman did, however, serve as a naval reserve officer and as an appointed civilian official. In both capacities, he was a public servant dedicated to the institutional and combat success of the U.S. Navy and U.S. Marine Corps.

Other great naval leaders have emerged from the reserve and civilian sectors. Admiral Vernon Clark, the twenty-seventh Chief of Naval Operations, spent the first four years of his naval career developing leadership skills as a reserve officer. Benjamin Stoddard, Theodore Roosevelt, Franklin Roosevelt, James Forrestal, and other Americans have distinguished themselves as civilian leaders in the Department of the Navy.

John Lehman shared many positive attributes with previous secretaries of the Navy but he also brought unique qualities to the job. He brought focus and decisiveness to issues great and small; aggressive determination to further the interests of the Department of the Navy; a vast professional knowledge of international security and naval affairs; fierce loyalty to those he liked and trusted; boundless enthusiasm and energy; articulate and forceful oratory skills; a zest for excitement and adventure; as well as initiative, drive, and great ambition.

From 1981 through 1987, John F. Lehman Jr. was the nation's sixty-fifth Secretary of the Navy—one of the youngest, brightest, and most colorful personalities to hold that office. Lehman proved from his first day in office to be a powerful—even ruthless—advocate for the U.S. Navy and Marine Corps. His own personal credentials—a reserve commission as a naval flight officer in the A-6E Intruder and the author of a book analyzing the role of carriers—placed him in good stead as a spokesman for the importance of U.S. naval power. Moreover, while he had come to the job at the very young age of thirty-nine, he was already armed with an Ivy League doctorate in international relations, a year's study at Cambridge University in Great Britain, a dozen years of experience in a variety of key policy jobs in Washington, and many powerful and loyal friends and mentors in the executive and legislative branches.

Like many great naval leaders, Lehman drove himself and those around him to achieve a set of clearly defined goals. His particular goals were fourfold: to articulate the need for U.S. naval power, to build a U.S. Navy of six hundred ships to wield that power, to slash the cost of those ships wherever possible, and to rekindle a sense of esprit and excitement on the waterfront and at sea. These goals fit comfortably with the agenda of President Ronald Reagan, who asserted, "America is back!" From the day Reagan took office, Lehman doggedly strove to put teeth into the administration's intentions and slogans through the realization of clear objectives.

Prodded by Lehman, the U.S. Navy and Marine Corps of the 1980s developed and publicized the *Maritime Strategy*, the object of which was to bottle up, box in, and kill the Soviet Fleet and other Soviet forces in time of war, while at the same time defending the NATO flanks in Europe and taking pressure off U.S. and allied army and air forces battling in Germany. John Lehman was not the *Maritime Strategy*'s originator. He was, however, a highly visible and effective advocate of the strategy and a mighty goad to uniformed U.S. Navy and Marine Corps strategists. He ensured that they too stayed focused on the mission.

The fleet that Lehman inherited in 1981 numbered some 479 battle force ships (including twelve carriers and twelve carrier air wings). President Reagan and Secretary Lehman thought these numbers were far too low to protect American interests in peacetime, deter or resolve crises, and prevail should war with the Soviets occur. The administration and Secretary

Lehman advocated a six-hundred-ship, fifteen-carrier U.S. Navy in response to the deficiency. Lehman worked to ensure that administration officials would approve such a force, senators and congressmen would fund it, and American captains of industry would build it. Lehman also fought for more U.S. Navy air wings and championed the AV-8B Harrier aircraft for the Marine Corps. By 1988, a year after he left office, the battle force had grown to 584 ships, including fourteen carriers and fourteen active (and two reserve) air wings—well on the way to six hundred.

John Lehman believed that even with the best rationale in the world, the American taxpayers and their representatives would not provide the required resources for a six-hundred-ship U.S. Navy if they thought that its leaders would squander those resources and indulge in waste, fraud, and abuse. Consequently, Lehman's third major effort as secretary was to contain and cut costs. Using the powers vested in his office and his immense political and bureaucratic skills, Lehman lowered the unit price of new aircraft, instituted firm fixed-price contracting, reduced overhaul backlogs, blocked expensive "gold-plating" of systems, increased competitive procurements, cut an entire command layer from the U.S. Navy's procurement structure, and shifted costs to private industry.

Lehman loved the excitement, adventure, and camaraderie of the operational U.S. Navy; he took every opportunity to steam and fly with fleet units. To the consternation of some senior officers, the secretary in his flight suit or flight jacket never stopped dropping in on ready rooms and mess decks. He wanted to find out what was really on Sailors' minds and how well they were carrying out his policies and programs. Secretary Lehman was especially comfortable with this approach, sometimes styled "management by walking around."

Unlike some of his predecessors and successors, John Lehman refused to serve solely as a figurehead or U.S. Navy business manager.

U.S. Naval Institute Photo Archive

Lehman forced the retirement of the legendary Admiral Hyman G. Rickover in 1982 because he believed that the admiral's ship design philosophy, personnel policies, and lack of accountability harmed the U.S. Navy. Lehman stretched the limits of the constitutional, legal, and political powers of the office of Secretary of the Navy but, in so doing, breathed new life into the office and into the U.S. Navy and the Marine Corps. The performance of the sea services in Libya, Lebanon, and Grenada benefited from his contributions. More importantly, his ardent post-event drives to institutionalize within the Department of the Navy the lessons learned from those operations ensured American naval success in the many campaigns of the late twentieth and early twenty-first centuries.

John Lehman served as Secretary of the Navy for more than six years—one of the longest terms on record. He then fashioned for himself a new career in private business and finance. From 2002 through 2004 he served on the National Commission on Terrorist Attacks Upon the United States (the "9/11 Commission"). Hardly retiring from public life, John Lehman produced a steady stream of provocative public speeches, articles, and books on naval topics. He was determined as a private citizen to continue helping to shape the naval services he once served in, headed, and still loved.

Suggested Reading

Hartmann, Frederick H. *Naval Renaissance: The U.S. Navy in the 1980s.* Annapolis, Md.: Naval Institute Press, 1990.

Lehman, John F., Jr. *Aircraft Carriers: The Real Choices.* Beverly Hills, Calif.: Sage, 1978.

———. *Command of the Seas.* 2nd ed. Annapolis, Md.: Naval Institute Press, 2001.

————. *Making War: The 200-Year-Old Battle Between the President and Congress Over How America Goes to War.* New York: Scribner's, 1992.

————. *On Seas of Glory: Heroic Men, Great Ships, and Epic Battles of the American Navy.* New York: Free Press, 2001.

About the Author

Captain Peter N. Swartz, USN (Ret.), is a senior analyst at the Center for Strategic Studies of the CNA Corporation, a nonprofit research and analysis organization that oversees the Center for Naval Analyses, the Navy Department's longtime Federally Funded Research and Development Center. He is a Vietnam War veteran and was a principal compiler of and spokesman for the U.S. Navy's maritime strategy of the 1980s. He received his commission through the NROTC program at Brown University, from which he graduated with a BA degree. He also holds master's degrees from Johns Hopkins and Columbia universities.

49

Leighton W. Smith

Integrity

Dr. John Darrell Sherwood

U.S. Naval Institute Photo Archive

On 28 August 1995, a Bosnian Serb mortar shell landed in Sarajevo's Mrkale Market, killing thirty-seven shoppers. A subordinate of Admiral Leighton W. "Snuffy" Smith, at work in his office, called out, "Admiral, check out your TV." What Smith saw disgusted him: innocent civilians lying dead and wounded in an open-air marketplace. The admiral—Commander in Chief, Allied Forces Southern Europe (a NATO command)—did not hesitate for a second. He picked up his phone and called the NATO commander in Sarajevo to confirm that Bosnian Serbs had fired the shell.

Once he received positive confirmation, Smith initiated Operation Deliberate Force— one of the most politically complex air operations in American history. Throughout the campaign, Smith carefully balanced competing political and military interests, while mindful of his troops and his political seniors. This campaign complemented a ground offensive by Croat and Bosnian Muslim troops and convinced the Serbian leadership to agree to peace talks that ultimately lead to the formation of the modern Bosnian state. Smith stands out as a model of military leadership in complex times.

Leighton Warren Smith came from a distinctly modest background. He spent his formative years on a small farm outside Mobile, Alabama, tending crops and caring for pigs. "My sisters and I slept in a room that's smaller than my walk-in closet right now." A terrible student, Smith barely graduated from Murphy High School in Mobile, but what he lacked in academic skills he compensated for in his dealings with people. The assistant principal of the school confessed to Smith's aunt that the boy "was the only person I've ever known that talked his way through high school."

Smith began his postsecondary education at the University of Alabama, but then secured an appointment to the U.S. Naval Academy. From that point on, Smith's sole goal was survival. "My English professor warned me before leaving

Alabama that I would never make it through the academy because I couldn't write." Smith, who never got far beyond algebra in high school, also did not have adequate preparation for his plebe math class. "During Plebe Summer, we went through about three years of math in about four weeks. I was completely and totally lost." By the middle of his first semester, Smith's academics had deteriorated to such an extent that he received a summons from the commandant of midshipmen, Captain William Floyd "Bush" Bringle.

Smith was immediately impressed when he marched into the captain's office. "He had a desk about an acre big. There was an American flag on one side, and the Navy flag on the other side. He was sitting there in his service dress blues. He had ribbons that went all the way up to his shoulder, topped by gold wings and just below that the Navy Cross. He had hair that went about six different directions and it was gray, and his teeth looked like somebody had tried to pull them out and didn't quite succeed. He had a face that looked like about a twenty-year-old football. He was a rugged looking man."

Smith learned an "incredible lesson in leadership." This Navy captain, in charge of day-to-day operations for the entire Naval Academy, was taking precious time out of his schedule "to reach down deep into that organization to drag an individual up who was having trouble and try to impose and instill in that individual a little bit of self-discipline and self-confidence." Bringle simply told Smith to improve his grades in ten days or else face another office counseling session.

Smith decided that he never wanted to see that office again. He knew that if he failed at the Naval Academy, he "had nothing to go home to but the pigs." Smith's encounter with Bringle inspired the midshipman to pour into his studies. He eventually graduated from the Naval Academy, earned a commission, and became an attack pilot.

The Vietnam War, during which Smith flew 280 combat missions and served three tours, taught the officer additional lessons about integrity and leadership. At one point, an intelligence officer suggested he claim a target he had not hit. The officer said, "I'm not allowed to put down that you missed the target. I've got to say you cratered the approaches to the bridge or something." Smith responded, "I didn't crater the approaches; I put the damn bombs in the water. I didn't do any damage at all. Now you put that down." The officer still refused to write a truthful report, so Smith told him to remove his name from the report and walked out. Smith remembered episodes like that more than his successes, which included helping destroy the famous "Dragon's Jaw" bridge at Thanh Hoa.

As commander in Bosnia many years later, Smith led NATO forces with the same sense of integrity and personal responsibility. "The military got bashed, big-time, in Vietnam for not being honest with the politicians, and so I was determined in that operation to be completely honest."

Although Operation Deliberate Force helped convince the Serbian leadership to come to the peace table, it was not designed as a "coercive air power campaign." Smith made it absolutely clear to his NATO and U.S. chains of command that the operation was designed only to enforce UN resolutions. The resolutions authorized NATO to employ close air support to defend designated safe havens, and if those havens were attacked, to punish the aggressors with offensive air strikes. Within these parameters, Smith allowed his air commander, Lieutenant General Michael Ryan, USAF, to use every appropriate weapon in his arsenal, including tactical air strikes and Tomahawk land attack missiles (TLAM). Ryan used these fearsome but precise sea-launched weapons against Serb positions near Banja Luka. The NATO forces soon ran out of worthwhile targets.

So effective were the TLAMs that Ambassador Richard Holbrooke, who was negotiating with the Serbs, wanted Smith's forces to keep employing the missiles and air strikes, even if it meant hitting old targets twice. Smith did not concur. Undoubtedly remembering his Vietnam experience, Smith observed, "You don't go back and hit old targets. You don't bomb holes in the ground. You lose all kinds of credibility with the forces you lead if you say, 'Hey, guys, we got to keep up this charade, this facade. Let's go bomb some more targets. And oh, by the way, don't worry about that exposure out there.'"

Smith held firm, and as a result of the air strikes combined with an offensive by Bosnian Muslim and Croat forces, the Serbs acceded to UN terms for ending the conflict. The twenty-two-day air campaign delivered 1,026 air-launched weapons against forty-eight targets in a strategically limited, tactically intense coalition air campaign. Every diplomat and senior commander interviewed by the air force's Balkan Air Campaign Study "believed that the air campaign distinctly affected the moral resistance of the Serb leaders and, consequently, the pace of negotiations."

Smith paid a price for his principled stand. Despite leading an especially successful air campaign, Smith was retired from the U.S. Navy in 1996. Smith's run-in with Holbrooke ended his promotion prospects during the Clinton Administration. What mattered more to Smith, however, was that he had obeyed his military directives and kept faith with his troops. As in Vietnam, Smith never let pressure from above undermine his integrity.

Suggested Reading

Owen, Robert. "The Balkans Air Campaign Study: Part I." *Airpower Journal* (Summer 1997), 4–25.

———. "The Balkans Air Campaign Study: Part II." *Airpower Journal* (Fall 1997), 6–27.

Sherwood, John Darrell. *Afterburner: Naval Aviators and the Vietnam War*. New York: New York University Press, 2004.

About the Author

John Darrell Sherwood is a historian in the Contemporary History Branch of the Naval Historical Center. He received a doctorate in history from George Washington University and is the author of three books: *Officers in Flight Suits: The Story of American Air Force Fighter Pilots in Korea* (New York University Press, 1998); *Fast Movers: Jet Pilots and the Vietnam War Experience* (Free Press, 1999); and *Afterburner: Naval Aviators and the Vietnam War* (New York University Press, 2004).

NATO

Afterword
Innovation Wins Wars

Lieutenant General Victor H. Krulak

Captain Grayson Merrill

The earliest nation to build an empire on new tools of war was Rome; first with the tactical concept of legions and then with armor, broadswords, chariots, and catapults. Britain came up with bows and arrows and sent the Romans packing. Today an effective military innovation can be a new weapon, platform, tactic, or strategy that yields a margin of superior power long enough to win a war before being overtaken by a countermeasure. History is prologue to the future.

America is presently the world's only superpower, thanks mostly to its timely innovation of nuclear-armed submarines and aircraft. Their incredible destructive power has deterred nuclear war since the Cuban Missile Crisis in 1962. On September 11, 2001, we awakened to the fact that a war on terrorism now faces us; neither weapons of mass destruction nor surgical strikes can win it.

We face an enemy made up of lawless criminals or religious zealots motivated by hate and hunger for power and money. Terrorists deliberately mix into populations of innocent civilians. Troops trained for a Geneva Convention war cannot identify and target terrorists from among their proximate civilians. Any innovative approach to solving this problem will be more psychological than technological, as we know high tech today. The end solution must win hearts and minds of the civilian majority and free them from fear of hijacking, kidnapping, torture, beheading, and more.

Currently, terrorism is blocking the formation of a democratic government in both Afghanistan and Iraq, warning us to do some mental gear shifting from warfighting to the destruction of terrorism. To the Navy this may seem like marketing flowers in a prison, but here's one innovation that suggests it's possible. By sincere but tough diplomacy, reinvigorate the United Nations to sponsor an International Spiritual Guide based on commonalities in member nations' religions. It should be started *now* so that it can be implemented when security is finally restored in the terrorist-infested nations of the Middle East.

Your humble coauthors have faced something like this before. We refer to the postwar problems that confronted Germany circa 1934, when we graduated from the U.S. Naval Academy in the midst of the Great Depression. The United States had insisted on reparations and paved the road to power for Adolph Hitler. The Marshal Plan was too little, too late.

After World War II most German weapons engineers overcame their fear of the Nazis and found ways to contact a Navy team that sought them as immigrants to America—capable of helping us win what finally became the Cold War. Their efforts, known as the "Paper Clip Program," brought some six hundred to the Navy alone. It was a great investment.

As Director of Tests at Point Mugu from 1945 to 1949, Grayson Merrill recruited some one-dozen German scientists from their "brainwashing" assignment at the Office of Naval Research to work on Bureau of Aeronautics (BuAer) post–World War II guided missiles. He soon learned the technical capabilities of Dr. Herbert A. Wagner and his colleagues, thus setting the stage for our story of innovation—"The Bootleg Development."

The "Bootleg Development" deals with a fairly common phenomenon at naval testing facilities that entails spinning off from assigned projects a new device or weapon not yet officially recognized by a written operational requirement. In this case, it was a close-air-support (CAS) system for all-weather, precision bombing by Marine Corps aircraft on enemy targets in a combat area. First used in Korea, its descendents enabled the surgical air strikes that resulted in quick, dramatic victory in the Iraqi Freedom war more than fifty years later.

In 1944, before Hiroshima, the Loon missile, a copy of the German buzz bomb, was under development by the U.S. Navy as its first submarine-launched missile aimed at Japanese beachhead fortifications. Its radar beacon was tracked by the sub's radar; course changes and a

dump command were sent by radio until the Loon dived into the target. For safety during tests off Point Mugu, we had an armed Marine F6F fighter escorting the missile.

The Marines were interested in the project because they would quite likely be near future targets, say an Iwo Jima beachhead. Consequently, they furnished a detachment of several fighters under the command of a colorful major named Marian C. Dalby.

Dalby was itching to get more involved with projects devoted to the Marine Corps, as was his cadre of talented enlisted technicians and officers. He was flying Loon simulation missions for Dr. Wagner, who was then modifying the SCR-584 radar. It used a Reeves Instrument Company plotting board to yield course changes, a warhead arming signal, and a dump command to the Loon.

Dalby reported that Dr. Wagner's air controller started with, "Climb to five thousand feet and fly course 213 degrees magnetic." When the radar confirmed Dalby had arrived at his location, the controller continued, "Change course to 202 magnetic." This would continue until Dalby saw Begg Rock dead ahead; then the controller's instructions were, in sequence, "Arm Loon" and "Dive Loon"—two commands Dalby obviously ignored. The second time Dalby did this, he wondered why the Americans should prefer Loon to a two-thousand-pound bomb.

What we were talking about was a CAS system the Marines had long dreamed about but not found. It's a frontline support concept with Marine troops at the front, and the enemy across the lines. If the weather is foul but flyable, the system is especially effective. Obviously, our American troops have close contact with the enemy, so they know where the targets are. Under the CAS concept, they are in charge of designating the targets and their coordinates to the ground radar crew. The crew's air controller then calls for attack aircraft support.

Once the fighters are airborne and acquired by the radar, the controller can use voice radio to direct an attack with relative safety at high altitude, in darkness or overcast. The effect is to replace the Loon with an attack aircraft and hit the target with a lethal bomb, instead of a Loon with its lesser TNT warhead.

Dr. Wagner, his air controller, and Dalby's leading enlisted technicians met. They all embraced the concept as being technically feasible. Modifications to the F6F fighters were relatively simple and clearly best left to Dalby and his cadre. Not so the SCR-584 radar and plotting board.

Wagner said he would like to enhance the accuracy of the system by adding an analog computer that would continuously process the radar's fighter position and motion data and automatically generate commands to be sent via the radio to the fighter through its existing voice radio link. The pilot would not hear course change commands but would see them being implemented by existing flight instruments. The improvement in accuracy depended primarily on Dr. Wagner's calculus-driven analog computer. Digital computers were only a distant dream at this point.

A go-ahead decision would be in violation of an unwritten BuAer policy that discourages in-house developments. Defense industries see these as their bread and butter. But here the right decision was to act on a unique, time-sensitive opportunity and deal with the objections later. Merrill made it so, ultimately mainstreamed the project with BuAer, and never heard a complaint.

Progress was later accelerated by the Hiroshima bomb that eliminated Japan as the enemy and so made the remaining Loons more available for the project. The average miss distance was about thirty-five yards CEP, or circular error probable. By 1949, Merrill was detailed back to BuAer and lost close contact with the project.

By coincidence Victor H. Krulak became the de facto sponsor for the system's deployment into the Korean War. This phase of the story is best told by excerpts from his book *First to Fight*.

By early 1950, the equipment was still an awkward-looking jungle of wires and breadboard-style panels. Even so, Dalby concluded that it was sufficiently reliable to risk exposing it to the . . . Marine Corps. In April, he took the contraption to the Marine Corps Base at Camp Pendleton in southern California, where he demonstrated it for a group of ground and air Marines. . . . We went to the demonstration because we were told to go. We had no idea what to expect.

In his orientation Dalby told us that he had two aircraft, flying at 18,000 feet and said, if everything worked, that his device would direct the course of the aircraft and release the bombs, which would fall within 150 yards of a target. He reemphasized that all of this would happen without the pilot ever seeing the target and that the equipment on the ground—not the pilot—would drop the bomb!

We were incredulous. Dalby invited me to select the first bombing target. I chose a terrain feature that was clearly visible. . . .

On the first run, two bombs landed within 50 yards of the target. Someone else chose another target, and on this run the bombs made a direct hit! After three more runs, all with similar results, there was no doubt: all-weather bombing had arrived in the Marine Corps.

This was only the first of many demonstrations and, as time passed, the system, named AN-MPQ-14 [A = Army, N = Navy, M = mobile, P = radar, Q = combination purpose, and 14 = 14th model/modification], gradually became more solid, more combat-compatible, and more efficient. . . .

By July 1951, the team was ready to go to war. The equipment had been finally hardened to meet the strains of combat. . . . When the unit arrived in Korea, the commanding general of the 1st Marine Aircraft Wing agreed to position it with the 1st Marine Division which, at that time, was involved in heavy fighting with the North Koreans a few miles south of the 38th Parallel.

The morale of the 1st Marine Aircraft Wing's Corsair night-fighter squadron,

VMF-513, was low because, in providing night support for the ground Marines, the pilots had to fly at low levels up dark Korean valleys, trying to find their targets under flares. They were suffering heavy casualties in the process. They say the great benefit of flying at altitudes of 15,000 to 20,000 feet, far above the enemy antiaircraft fire, is having greater success hitting the target. . . .

In truth, a new era had dawned. The Marines on the ground, the direct beneficiaries of the night and all-weather bombing, were enthusiastic in their praise and vocal in their calls for more systems of the same type.

In the Vietnam War that followed, the Marines had organized Air Support Radar Teams equipped with a new generation of CAS system, then-designated AN TPQ-10 (A = Army, N = Navy, T = ground transportable, P = radar, Q = combination purpose, and 10 = 10th model/modification), which was especially valuable in the unfavorable weather of that war. That versatile system could handle as many as 105 missions a day at Khe Sanh and stood tall as evidence of the creativity, determination, and technical diversity of Major Dalby, Dr. Wagner, and those who helped with the Bootleg Development.

Dalby was a first-class doer, and the whole aeronautical world owes him a debt of gratitude.

About the Authors

Lieutenant General Victor H. Krulak served in the Marines Corps from 1934 to 1968, distinguishing himself in a career that spanned three wars, during which he commanded everything from combat platoons to a fleet Marine force. A 1934 graduate of the U.S. Naval Academy, he later earned a PhD from the University of San Diego, and in 2004, he was selected as a Distinguished Graduate by the Naval Academy. He is known as the "father of the LCVP landing craft" and is the author of *First to Fight: An Inside View of the U.S. Marine Corps* (Naval Institute Press, 1984).

Captain Grayson Merrill graduated from the Naval Academy in 1934 and subsequently served in battleships and destroyers before he became a naval aviator. He is best known for his work on guided missiles; he was instrumental in the late 1940s in establishing the Naval Air Missile Test Center at Point Mugu, California, where a building is now named in his honor. In the mid-1950s he was selected as the first technical director for the Polaris program. Following his 1957 retirement from the Navy, Merrill worked in the defense industry and edited a series of books on guided missiles.

Appendix A
Naval Historical Center

The Naval Historical Center, located in the Washington Navy Yard not far from the U.S. Capitol, holds the keys to the history and heritage of the U.S. Navy from its creation in 1775 to the present.

One of those keys is the center's Web site (http://www.history.navy.mil), which enables Sailors to learn about the history of their ship or aircraft squadron, naval customs and traditions, key dates in the U.S. Navy's history, biographies of naval leaders and heroes, and information on the Navy's birthday and Midway Night celebrations. A "frequently asked questions" feature provides some answers to the sinking of USS *Maine* in 1898, the loss at sea of famous aviator Amelia Earhart, the surprise attack on Pearl Harbor, the Tonkin Gulf Incident of the Vietnam War, and much more.

Available for downloading are a summary history of the U.S. Navy, descriptions of battles and operations from the War for Independence to Operation Desert Storm, and ten thousand individual ship entries from the *Dictionary of American Naval Fighting Ships*. The Web site helps users obtain U.S. Navy Heritage Mini-Series Videos on the Civil War fight between USS *Monitor* and CSS *Virginia*, the Battle of Midway, the Cuban Missile Crisis, naval heroes in action, and other subjects. Also presented are instructions for obtaining copies of *Naval Aviation News*, a full-color, bimonthly magazine of the naval aviation community.

Ordering information is also provided for works produced by the center, sometimes in cooperation with commercial publishers, including the following.

Narrative Histories

Sea Raiders of the American Revolution: The Continental Navy in European Waters
Against All Odds: U.S. Sailors in the War of 1812
By Sea, Air, and Land: An Illustrated History of the U.S. Navy and the War in S.E. Asia
Forged in War: The Naval-Industrial Complex and American Submarine Construction

Revolt of the Admirals: The Fight for Naval Aviation, 1945–1950

Where the Fleet Begins: A History of the David Taylor Research Center

Shield and Sword: The United States Navy and the Persian Gulf War

Black Shoes and Blue Water: Surface Warfare in the United States Navy, 1945–1975

Serving Proudly: A History of Women in the U.S. Navy

An Ocean in Common: American Naval Officers, Scientists, and the Ocean

Afterburner: Naval Aviators and the Vietnam War

The Washington Navy Yard: An Illustrated History

On Course to Desert Storm: The United States Navy and the Persian Gulf

The U.S. Navy in the Modern World Series

Cordon of Steel: The U.S. Navy and the Cuban Missile Crisis

"Swift and Effective Retribution": The U.S. Sixth Fleet and the Confrontation with Qaddafi

Project HULA: Soviet-American Cooperation in the War against Japan

From Dam Neck to Okinawa: A Memoir of Antiaircraft Training

The U.S. Navy in the Korean War Series

Assault from the Sea: The Amphibious Landing at Inchon

Naval Leadership in Korea: The First Six Months

Fleet Operations in a Mobile War, September 1950–June 1951

Long Passage to Korea: Black Sailors and the Integration of the U.S. Navy

Attack from the Sky: The Naval Air War in Korea

The Sea Services in the Korean War, 1950–1953 (CD-ROM)

Documentary Histories

Naval Documents of the American Revolution (10 vols.)

The Naval War of 1812: A Documentary History (3 vols.)

Reference Works

Dictionary of American Naval Fighting Ships (online)

Dictionary of American Naval Aviation Squadrons (CD-ROM)

United States Naval Aviation, 1910–1995

The Guide to Naval History Organizations, Programs, and Resources, posted on the Web site, presents an owners' and operators' manual that describes not only the center but the twelve official U.S. Navy museums, other Navy and Marine Corps historical programs, and nongovernmental organizations that value the U.S. Navy's historical legacy.

With good reason, the Naval Historical Center has been called "the Navy's Smithsonian Institution." The Navy Department Library, Curator, Navy Art, and U.S. Navy Museum branches maintain 150,000 books; 130,000 artifacts; 200,000 photographs; and 10,000 paintings. The Operational Archives holds 19,000 cubic feet of the Navy's most important records from 1946 to the present. The center administers the Navy's Command History and more recent Commander's War Diary programs.

The center's Underwater Archaeology Branch helps preserve thousands of U.S. Navy ship and aircraft wrecks located around the world and recently managed the project that raised Confederate submarine *H. L. Hunley* from the harbor of Charleston, South Carolina. The center administers and helps maintain the U.S. Navy's oldest and most historic warship, USS *Constitution,* located in Boston, Massachusetts. Finally, in support of the operating forces and their global mission, civilian staff historians, curators, and artists deploy with uniformed members of Naval Reserve Combat Documentation Detachment 206 to capture the vital history of the U.S. Navy in the twenty-first century.

Appendix B
The U.S. Marine Corps History and Museums Division

Mission

The U.S. Marine Corps' History and Museums Division collects documents, artifacts, interviews, and works of art; preserves them; and presents the history of the Marine Corps through publications, museum exhibits, and other activities. In order to aid decision making, the division supports professional military education, motivates Marines, and informs the American public.

This mission is accomplished through three interrelated branches: history, museums, and field operations. In 1950, reflecting on the experience of World War II, Colonel Robert D. Heinl articulated the primary functions of the modern historical program as follows:

1. Maintenance of historical archives
2. Preparation and publication of definitive official narratives
3. Operation of a working reference collection
4. Applied research to provide answers to historical questions that originate either within the service or the general public
5. Encouragement of semiofficial or private historical research of military value
6. Arrangement for collection, preservation, and display of historical objects
7. Establishment of a specialist Reserve historical component

The location and command relations of the History and Museums Division (HD) have varied over time as Headquarters Marine Corps (HQMC) has changed. On 1 October 2002, the History and Museums Division became a part of Marine Corps University. Part of the division, including the current Marine Corps Museum, occupies Building 58 at the Washington Navy Yard (hours, reservations, and information at 202-433-3840 or -3401). The other elements of HD at Building 58 are the library, reference, archives, oral history, art, history writing, and photographic sections. Researchers may make arrangements to use these resources during normal business hours by calling 202-433-3840 or

-3483. Among the services and products provided by HD are command chronologies on CD-ROM that can be requested by individual veterans for their unit and period of service. (These have proven extremely helpful to Vietnam veterans claiming benefits.)

In 2003, the Air-Ground Museum on the Marine Corps Base at Quantico, Virginia, was closed in anticipation of the 2006 opening of the new National Museum of the Marine Corps. Now under construction outside the gates of the base, the new museum will provide more convenient access to the public, just off the interstate highway. Large artifacts, such as aircraft, armored vehicles, crew-served weapons, and the like, are being stored in the former museum buildings. Other Museum Branch activities (curators, exhibits, and restoration) are located in various buildings around Quantico; for more information, call 702-784-2606.

The Field History Branch is composed of reservists formed as an Individual Mobilization Augmentee detachment. They are trained and available to deploy with the operating forces in order to provide historical coverage of peacetime and wartime activities. They collect official documents, conduct interviews of key participants, identify artifacts for retention, and make a visual record via still and motion picture photography and combat art.

Related background on the division, HQMC, and Quantico activities can be found in a number of division publications including: Kenneth W. Condit, et al., *A Brief History of Headquarters Marine Corps Staff Organization* (Washington, D.C.: Historical Division, 1971); Charles A. Fleming, et al., *Quantico: Crossroads of the Marine Corps* (Washington, D.C.: History and Museums Division, 1978); Kenneth J. Clifford, *Progress and Purpose: A Developmental History of the U.S. Marine Corps* (Washington, D.C.: History and Museums Division, 1973).

For more information on the division and a wide range of topics relating to the traditions, culture, and history of the U.S. Marine Corps, please see the Web site at http://www.history.usmc.mil/.

The Marine Corps Heritage Foundation, a 501(c)3 nonprofit, supports many programs offered by HD. The foundation sponsors internships, fellowships, grants, and awards to ensure continued excellence in researching, recording, and publishing Marine Corps history. Located in Quantico, the foundation is also the cosponsor of the National Museum of the Marine Corps. With a loyal and enthusiastic membership numbering in the tens of thousands, the foundation raises funds to support the educational and public programs that do not receive government funding. More information may be obtained at http://www.marineheritage.org/ or by calling 1-800-397-7585.

The Marine Corps' Motto

"Semper Fidelis" (always faithful) is the motto of the Corps. That Marines have lived up to this motto is proved by the fact that there has never been a mutiny among U.S. Marines. "Semper Fidelis" was adopted about 1883 as the motto of the Corps. Before that, there had been three mottoes, all traditional rather than official. The first, antedating the War of 1812, was "Fortitudine" ("with fortitude"). The second, "By sea and by land," was obviously a translation of the Royal Marine's "Per mare, per terram." Until 1848, the third motto was "To the shores of Tripoli," in commemoration of O'Bannon's capture of Derna in 1805. In 1848, after the return to Washington of the Marine battalion that took part in the capture of Mexico City, this motto was revised to: "From the Halls of the Montezumas to the Shores of Tripoli"—a line now familiar to all Americans. This revision of the Corps motto in Mexico has encouraged speculation that the first stanza of "The Marines' Hymn" was composed by members of the Marine battalion that stormed Chapultepec Castle.

Brief History of the U.S. Marine Corps

On 10 November 1775, the Continental Congress meeting in Philadelphia passed a resolution stating that "two battalions of Marines be raised" for service as landing forces with the fleet. This resolution established the Continental Marines and marked the birth date of the U.S. Marine Corps. Serving on land and at sea, these first Marines distinguished themselves in a number of important operations, including their first amphibious raid into the Bahamas in March 1776, under the command of Captain (later Major) Samuel Nicholas. Nicholas, the first commissioned officer in the Continental Marines, remained the senior Marine officer throughout the American Revolution and is considered to be the first Marine Commandant. The Treaty of Paris in April 1783 brought an end to the Revolutionary War and, as the last of the Navy's ships were sold, the Continental Navy and Marines went out of existence.

Following the Revolutionary War and the formal reestablishment of the Marine Corps on 11 July 1798, Marines saw action in the quasi-war with France, landed in Santo Domingo, and took part in many operations against the Barbary pirates along the "shores of Tripoli." Marines participated in numerous naval operations during the War of 1812, including contributing to the defense of Washington at Bladensburg, Maryland, and fighting alongside Andrew Jackson in the defeat of the British at New Orleans. The decades following the War of 1812 saw the Marines protecting American interests around the world: in the Caribbean, at the Falkland Islands, in Sumatra, off the coast of West Africa, and close to home in the operations against the Seminole Indians in Florida.

During the Mexican War (1846–48), Marines seized enemy seaports on both the Gulf and Pacific coasts. A battalion of Marines joined General Scott's army at Pueblo and fought all the way to the "Halls of Montezuma," Mexico City. Marines also served ashore and afloat in the Civil War (1861–65). Although most service was with the U.S. Navy, a battalion fought at Bull Run and other units saw action with the blockading squadrons and at Cape Hatteras, New Orleans, Charleston, and Fort Fisher. The last third of the nineteenth century saw Marines making numerous landings throughout the world, especially in the Orient and the Caribbean.

Following the Spanish-American War (1898), in which Marines performed with valor in Cuba, Puerto Rico, Guam, and the Philippines, the Corps entered an era of expansion and professional development. It saw active service in the Philippine Insurrection (1899–1902), the Boxer Rebellion in China (1900), and in numerous other nations, including Nicaragua, Panama, Cuba, Mexico, and Haiti.

In World War I, the Marine Corps distinguished itself on the battlefields of France as the 4th Marine Brigade earned the title of "Devil Dogs" for heroic action during 1918 at Belleau Wood, Soissons, Saint-Mihiel, Mont Blanc, and in the final Meuse-Argonne offensive. Marine aviation, which dates from 1912, also played a part in the war effort; Marine pilots flew day bomber missions over France and Belgium. More than thirty thousand Marines served in France and more than a third were killed or wounded in six months of intense fighting.

During the two decades before World War II, the Marine Corps began to develop in earnest the doctrine, equipment, and organization needed for amphibious warfare. The success of this effort was proven first on Guadalcanal, then on Bougainville, Tarawa, New Britain, Kwajalein, Eniwetok, Saipan, Guam, Tinian, Peleliu, Iwo Jima, and Okinawa. By the end of the war in 1945, the Marine Corps had grown to include six divisions, five air wings, and supporting troops. Its strength in World War II peaked at 485,113. The war cost the Marines nearly eighty-seven thousand dead and wounded. Eighty-two Marines earned the Medal of Honor.

While Marine units took part in the postwar occupation of Japan and North China, studies were undertaken at Quantico, Virginia, which concentrated on attaining a "vertical envelopment" capability for the Corps through the use of helicopters. Landing at Inchon, Korea, in September 1950, Marines proved that the doctrine of amphibious assault was still viable and necessary. After the recapture of Seoul, the Marines advanced to the Chosin Reservoir only to see the Chinese Communists enter the war. After years of offensives, counteroffensives, seemingly endless trench warfare, and occupation duty, the last Marine ground troops were withdrawn in March 1955. More than twenty-five thousand Marines were killed or wounded during the Korean War.

In July 1958, a brigade-size force landed in Lebanon to restore order. During the Cuban Missile Crisis in October 1962, a large amphibious force was marshaled but not landed. In April 1965, a brigade of Marines landed in the Dominican Republic to protect Americans and evacuate those who wished to leave.

The landing of the 9th Marine Expeditionary Brigade at Da Nang in 1965 marked the beginning of large-scale Marine involvement in Vietnam. By summer 1968, after the enemy's Tet Offensive, Marine Corps strength in Vietnam rose to a peak of approximately eighty-five thousand. The Marine withdrawal began in 1969 as the South Vietnamese began to assume a larger role in the fighting; the last ground forces were out of Vietnam by June 1971. The Vietnam War, longest in the history of the Marine Corps, exacted a high cost as well with over thirteen thousand Marines killed and more than eighty-eight thousand wounded. In the spring of 1975, Marines evacuated embassy staffs, American citizens, and refugees in Phnom Penh, Cambodia, and Saigon, Republic of Vietnam. Later, in May 1975, Marines played an integral role in the rescue of the crew of the USS *Mayaguez*, which was captured off the coast of Cambodia.

The mid-1970s saw the Marine Corps assume an increasingly significant role in defending NATO's northern flank as amphibious units of the 2nd Marine Division participated in exercises throughout northern Europe. The Marine Corps also played a key role in the development of the Rapid Deployment Force, a multiservice organization created to ensure a flexible, timely military response around the world when needed. The Maritime Prepositioning Ships (MPS) concept was developed to enhance this capability by prestaging equipment needed for combat in the vicinity of the designated area of operations and reduce response time as Marines travel by air to link up with MPS assets.

The 1980s brought an increasing number of terrorist attacks on U.S. embassies around the world. Marine Security Guards, under the direction of the State Department, continued to serve with distinction in the face of this challenge. In August 1982, Marine units landed at Beirut, Lebanon, as part of the multinational peacekeeping force. For the next nineteen months, these units faced the hazards of their mission with courage and professionalism. In October 1983, Marines took part in the highly successful, short-notice intervention in Grenada. As the decade of the 1980s came to a close, Marines were summoned to respond to instability in Central America. Operation Just Cause was launched in Panama in December 1989 to protect American lives and restore the democratic process in that nation.

Less than a year later, in August 1990, the Iraqi invasion of Kuwait set in motion events that would lead to the largest movement of Marine Corps forces since World War II. Between August 1990 and January 1991, some twenty-four infantry battalions, forty squadrons, and more than ninety-two thousand Marines deployed to the Persian Gulf as part of Operation Desert Shield. Operation Desert Storm was launched 16 January 1991, the day the air campaign began. The main attack came overland beginning 24 February when the 1st and 2nd Marine Divisions breached the Iraqi defense lines and stormed into occupied Kuwait. By the morning of 28 February, one hundred hours after the ground war began, almost the entire Iraqi army in the Kuwaiti theater of operations had been encircled with four thousand tanks destroyed and forty-two divisions destroyed or rendered ineffective.

Overshadowed by the events in the Persian Gulf during 1990–91 were a number of other significant Marine deployments demonstrating the Corps' flexible and rapid response. Included among these were noncombatant evacuation operations in Liberia and Somalia and humanitarian lifesaving operations in Bangladesh, the Philippines, and northern Iraq. In December 1992, Marines landed in Somalia, marking the beginning of a two-year humanitarian relief operation in that famine-stricken and strife-torn nation. In another part of the world, Marine Corps aircraft supported Operation Deny Flight in the no-fly zone over Bosnia-Herzegovina. During April 1994, Marines once again demonstrated their ability to protect American citizens in remote parts of the world when a Marine task force evacuated U.S. citizens from Rwanda in response to civil unrest in that country. Closer to home, Marines went ashore in September 1994 in Haiti as part of the U.S. force participating in the restoration of democracy in that country. During this same period Marines were actively engaged in providing assistance to the nation's counter-drug effort, assisting in battling wild fires in the western United States, and aiding in flood and hurricane relief operations.

During the late 1990s, Marine Corps units deployed to several African nations, including Liberia, the Central African Republic, Zaire, and Eritrea, in order to provide security and assist in the evacuation of American citizens during periods of political and civil instability in those nations. Humanitarian and disaster relief operations were also conducted by Marines during 1998 in Kenya and in the Central American nations of Honduras, Nicaragua, El Salvador,

and Guatemala. In 1999, Marine units deployed to Kosovo in support of Operation Allied Force. Soon after the September 2001 terrorist attacks on New York City and Washington, D.C., Marine units deployed to the Arabian Sea and in November set up a forward operating base in southern Afghanistan as part of Operation Enduring Freedom.

The Marine Corps has continued its tradition of innovation to meet the challenges of a new century. The Marine Corps Warfighting Laboratory was created in 1995 to evaluate change, assess the impact of new technologies on warfighting, and expedite the introduction of new capabilities into the operating forces of the Marine Corps. Exercises such as "Hunter Warrior" and "Urban Warrior" were designed to explore future tactical concepts and to examine facets of military operations in urban environments.

Today's Marine Corps stands ready to continue in the proud tradition of those who so valiantly fought and died at Belleau Wood, Iwo Jima, the Chosin Reservoir, and Khe Sanh. Combining a long and proud heritage of faithful service to the nation with the resolve to face tomorrow's challenges will continue to keep the Marine Corps the "best of the best."

Appendix C
Selected Annotated Bibliography on Naval Leadership

Adorno, Theodor W., Else Frenkel-Brunswick, Daniel J. Levinson, and R. Nevitt Sanford. *The Authoritarian Personality*. New York: Harper, 1950. Study in human behavior and nature that focuses specifically on its manifestation in Nazi Germany while generally extrapolating it.

Alden, Carroll S., and Ralph Earle. *Makers of Naval Tradition*. Boston: Ginn, 1942. Reprinted 1972 by Books for Libraries. A collection of twelve biographies of outstanding American naval officers from John Paul Jones to William Sampson.

Avolio, Bruce J. *Full Leadership Development: Building the Vital Forces in Organizations*. Thousand Oaks, Calif.: Sage, 1999. Approaches the concept of leadership as a system comprised of people, timing, resources, the context of interaction, and the expected results in performance and motivation.

Barge, J. Kevin. *Leadership: Communication Skills for Organizations and Groups*. New York: St. Martin's, 1994.

Bass, Bernard M. *Bass and Stogdill's Handbook of Leadership: A Survey of Theory and Research*. New York: Free Press, 1990. Reference on various aspects of leadership.

———. *Leadership and Performance Beyond Expectations*. New York: Free Press, 1985. Reviews the theory and research on transformational leadership.

Bass, Bernard M., and Avolio, Bruce J., eds. *Improving Organizational Effectiveness Through Transformational Leadership*. Thousand Oaks, Calif.: Sage, 1994. Chapters explore the effects of transformational leadership on delegation, teamwork, decision making, total quality management, and corporate reorganization.

Bennis, Warren G. *On Becoming a Leader: The Leadership Classic*. Cambridge, Mass.: Perseus, 2003. Examines the qualities that define leadership, the people who exemplify it, and the strategies that anyone can apply to become an effective leader.

Bennis, Warren G., and Burt Nanus. *Leaders:*

The Strategies for Taking Charge. New York: Harper and Row, 1985. This study of corporate America focuses on "attention through vision, meaning through communication, trust through positioning, and the deployment of self."

Blanchard, Kenneth H., and Spencer Johnson. *The One Minute Manager.* New York: William Morrow, 1982. Guide for managers that demonstrates techniques and includes medical and behavioral science studies.

Blank, Warren. *The 9 Natural Laws of Leadership.* New York: American Management Association, 1995. Proposes a leadership model based on the science of quantum physics.

Bolman, Lee G., and Terrence E. Deal. *Reframing Organizations.* San Francisco: Jossey-Bass, 1991. Views organizations as factories, families, jungles, and theaters or temples.

Bradford, James C., ed. *Admirals of the New Steel Navy: Makers of the American Naval Tradition, 1880–1930.* Annapolis, Md.: Naval Institute Press, 1990. Individual essays on the flag officers who helped build the powerful U.S. Fleet that served the nation during the Spanish-American War and World War I.

———. *Captains of the Old Steam Navy: Makers of the American Naval Tradition, 1840–1880.* Annapolis, Md.: Naval Institute Press, 1986. Individual essays by noted historians on officers who led the U.S. Navy before, during, and after the Civil War.

———. *Command Under Sail: Makers of the American Naval Tradition, 1775–1850.* Annapolis, Md.: Naval Institute Press, 1985. Well-written, informative essays on the men who led the U.S. Navy from its birth to the years before the Civil War.

Bridges, William. *Managing Transitions.* Reading, Mass.: Addison-Wesley, 1991. Focuses on the human side of organizational change.

Bryman, Alan. *Charisma and Leadership in Organizations.* London: Sage, 1992.

Buckingham, Marcus, and Donald O. Clifton. *Now Discover Your Strengths: How to Develop Your Talents and Those of the People You Man-age.* New York: Simon and Schuster Adult Publishing Group, 2001. Helps readers identify their talents, build them into strengths, and enjoy consistent performance.

Buckingham, Marcus, and Curt Coffman. *First Break All the Rules: What The World's Greatest Managers Do Differently.* New York: Simon and Schuster Adult Publishing Group, 1999. Study of great managers in a wide variety of situations: leadership positions, front-line supervisors, Fortune 500 companies, and key players in small, entrepreneurial companies.

Buell, Thomas B. *The Quiet Warrior: A Biography of Admiral Raymond A. Spruance.* Boston: Little, Brown, 1974.

Burns, John M. *Leadership.* New York: Harper and Row, 1978. Examines the role of leadership in American history.

Campbell, James. *The Hero with a Thousand Faces.* Princeton, N.J.: Princeton University Press, 1949. Combines the spiritual and psychological aspects of psychoanalysis with the archetypes of world mythology.

Ciulla, Joanne B., ed. *Ethics, the Heart of Leadership.* Westport, Conn.: Quorum Books, 1998. Explores the ethical dynamic of leadership in business and society.

Cogar, William B. *Dictionary of Admirals of the U.S. Navy.* 2 vols. Annapolis, Md.: Naval Institute Press, 1989.

Coletta, Paolo E., ed. *American Secretaries of the Navy.* 2 vols. Annapolis, Md.: Naval Institute Press, 1980. Coletta and twenty other scholars have contributed biographies of the sixty secretaries of the Navy from Stoddert to Chafee.

Collins, Arthur S. *Common Sense Training: A Working Philosophy for Leaders.* Novato, Calif.: Presidio, 1998. Presents a military training philosophy encompassing the platoon to division level.

Collins, James C., and Jerry I. Porras. *Built to Last: Successful Habits of Visionary Companies.* New York: HarperCollins, 2002. A management study that shows how great companies succeed and how long-term sustained performance can be engineered into an enterprise from the outset.

―――. *Good to Great: Why Some Companies make the Leap . . . and Others Don't.* New York: HarperCollins, 2001. Compares and contrasts management strategy and practice of companies.

Connelly, Owen. *On War and Leadership: The Words of Combat Commanders from Frederick the Great to Norman Schwarzkopf.* Princeton, N.J.: Princeton University Press, 2002. Distills military leadership and wartime experience by examining combat leaders.

Cox, Taylor, Jr. *Cultural Diversity in Organizations: Theory, Research, and Practice.* San Francisco: Berrett-Koehler, 1993. Analyzes the importance of valuing diversity.

Csikszentmihalyi, Mihaly. *The Evolving Self: A Psychology for the Third Millennium.* New York: HarperCollins, 1993. A guide to life in the future.

Depree, Max. *Leadership Is an Art.* New York: Doubleday, 2004. Emphasizes humanitarian management through persuasion and democratic participation.

―――. *Leadership Jazz.* New York: Dell, 1992. Connects business leadership to the art of jazz.

Fehrenbach, T. R. *This Kind of War: The Classic Korean War History.* Washington, D.C.: Brassey's, 2000. Account of the Korean War from individual soldiers.

Fiedler, Fred Edward. *A Theory of Leadership Effectiveness.* New York: McGraw-Hill, 1967.

Fiedler, Fred Edward, and Martin M. Chemers. *Leadership and Effective Management.* Glenview, Ill.: Scott, Foresman, 1974.

Fischer, David Hackett. *Washington's Crossing.* New York: Oxford University Press, 2004. Discussion of tactical, operational, and strategic factors involved in Washington's crossing of the Delaware and the following destruction of the Hessian garrison of Trenton and defeat of a British brigade at Princeton.

Gardner, Howard, and Emma Laskin. *Leading Minds: An Anatomy of Leadership.* New York: Basic Books, 1995. Addresses the role of the mind and creativity in leadership.

―――. "The Nature of Leadership." Leadership Papers. *The Independent Sector* 1 (January 1986): 116–238.

Gardner, John W. *On Leadership.* New York: Free Press, 1990. Proposes and illustratively supports his theory on leadership and vision.

Gergen, David. *Eyewitness to Power: The Essence of Leadership, Nixon to Clinton.* New York: Simon and Schuster Adult Publishing Group, 2001. Presents accounts of the Nixon, Ford, Reagan, and Clinton administrations and their struggles to exercise power in addition to key lessons drawn from them for leaders of the future.

Grant, Ulysses S. *Personal Memoirs of U. S. Grant.* New York: Dover, 1995. Autobiographical chronicle of Grant's campaigns and battles.

Greenleaf, Robert K. *Servant Leadership: A Journey into the Nature of Legitimate Power and Greatness.* New York: Paulist, 1977.

Gross, Ronald. *Peak Learning.* Los Angeles: Tarcher, 1991. Presents a program to aid in better learning.

Heifetz, Ronald A. *Leadership Without Easy Answers.* Cambridge, Mass.: Harvard University Press, 1994. Identifies strategies of leadership through problem diagnosis.

Hickman, Gill Robinson, ed. *Leading Organizations: Perspectives for a New Era.* Thousand Oaks, Calif.: Sage, 1998. Provides a view of leadership across an organization.

Hollander, Edwin P. *Leadership Dynamics.* New York: Free Press, 1964. Emphasizes the role of transactional leadership.

Howarth, Stephen, ed. *Men of War: Great Naval Leaders of World War II.* New York: St. Martin's, 1993. Covers the combat performance of the U.S. naval officers who changed the course of World War II.

Hughes, Richard L., Robert C. Ginnett, and Gordon J. Curphey. *Leadership: Enhancing the Lessons of Experience.* Homewood, Ill.: Irwin, 1993. Provides advice for advanced leadership skills, applying theory and research to real-life experience.

Hunt, James G., and Lars L. Larson, eds. *Leadership: The Cutting Edge.* Carbondale: Southern Illinois University Press, 1976.

Jenks, James M., and John M. Kelly. *Don't Do: Delegate!* New York: Ballantine, 1985. Provides instruction on the specifics of delegation.

Johnson, Paul M. *Modern Times: The World from the Twenties to the Nineties.* New York: HarperCollins, 2001. A world history of the events, ideas, and personalities of the twentieth century.

Jung, Carl G. *Psychological Types.* New York: Harcourt and Brace, 1923. Work upon which the Myers-Briggs Type Indicator is based.

Kanungo, Rabindra N., and Manuel Mendonca. *Ethical Dimensions of Leadership.* Thousand Oaks, Calif.: Sage, 1996. Offers practical strategies for effective leadership, such as employee empowerment, together with suggestions about how leaders can prepare for ethical leadership. Also considers non-Western sociocultural environments.

Keegan, John. *The Face of Battle.* New York: Penguin, 1983. Conveys military history of the battlefield with an emphasis on the participants' experience. Surveys three battles: Agincourt, Waterloo, and Somme.

———. *The Mask of Command.* New York: Penguin, 1988. Keegan considers what makes a great military leader by examining four influential commanders: Alexander the Great, the Duke of Wellington, Ulysses S. Grant, and Adolph Hitler.

Kinlaw, Dennis C. *Superior Teams: What They Are and How to Develop Them.* Hampshire, U.K.: Grove, 1998.

Koestenbaum, Peter. *Leadership: The Inner Side of Greatness.* San Francisco: Jossey-Bass, 1991. Discusses the fundamental nature of leadership and how to become an exceptional and compassionate leader in today's complex world.

Kotter, John P. *A Force for Change: How Leadership Differs from Management.* New York: Free Press, 1990. Emphasizes the synthesis of leadership and management; examines leadership as a process that invokes change.

Kouzas, James M., and Barry Z. Posner. *The Leadership Challenge.* San Francisco: Jossey-Bass, 2003. Emphasizes the consistency of leadership fundamentals.

Likert, R. *New Patterns of Management.* New York: McGraw-Hill, 1961.

Love, Robert W., ed. *The Chiefs of Naval Operations.* Annapolis, Md.: Naval Institute Press, 1980. Chapters on each of the Navy's CNOs from 1915 to 1974, including Admirals King, Nimitz, and Burke.

Lowenherz, David H., ed. *50 Greatest Letters from America's Wars.* New York: Crown, 2002. Collected letters written by military personnel from the Revolution to operations in Afghanistan.

Marolda, Edward J., ed. *FDR and the U.S. Navy.* New York: St. Martin's, 1998. Papers by distinguished scholars on Franklin D. Roosevelt's association with naval leaders and the development of strategy in World War I, the interwar years, and World War II.

Marshall, George C. *The War Reports.* Philadelphia: Lippincott, 1947.

McDonough, James R. *Platoon Leader: A Memoir of Command in Combat.* New York: Random House, 2003. Memoir of small unit leadership in Vietnam.

McFarland, Lynne Joy, Larry E. Senn, and John R. Childress. *Twenty-First-Century Leadership: Dialogues with 100 Top Leaders.* New York: Leadership Press, 1993.

McGrath, J. E. *Leadership Behavior: Some Requirements for Leadership Training.* Washington, D.C.: U.S. Civil Service Commission, 1964.

Montgomery, Bernard L. *The Memoirs of Field-Marshal Montgomery.* New York: Dell Books, 1958.

Montor, Karel, et al. *Naval Leadership: Voices of Experience.* Annapolis, Md.: Naval Institute Press, 1987. Insights on leadership from senior U.S. and foreign naval officers.

Morrell, Margot, and Stephanie Capparell. *Shackleton's Way: Leadership Lessons from the Great Antarctic Explorer.* New York: Penguin, 2002. Antarctic explorer Shackleton's leadership style and principles translated for the modern business world from anecdotes, the diaries of the men in his crew, and Shackleton's own writing.

Nanus, Burt. *Visionary Leadership.* San Francisco: Jossey-Bass, 1990. Shows vision as the key to leadership and demonstrates the process for defining vision.

Northouse, Peter G. *Leadership: Theory and Practice.* 2nd ed. Thousand Oaks, Calif.: Sage, 2001. Bridges research and practical uses of leadership.

Nye, Joseph, Jr. *Bound to Lead: The Changing Nature of American Power.* New York: Basic Books, 1990. Demonstrates the power of the United States and addresses management of the transition to global interdependence.

Nye, Roger H. *The Challenge of Command: Reading for Military Excellence.* New York: Perigee Trade, 2002. Discusses the ideal leader through philosophy, ethics, and morality.

Paine, Thomas. *Common Sense.* Edited by I. Kramnick. New York: Penguin, 1976. Kramnick's introduction examines Paine's life and work within the context of the political and social changes taking place in Europe and America in the late eighteenth century.

Parker, Glenn M. *Team Players and Teamwork.* San Francisco: Jossey-Bass, 1990. Draws on stories of more than fifty team-driven organizations, including Xerox, Honeywell, General Motors, and 3M, to provide evidence of the qualities of high performing teams.

Peters, Thomas J., and Nancy Austin. *A Passion for Excellence.* New York: Random House, 1985. Highlights methods and accomplishments of organizational leaders.

Peters, Thomas J., and Robert H. Waterman Jr. *In Search of Excellence: Lessons from America's Best-Run Companies.* New York: Warner Books, 1984. Presents common management principles.

Phillips, Don T. *Lincoln on Leadership: Executive Strategies for Tough Times.* New York: Warner Books, 1992. Considers the national transformation resulting from Lincoln's expertise and the incorporation of his examples and wisdom into today's society.

Robbins, Anthony. *Awaken the Giant Within.* New York: Summit Books, 1991. Describes the control unconscious beliefs have on behavior and how to change the effects to accomplish goals.

———. *Unlimited Power.* New York: Fawcett Columbine, 1986. Teaches goal definition, focused action, results gauging, and behavior adjustment.

Roosevelt, Eleanor. *The Autobiography of Eleanor Roosevelt.* New York: Da Capo, 1992. A portrait of Eleanor Roosevelt.

———. *You Learn by Living.* New York: Harper and Brothers, 1960.

Roosevelt, Franklin D. *Nothing to Fear: The Selected Addresses of Franklin Delano Roosevelt: 1932–1945.* Edited by B. D. Zeving. Cambridge, Mass.: Riverside, 1946. Examines the leadership qualities of Franklin Delano Roosevelt.

Rustow, Dankwart A., ed. *Philosophers and Kings: Studies in Leadership.* New York: Braziller, 1970. Compilation of studies of individual leaders.

Schwartz, Peter. *The Art of the Long View: Planning for the Future in an Uncertain World.* New York: Doubleday, 1996. Provides tools for developing a strategic vision.

Simonton, Dean Keith. *Genius, Creativity, and Leadership: Historiometric Inquiries.* Cambridge, Mass.: Harvard University Press, 1984. Uses historiometry to examine creativity and leadership simultaneously.

Slim, William. *Defeat into Victory.* New York: Buccaneer Books, 1991. A testament of battling Japan in Burma and India in 1942–45.

Smith, Perry M. *Taking Charge: A Practical Guide for Leaders.* Collingdale, Pa.: DIANE, 1995. Provides a practical guide for leaders who head large and complex organizations. Contains case studies, checklists, helpful hints, rules of thumb, and other techniques.

Spiller, Roger J., Joseph G. Dawson, and T. Harry Williams, eds. *Dictionary of American Military Biography*. 3 vols. Westport, Conn.: Greenwood, 1984. Includes biographical essays on seventy-five Navy and Marine Corps officers distinguished for their service from the American Revolution to the present.

Stockdale, James B. *A Vietnam Experience: Ten Years of Reflection*. Palo Alto, Calif.: Hoover Institution Press, 1991.

Sweetman, Jack, ed. *Great Admirals: Command at Sea, 1587–1945*. Annapolis, Md.: Naval Institute Press, 1997. Presents essays by distinguished scholars on key figures in world naval history, including the American flag officers Farragut, Dewey, and Halsey.

Tead, Ordway. *The Art of Leadership*. New York: Whittlesly House, 1935. Argues the role of character and values in leadership.

Tichy, Noel M., and Mary Anne Devanna. *The Transformational Leader*. New York: Wiley, 1990. Shows how leaders of companies like Chase, GE, and Chrysler have transformed their companies.

Wills, Garry. *Certain Trumpets: The Call of Leaders*. New York: Simon and Schuster, 1994. Examines history through history and biography.

Winston, Stephanie. *The Organized Executive: Top Executives and CEOs Reveal the Organizing Principles That Helped Them Reach the Top*. New York: Crown, 2004.

Wooden, John. *They Call Me Coach*. Waco, Tex.: Word Books, 1972. Personal history on Wooden's life, career, and players.

Yukl, Gary. *Leadership in Organizations*. 3rd ed. Englewood Cliffs, N.J.: Prentice Hall, 1994. Surveys major theories and research on leadership and managerial effectiveness in organizations and includes practical suggestions for improving skills.

Zuker, Elaina. *The Seven Secrets of Influence*. New York: McGraw-Hill, 1991.

About the Editor

Lieutenant Colonel Joseph J. Thomas is currently a battalion officer and ethics instructor at the U.S. Naval Academy. Some of his past assignments include 1st and 2nd Marine Aircraft Wings, 26 Marine Expeditionary Unit (Special Operations Capable), Marine Aviation Weapons and Tactics Squadron One, Marine Corps Training and Education Command, and Marine Officer Instructor at the University of Notre Dame. He is a past recipient of the General Merritt Edson Leadership Award, the Marine Corps Association's Research and Writing Award, and the Colonel Donald G. Cook Distinguished Graduate Award from Command and Control Systems School. Lieutenant Colonel Thomas holds a bachelor's degree from Muhlenberg College, is a graduate of Marine Corps Command and Staff College, and holds master's degrees from Syracuse University and the U.S. Army War College. He also holds a PhD from George Mason University. Lieutenant Colonel Thomas and his wife, Jackie, have three sons: Joseph Jr., Andrew, and Robert.

The Naval Institute Press is the book-publishing arm of the U.S. Naval Institute, a private, nonprofit, membership society for sea service professionals and others who share an interest in naval and maritime affairs. Established in 1873 at the U.S. Naval Academy in Annapolis, Maryland, where its offices remain today, the Naval Institute has members worldwide.

Members of the Naval Institute support the education programs of the society and receive the influential monthly magazine *Proceedings* and discounts on fine nautical prints and on ship and aircraft photos. They also have access to the transcripts of the Institute's Oral History Program and get discounted admission to any of the Institute-sponsored seminars offered around the country. Discounts are also available to the colorful bimonthly magazine *Naval History.*

The Naval Institute's book-publishing program, begun in 1898 with basic guides to naval practices, has broadened its scope to include books of more general interest. Now the Naval Institute Press publishes about one hundred titles each year, ranging from how-to books on boating and navigation to battle histories, biographies, ship and aircraft guides, and novels. Institute members receive significant discounts on the Press's more than eight hundred books in print.

Full-time students are eligible for special half-price membership rates. Life memberships are also available.

For a free catalog describing Naval Institute Press books currently available, and for further information about joining the U.S. Naval Institute, please write to:

Membership Department
U.S. Naval Institute
291 Wood Road
Annapolis, MD 21402-5034
Telephone: (800) 233-8764
Fax: (410) 269-7940
Web address: www.navalinstitute.org